The history of the present English subjunctive

A corpus-based study of mood and modality

Lilo Moessner

EDINBURGH
University Press

Edinburgh University Press is one of the leading university presses in the UK. We publish academic books and journals in our selected subject areas across the humanities and social sciences, combining cutting-edge scholarship with high editorial and production values to produce academic works of lasting importance. For more information visit our website: edinburghuniversitypress.com

© Lilo Moessner, 2020, 2022

First published in hardback by Edinburgh University Press 2020

Edinburgh University Press Ltd
The Tun – Holyrood Road,
12(2f) Jackson's Entry,
Edinburgh EH8 8PJ

Typeset in Sabon by
Servis Filmsetting Ltd, Stockport, Cheshire,
and printed and bound in Great Britain by
CPI Group (UK) Ltd, Croydon CR0 4YY

A CIP record for this book is available from the British Library

ISBN 978 1 4744 3799 8 (hardback)
ISBN 978 1 4744 3800 1 (paperback)
ISBN 978 1 4744 3801 8 (webready PDF)
ISBN 978 1 4744 3802 5 (epub)

The right of Lilo Moessner to be identified as the author of this work has been asserted in accordance with the Copyright, Designs and Patents Act 1988, and the Copyright and Related Rights Regulations 2003 (SI No. 2498).

The history of the present English subjunctive

Contents

List of Figures

List of Tables

Acknowledgements

During the work on this book I had the help from many colleagues and friends, which I gratefully acknowledge. I profited from useful comments by the reviewers of the first versions, from discussions about individual issues at many conferences where I read papers on topics related to or inspired by my research on the subjunctive. Special thanks go to Bas Aarts, who read and commented on several draft versions of my manuscript, to Christian Mair, who put me up to date on recent developments of the ARCHER corpus, to David Yerkes, who made parts of his doctoral dissertation accessible to me, to Martti Mäkinen, who shared his knowledge about medieval medical terminology with me, and to Laura Williamson and her editorial team at Edinburgh University Press, who patiently and competently accompanied the whole production process. Last, but not least, I sincerely thank my friend Christa Schmidt, without whose never-failing moral support, encouragement in difficult periods, critical reading of the whole text, and editorial expertise this book would never have been completed. All shortcomings are, of course, mine.

Denzlingen, September 2019

I

Introduction

1.1 Motivations for the aim and scope of the book

From the last quarter of the twentieth century onwards more and more linguists have been refuting Fowler's famous claim (1965: 595) that the English subjunctive was dying (Collins 2015, Collins et al. 2014, Crawford 2009, Hoffmann 1997, Hundt 1998a, 1998b, 2009, 2018, 2019, Hundt and Gardner 2017, Johansson and Norheim 1988, Kastronic and Poplack 2014, Kjellmer 2009, Leech et al. 2009, Övergaard 1995, Peters 1998, 2009, Sayder 1989, Schneider 2000, 2005, 2007, 2011, Serpollet 2001, Waller 2017). Only Ruohonen (2017) casts some doubt on the hypothesis of a revival of the subjunctive continuing into the twenty-first century. These studies are based on corpus-linguistic evidence and deal with the so-called mandative subjunctive, i.e. with subjunctive use in subordinate clauses depending on expressions of 'demand, recommendation, proposal, resolution, intention, etc.' (Quirk et al. 1985: 156). Their general message is that the subjunctive enjoys a healthy life and shows an increasing frequency in many diatopic varieties. The same construction type was also at issue in some studies on differences of subjunctive use in British and American English (Algeo 1988, 1992, Greenbaum 1977, Johansson 1979, Turner 1980, Nichols 1987). They are based on elicitation tests and also come to the conclusion that the subjunctive is very much alive in the second half of the twentieth century. How can we explain Fowler's pessimistic outlook? Its assumption is that in the past the subjunctive was frequently used, but then lost its popularity.

Extensive research on the subjunctive in Old English (OE) dates from the first half of the twentieth century, but the relevant publications cover only poetry (Behre 1934), only dependent clauses (Glunz 1929, Vogt 1930, Wilde 1939/1940) or only special adverbial clauses (Callaway 1931, 1933), and they do not provide quantitative results.[1]

---

[1] Even more restricted is the scope of studies of the OE subjunctive in individual texts: in Bede's *Ecclesiastical History* (Faulkner, diss. 2004), in the English

Subjunctive constructions in Middle English (ME) have not received much attention. López-Couso and Méndez-Naya (1996, 2006) and Moessner (2007, 2010a) describe the use of subjunctives and alternative constructions in noun clauses after suasive verbs. The use of the subjunctive in ME conditional clauses is dealt with in Kihlbom (1939) and in Moessner (2005). The general information to be gleaned from these studies is that the development of subjunctive frequency was not uniform across construction types (frequency rise in conditional clauses, frequency drop in noun clauses) and across text categories (instructive text types preserve the subjunctive longer than narrative text types).

Studies on the subjunctive in the Early Modern English (EModE) period also focus on the construction types noun clause (Fillbrandt 2006, Rütten 2014, 2015) and adverbial clause (Moessner 2006). They show that in EModE, too, the development of subjunctive frequency is influenced by a number of factors, e.g. diatopic variety, construction type and text category.

Subjunctive use in individual periods is also described in reference works on these periods (OE: Mitchell 1985, Traugott 1992; ME: Fischer 1992, Mustanoja 1960; EModE: Barber 1997, Görlach 1991, Nevalainen 2006, Rissanen 1999; Present-Day English (PDE): Huddleston and Pullum 2002, Quirk et al. 1985). Since they are not exclusively based on corpus data, they do not contribute exact quantitative results.

Two articles by Éva Kovács promise an overview of subjunctive constructions in OE and ME (2010) and from EModE to PDE (2009). Yet they turn out to be summaries of handbook wisdom, and they do not take notice of the many specialised studies published before.

The only diachronic investigation of subjunctive use which covers more than one period is by Wayne Harsh (1968). He examines data from all periods of the English language, and he includes all construction types in which the subjunctive can occur. In his analysis he uses a complex classification system with thirteen 'syntactic categories'. Yet each of his five chapters deals with a different aspect of subjunctive use. Therefore, it is not possible to derive a comprehensive history of the English subjunctive from the figures in the individual chapters. Chapter 2 traces the development of subjunctive frequency in six translations of the *New Testament* from OE to PDE. Chapter 3 compares subjunctive use in the original texts of the *Peterborough Chronicle* and two of Chaucer's *Canterbury Tales* with their modern translations. Chapter 4 focuses on differences between verse and prose texts and on diatopic variation in ME, and Chapter 5 describes subjunctive use in twenty-four British and American plays from the fifteenth to the twentieth centuries. The results

---

translation of Gregory's *Cura Pastoralis* (Fleischhauer 1886), in *The Anglo-Saxon Gospels* (Henshaw 1894) or in *Beowulf* (Mourek 1908).

of the individual chapters are summarised in the introduction as two parallel trends: '(1) a decline in the use of inflected subjunctive forms, and (2) an increasing use of a variety of grammatical structures in place of such forms' (Harsh 1968: 12). Among these grammatical structures are indicative forms, imperative forms, modal constructions, infinitive constructions and participle constructions.

Visser's historical syntax (1963–1973) and Jespersen's historical grammar (1909–1949) are helpful reference works which provide authentic examples of subjunctive use in all construction types in the different periods, but they do not present a systematic description of subjunctive use in the history of the English language either. This is a long-standing gap in the research landscape of the English subjunctive, and it is the aim of the present book partly to fill it.

Ideally, a systematic history of English subjunctive use should start with the analysis of the oldest English texts, describe – and possibly explain – changes in its use in all construction types across the different periods until the present day, and it should be based on corpus evidence. In section 1.3 I will clarify where my study has to fall short of this ideal at present.

1.2 The subjunctive and its relation to the categories mood and modality

Subjunctive is a controversial term in English linguistics. In the tradition of the part of speech theory it is used as one of the realisations of the inflectional category mood of the verb, the others being indicative and imperative, and this is how the term subjunctive will be used in this book. A subjunctive is identified via its form. The underlying claim here is that this is an adequate descriptive model not only for the historical periods of English, but for all periods including PDE. The controversy about the subjunctive arises from the fact that some linguists deny the existence of the category mood in PDE (Aarts 2012, Palmer 1974) or accept only the form *were* in the first and third person singular past as the realisation of an irrealis mood (Huddleston and Pullum 2002). Palmer (1974: 48) even claims that 'the notion of a subjunctive mood is a simple transfer from Latin'.

For the historical periods it is generally acknowledged that the subjunctive as a marker of the category mood is a viable definition, because English had a fully-fledged inflectional verbal system with formal differences between indicative and subjunctive in present and in past tense.[2] The amount of syncretism grew steadily from OE to ME. Whereas in OE the

---

[2] Cf. the description of verbal morphology in OE grammars and reference works (Campbell 1959: §§730, 748, 754, 762, Hogg 1992: 3.4.2.1–3.4.2.3, Pilch 1970: §33) and in ME handbooks and in the relevant parts of language histories (Burrow

indicative : subjunctive contrast was only non-existent in the first person singular present tense of lexical verbs, it was given up in ME in the plural present tense and in the second person singular past of strong verbs and in the first and third person singular past of weak verbs. From EModE onwards we find different descriptions of verbal morphology. While Lass (1999: 161), Nevalainen (2006: 96–97) and Rissanen (1999: 227–231) explicitly use the category mood with an indicative : subjunctive contrast for present and past, Barber (1997: 164–180) posits a seven-form verb system and then outlines in detail the forms used for the second and third person singular and for plural present, before he adds a paragraph on the subjunctive where he notes that the indicative : subjunctive contrast in EModE is restricted to the second and third person singular of the present tense. The verb *be* preserved more indicative : subjunctive contrasts in all periods. The further reduction of the indicative : subjunctive contrast to the third person singular present tense after the loss of the pronoun *thou* for the second person singular admittedly made mood a minor category of the English verb today. This is probably the reason for the rejection of the category mood as outlined above. If, however, the reduction of the realisation possibilities of a category were a valid argument for abolishing the category itself, it would follow that the category case no longer existed in PDE substantives, because the original five-form system in singular and plural has been reduced to a two-form system in singular and a one-form system in plural. Yet PDE grammars contain detailed treatments of case in substantives (cf. Huddleston and Pullum 2002: 455–483, Quirk et al. 1985: 318–331).

The discussion about the definition of the subjunctive in modern linguistics started with the introduction of the category modality by Palmer in his book *Modality and the English Modals* (1979) and its further elaboration in more recent publications (e.g. Palmer 2001). He distinguishes the notional category modality from grammatical categories like mood. Modality captures the status of a proposition which describes an event or a situation, and it is usually marked in the verbal syntagm through mood or through modal systems.[3] Most languages use either mood or a modal system, but there are languages where both coexist. Yet Palmer observes that in these languages 'one will, in time, replace the other' (Palmer 2001: 104). It may be argued that English is a case in point with its mood system shrinking and its modality system expanding. Unfortunately, Palmer is inconsistent in the application of his category modality and its realisations when it comes to the description of the subjunctive in PDE. He lists the three constructions which Quirk et al. (1985) call the

and Turville-Petre 1992: 31–37, Lass 1992: 2.9.2, Moessner and Schaefer 1987: 111–126).

[3] Other markers of modality are e.g. modal adverbs like *certainly, probably, possibly*.

were-subjunctive, the mandative subjunctive and the putative *should*-construction and rejects all of them as subjunctives: the first because it is restricted to conditional clauses, the second because it is rare in British English, and the last because *should* is a modal verb. The arguments put forward against the analysis of the first two constructions as subjunctives are invalid, because they rest on frequency alone. If frequency were a valid argument for denying the existence of a construction type, the construction type *may have been being examined* (Quirk et al. 1985: 151) should be denied its existence in PDE, too.

The authors of the *Cambridge Grammar* take up Palmer's concept of modality and set it off explicitly against the category mood: 'The distinction between mood and modality is like that between tense and time, or aspect and aspectuality: mood is a category of grammar, modality a category of meaning. Mood is the grammaticalisation of modality within the verbal system' (Huddleston and Pullum 2002: 172). They accept the traditional terms indicative, subjunctive and imperative as realisations of mood in the inflectional system of verbs, but concerning PDE they note that 'historical change has more or less eliminated mood from the inflectional system, with irrealis mood confined to 1st/3rd person singular *were*' (ibid.).[4] Very idiosyncratically they apply the term mood to the system of PDE modal auxiliaries.[5] By contrast their concept of modality is not so neatly defined. The authors admit that 'it is rather broad and finds expression in many areas of the language besides mood; it is, moreover, not sharply delimited or subdivided' (ibid.). In their list of linguistic expressions of modality we find past tense as an expression of modal remoteness, the clause types imperative and interrogative as expressions of directives and questions respectively, as well as subordination as an expression of non-factuality.[6] So far, the message of the *Cambridge Grammar* is that the subjunctive as realisation of the inflectional category mood does not exist in PDE except for the form *were* in the first and third person singular past of the verb *be*. The subjunctive is, however, reintroduced by the backdoor via subordination as a linguistic expression of the modality 'necessity or desirability of actualisation' (2002: 174). Since the model of the *Cambridge Grammar* does not allow the use of the term subjunctive for an inflectional form of the verb, the form *be* in the example *It's essential that he be told* is analysed as the plain form of

---

[4] According to the terminology used before, 'irrealis' should be replaced by 'subjunctive'.

[5] The authors are aware of their unusual terminology, which they justify in a footnote: 'we take the extension of the term to analytic systems to be parallel to the use of tense and aspect for analytic systems as well as inflectional ones' (Huddleston and Pullum 2002: 172, fn 47).

[6] The clause type declarative is described as the default clause type, which is associated with factual statements and therefore regarded as unmodalised.

the verb *be*. From the previous definition of the plain form as a secondary form of the inflectional paradigm of verbs (Huddleston and Pullum 2002: 83) it follows that the rejection of the term subjunctive for the form *be* in the above example is a mere matter of terminology. In chapter 10 of the *Cambridge Grammar*, on 'Clause type and illocutionary force', there is less hesitation to use the term subjunctive for examples like *God save the Queen*. They represent one of the minor optative clause types, they express the modality wish and they are realised by subjunctive constructions. In sum, the authors of the *Cambridge Grammar* make every effort to abolish mood as an inflectional category of the English verb and subjunctive as one of its realisations, but they do so at the expense of using an idiosyncratic definition of mood and of defining subjunctive as a clause type/construction type. The only linguistic property by which it is defined is that it contains a verb in its plain form. This is not a sufficient property, however, because the subjunctive clause type shares it with the imperative clause type. The concept of plain form in addition to the form of present tense plain involves the additional problem that in a given utterance the verb form can only be identified once the clause type is identified, but the identification of the latter relies on that of the former. In the utterance *They save the Queen* the verb form *save* can only be identified as present tense plain when the utterance has been identified as a declarative clause type, and the identification of the utterance as a realisation of the clause type declarative relies on the prior identification of the verb form as present tense plain. Similarly, in the utterance *God save the Queen* the verb form *save* can only be identified as plain form when the utterance has been identified as a subjunctive clause type and vice versa.

The idea of subjunctive as a clause type was elaborated by Bas Aarts. Starting from the assumption that Palmer's 1974 claim that the notion of a subjunctive mood had no place in English grammar was 'generally accepted in most modern descriptive frameworks' and that other studies failed to provide an alternative adequate description of English grammar, he proposes to fill this gap by positing 'a "subjunctive clause type", along with declaratives, interrogatives, imperatives and exclamatives' (Aarts 2012: 1). Before going into the details of this new model, he reviews other modern approaches to the analysis of the subjunctive (Anderson 2001, Huddleston and Pullum 2002, Quirk et al. 1985, Radford 1988). He points out that they disagree on whether subjunctive verbs and clauses containing these should be described as finite or non-finite. The reason for their disagreement is the use of different morphosyntactic properties or the different interpretation of the same morphosyntactic property in the decision about finiteness.[7] Then Aarts presents his own solution

---

[7] Radford (1988) uses the properties of an obligatory subject and of case-marking on the subject as markers of finiteness. Quirk et al. (1985) use a scale of finiteness

of what he calls the 'subjunctive conundrum' in the title of his article. He establishes subjunctive as a separate construction whose degree of finiteness is determined by its position on a scale of finiteness, which he acknowledges as a recast and extended version of Quirk et al.'s scale of finiteness. It contains the following properties: possible occurrence in an independent clause (a), tense contrast (b), person and number concord with the subject (c), *do*-support in negative and interrogative clauses (d), an obligatory subject (e), particular subordinators, typically *that* (f), and alternation with finite clauses (g). The prototypical finite clause is marked '+' for all these properties, while subjunctive clauses turn out to be peripherally finite on this scale. The corresponding subjunctive clause type is defined by its distinctive morphosyntactic properties: (1) no *do*-support when negated, (2) no syntactic independence (with a few formulaic exceptions), (3) no person/number concord, (4) no tense contrast. These properties also figure on Quirk et al.'s and on Aarts's scales of finiteness, on which subjunctive verb phrases/subjunctive clauses can be measured. Aarts's finiteness analysis seems to differ from Quirk et al.'s concerning properties (2) and (4). Yet this is not a categorical but only a gradual difference. Aarts acknowledges that subjunctive constructions also occur in independent clauses, although they are 'formulaic exceptions'. On the other hand Quirk et al. do not deny the occurrence of subjunctive verb phrases in subordinate clauses.[8] Although tense contrast is questioned/denied as a property of the subjunctive verb phrase/ the subjunctive clause type, both Quirk et al. and Aarts are aware of the so-called *were*-subjunctive, and they agree that it plays only a marginal role in PDE. It is also important to note that properties (e)–(g) of Aarts's scale of finiteness do not figure in his definition of the subjunctive clause type. The conclusion to be drawn is that the subjunctive clause type is defined on the basis of the morphosyntactic properties of its verb phrase. Yet Aarts neglects this point and argues that his subjunctive clause type fits nicely into a model with the other clause types of declarative, interrogative, imperative, exclamative.[9] In this model the

with five properties: finite verb phrases can occur in independent clauses (a), they have tense contrast (b), person and number concord with the subject (c), the first element in a finite verb phrase is an operator or a simple present or past form (d), finite verb phrases have mood, which indicates the status of the predication (e). On the basis of property (a), subjunctive verb phrases are analysed as finite in Quirk et al.'s grammar and by Radford (1988), whereas they are analysed as non-finite by Anderson (2001, 2007), because he denies them the capacity to license an independent predication.

[8] Cf. the formulation of the corresponding property: 'Finite verb phrases <u>can</u> occur as the verb phrase of independent clauses' (Quirk et al. 1985: 149) [my underlining]

[9] The subjunctive clause type is reminiscent of one of the *Cambridge Grammar*'s optative clause types which expresses the modality wish and is realised by a subjunctive construction, i.e. contains a verb in its plain form.

category mood has no place (with perhaps the exception of the indicative), the clause types are characterised by their typical uses. The correspondences are declarative/statement, interrogative/question, imperative/directive, exclamative/exclamation, subjunctive/directive. In this model, subjunctive clauses and imperative clauses cannot be distinguished by their typical use. The ambiguity is not removed either when we turn to the morphosyntactic properties that allegedly distinguish the two clause types. Aarts argues that the subjunctive clause type cannot occur in main clauses and the imperative clause type cannot occur in subordinate clauses. Yet he also said that subjunctive clauses do occur (exceptionally) in main clauses, and examples of the type *He answered: 'Leave me alone!'* document that imperative clauses can function as subordinate clauses.

For PDE, Aarts's subjunctive clause type might be saved by the feature 'obligatory subject', which figures only on his scale of finiteness, but not as one of the distinctive morphosyntactic properties of his subjunctive clause type. In this respect, PDE subjunctive clauses and imperative clauses differ. Obligatoriness of the subject is, however, not a feature of finite clauses in the historical periods of English. Since it was required at the outset that the model of the subjunctive to be used in this book should be valid for all periods of English, the obvious solution was to use mood in its traditional sense as an inflectional category and define subjunctive as one of its realisations.

The concept of the subjunctive as a realisation of the category mood is incomplete if it does not include the shades of meaning that this form contributes to an utterance. This is in line with Portner's definition of verbal mood (2012: 1262) as 'a distinction in form among clauses based on the presence, absence, or type of modality in the grammatical context in which they occur'.

The meaning aspect appears under many guises in earlier descriptions of the subjunctive. For Behre (1934: 1) the subjunctive 'is capable of serving to indicate certain mental attitudes on the part of the speaker towards the verbal activity . . .'. Among these mental attitudes two are especially prominent, namely will and wish. The former is given when the realisation of an action depends on the authority of the speaker, the latter when it depends on factors beyond the speaker's control. In the first case the subjunctive is used to express 'exhortation, command, demand, instruction, etc.', in the second it expresses 'prayer, humble petition or request . . . hope or longing, etc.' (1934: 9). In his chapter on the subjunctive Visser (1963–1973: §§834–895) avoids the term subjunctive and uses 'modally marked form' instead. The modality which he associates with the subjunctive is 'non-fact', and he adds the specifications 'wish, imagination, contingency, doubt, diffidence, uncertainty, supposition, potentiality, etc.' (§834). Yet the subjunctive is not the only marker of non-fact modality. Among Visser's list of other non-fact modality markers are subordinating conjunctions, modal auxiliaries, matrix verbs like *desire*, modal adverbs and word order (type 'go we').

Visser draws attention to the importance of the element 'form' in his term 'modally marked form', because he is aware of possible misinterpretations of the term 'subjunctive', which he detected already in the works of 'the earliest English grammarians', where the subjunctive was introduced as a form of the verb, but understood as a meaning of the verb. It is not quite clear to which grammarians Visser refers, but the tendency to interpret subjunctive as a meaning is quite obvious in grammars of the EModE period. Bullokar in his *Bref Grammar for English* (1586: 28) and Joshua Poole in *The English Accidence* (1646: 13) claim that the subjunctive has the same forms as the indicative. Charles Butler in *The English Grammar* (1634: 46) and Jeremiah Wharton in his *English Grammar* (1654: 43), who use the term 'potential' instead of subjunctive, describe its form as a sequence of a modal auxiliary and the infinitive.[10] The foregrounding of the meaning aspect is also visible in the treatment of mandative constructions in the *Cambridge Grammar* (Huddleston and Pullum 2002: 995), where noun clauses with indicative verbs like *They demand that the park remains open* are interpreted as mandative because they express deontic modality.

Although the term modality is not used, the conditions for the use of the so-called mandative subjunctive are spelled out in semantic terms in more recent publications as well: it can be used 'with any verb in a *that*-clause ... introduced by an expression of demand, recommendation, proposal, resolution, intention, etc.' (Quirk et al. 1985: 156), after 'verbs and nouns which express, or signify, volition' (Övergaard 1995: 92), and 'after suasive verbs, nouns and emotive adjectives such as *demand, order, imperative*, and *necessary*' (Hoffmann 1997: 13).

In the only book-length publication on the meaning of the English subjunctive James (1986: 13) defines modality as 'a linguistic term for manner of representation'. He posits two manners of representation of the state of affairs in the world. The first manner of representation intends that it matches the state of affairs in the world. This is the case for example when an architect draws a sketch of a house after it has been built. The second manner of representation intends that the state of affairs in the world match its representation. This is the case when the architect draws a sketch of a house that he intends to build. These constellations are reminiscent of Searle's (1976: 3) two directions of fit between words and the world to which James refers. Both authors use the term epistemic modality for the first manner of representation and root

[10] Cf. also Dons (2004: 98–109).

modality for the second manner of representation. Epistemic modality is given in assertions, explanations, statements, descriptions, etc. (e.g. *John knows that his future wife is a good cook*), and root modality is given in requests, commands, vows, promises, etc. (e.g. *John wishes that his future wife be a good cook*). This terminology corresponds to Visser's dichotomy fact and non-fact modality.

Root modality can be expressed by the subjunctive. However, it can also be expressed by imperatives and by more complex verbal syntagms, especially by those of the form 'modal/semi-modal auxiliary + infinitive'. The analysis of modality is complicated by the fact that some modal auxiliaries can express root modality and epistemic modality. Depending on the context the sentence *John may go to the party* can mean that he is allowed to go to the party or that it is likely that he will go to the party. In the first case *may* expresses the root modality permission, in the second it expresses the epistemic modality possibility/probability. Since James is only concerned with the semantics of the subjunctive, he does not discuss the ambiguity of modal auxiliaries.

In another approach to semantics modality is decribed in terms of quantification over possible worlds (Hintikka 1962). In possible world semantics the number of modalities is not restricted by the direction of fit criterion, but an indefinite number of modalities is posited. They are classified along the dimensions 'force' (necessity vs. possibility) and 'flavour'. The flavour of an element expressing modality is determined by the sets of possible worlds with which it is compatible. If an expression of modality quantifies over worlds compatible with a body of rules, it has the flavour deontic, if it quantifies over worlds compatible with a set of wishes, it has the flavour bouletic, and if it quantifies over worlds compatible with the available evidence, it has the flavour epistemic, etc. (Hacquard 2012: 1486). The ambiguity of modal auxiliaries plays a prominent role in standard possible world semantics.

In Kratzer's model of modality in possible worlds semantics the problems stemming from this ambiguity are solved by adding the variables 'context of use' and 'conversational background' (Kratzer 1991: 640–641). This makes modality a category of pragmatics. Kratzer argues that the epistemic interpretation of the sentence *John may go to the party* derives from its context of use, which is specified by expressions such as *given that John loves parties, that he is a good friend of the person who organised the party, that on the day of the party he will be back from his stay abroad*, etc. These and other pieces of information form the conversational background of the sentence. It can be paraphrased as *in view of the available evidence*, and in possible world semantics it is formally represented as a function that relates worlds to sets of propositions. So, the conversational background explains why a modal auxiliary in a given sentence receives a particular modal interpretation, and it is not necessary to postulate an inherent ambiguity for some modal auxiliaries. When the sentence *John may go to the party* is interpreted as expressing deontic modality, it is also related to a world that is compatible with the speaker's experience. Yet the world of experience which is at issue here contains elements such as *John's mother persuaded her husband to apply less strict rules in the education of their son* or *John did his father a favour for which he wants to reward his son* or *the party was organised by John as a birthday present for his father*, etc. The conversational background of the deontic interpretation can be paraphrased as *in view of the rules holding in John's family*.

Hacquard (2012: 1495) rightly points out that the standard version of possible world semantics fails to account for several systematic differences (e.g. speaker-orientedness vs. subject-orientedness) between epistemic modality and non-epistemic ('circumstantial modality' in Kratzer's terminology, 'root modality' in James's terminology) modality. Kratzer (1991: 643) deals with this problem by introducing the concept of graded modality. Graded modality implies two types of conversational background, one from which the 'modal base' is derived (in the case of epistemic modality paraphrased as *in view of the available evidence*), which determines the type of modality, and a second conversational background, which introduces an ordering. It is called the 'ordering source', and it ranges from necessity to possibility. The modal base of circumstantial modality is derived from the conversational backgrounds that are paraphrased as *in view of a set of rules, in view of the speaker's wishes*, etc. The two kinds of modal bases which Kratzer posits for English (1991: 646) are distinguished by their conversational backgrounds:

> . . . circumstantial and epistemic conversational backgrounds involve different kinds of facts. In using an epistemic modal, we are interested in what else may or must be the case in our world given all the evidence available. Using a circumstantial modal, we are interested in the necessities implied by or the possibilities opened up by certain sorts of facts.

My understanding of modality combines aspects from Searle-type semantics and from possible world semantics. I consider the direction of fit between words and the world as the most important classification criterion of modality. Epistemic modality is given when an illocutionary act is intended to get words to match the world. The conversational background of sentences expressing epistemic modality can be paraphrased as *in view of what the speaker knows* or *in view of what the speaker derives from all available evidence*. When epistemic modality is expressed by the verbal syntagm, the available forms are the indicative and combinations of modal auxiliaries/semi-auxiliaries with the infinitive of lexical verbs.[11] Epistemic modality realised by indicatives reflects a position near the necessity pole of the ordering source, epistemic modality realised by combinations of modal auxiliaries/semi-auxiliaries with infinitives reflects positions towards the possibility pole of the ordering source. Root modality is given when an illocutionary act is intended to get the world to match the words. Depending on the type of root modality, the conversational background of sentences expressing root modality can be paraphrased as *in view of the speaker's orders* (deontic modality) and *in view of the speaker's wishes* (bouletic modality), etc. When root modality is expressed by the verbal syntagm, the available forms are the subjunctive, the imperative and combinations of modal auxiliaries/semi-auxiliaries with the infinitive of lexical verbs. The different realisations also reflect different positions on the ordering source with the imperative nearest to the necessity pole of the ordering source.

The model of the subjunctive which I will use in this book integrates its formal aspect described in terms of the morphological category mood and its meaning aspect described in terms of the semantic/pragmatic category modality. It is illustrated by Figure 1.1.

The forms of the verbal syntagm which compete with the subjunctive depend on the construction type involved; the number of forms in the verbal syntagm in which the subjunctive is overtly marked depends on the language period, e.g. in relative clauses the imperative does not compete with the subjunctive, and in OE only the first person singular is not overtly marked for mood.

The expression of modality in the verbal syntagm also depends on the construction type involved. Since in simple sentences only one verbal syntagm is involved, it necessarily expresses modality. In complex sentences, where several verbal syntagms are involved, modality can be expressed in one or more than one verbal syntagm.

1.3 Corpus considerations

One of the key issues in corpus linguistics is the representativeness of a corpus (Biber 1993, Biber et al. 1998, Bungarten 1979, Leech 2007, Rieger 1979). Before the compilation of the first electronic corpora in the 1970s, representativeness was not discussed in linguistics. Descriptions of large amounts of data existed (e.g. Jespersen 1909–1949, Visser 1963–1973), but it was tacitly assumed that these data faithfully represented the language use of the periods under investigation.

---

[11] This is where my concept of modality differs from that advocated in the *Cambridge Grammar*: 'The default clause type, the declarative, is associated with factual statements and . . . can (in the absence of any other relevant marking) be regarded as unmodalised' (Huddleston and Pullum 2002: 174).

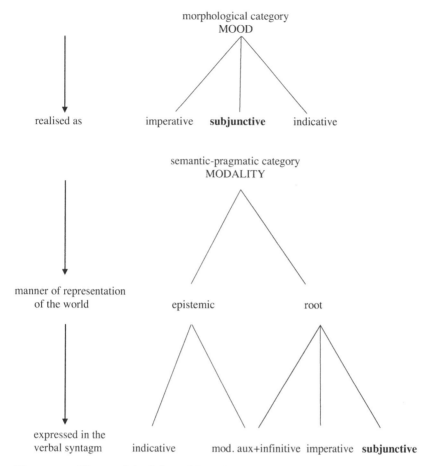

morphological category
MOOD

realised as   imperative   **subjunctive**   indicative

semantic-pragmatic category
MODALITY

manner of representation
of the world   epistemic   root

expressed in the
verbal syntagm   indicative   mod. aux+infinitive imperative **subjunctive**

Figure 1.1 The model of the subjunctive

The compilers of the *Brown Corpus*, by contrast, were aware of the desirability of representativeness. Francis described a linguistic corpus as 'a collection of texts assumed to be representative of a given language, dialect, or other subset of a language, to be used for linguistic analysis' (Francis 1979: 110). The universe of texts from which the samples of the *Brown Corpus* were taken was determined as 'edited English prose printed in the United States during the calendar year 1961' (*Brown Corpus Manual*). The text categories and the number and size of the texts to be included in each category were decided upon during a conference at Brown University in 1963. It was clear at the outset that the corpus to be sampled under these conditions could not be fully random and thus could not really be representative of twentieth-century American English.

A similar restricted representativeness was also acknowledged by the compilers of the *LOB Corpus*: '. . . the present corpus is not representative in a strict statistical sense . . . The true "representativeness" of the present corpus arises from the deliberate attempt to include relevant categories and subcategories of texts rather than from blind statistical choice' (Johansson 1978: 14). The same compilation strategies were also followed for the FLOB and Frown corpora to make them compatible with their predecessors.

Even more problems are involved in the compilation of diachronic corpora, especially when they are to cover the earliest periods of the English language. The amount of available data becomes smaller the further we go back in time, their quality is poorer and some text types simply did not exist in earlier periods. The compilers of the *Helsinki Corpus* (HC) were aware of these limitations, and they devised a complex system of text classification with a wider grid of seven prototypical text categories and a narrower grid of thirty-four text types (Kytö 1996: 46; Kytö and Rissanen 1993: 10–14; Rissanen 1994: 76–77). This does not make the HC fully representative, but on a scale of representativeness it occupies a rather high position. It is certainly because of its sophisticated text classification system that the HC has become the standard corpus for the analysis of linguistic features of the historical periods of the English language. Therefore, it was only natural that the data for the present book should come from this corpus. Unfortunately, the HC stops at the end of the EModE period.

It was tempting to use ARCHER (*A Representative Corpus of Historical English Registers*), the other multi-purpose historical corpus of the English language, for the following periods up to the twentieth century. Here another crucial property of linguistic corpora needs to be considered, namely the comparability of corpora. As Leech (2007: 142) points out, 'comparability, like representativeness, can be conceptualised as a scale, rather than as a goal to be achieved 100 per cent'. Biber et al. (1994: 1), one of the compilers of ARCHER, explains that it was 'designed to investigate the diachronic relations among oral and literate registers of English between 1650 and the present'. From his description of its aims it becomes clear that it was designed as a self-contained corpus with a particular focus on the differences between written and oral registers and between British and American English. Another aim was to allow the investigation of the changing writing styles in the representative journals *Philosophical Transactions of the Royal Society* and *Edinburgh Medical Journal*. These aims explain ARCHER's make-up. In its original version (ARCHER-1), which was compiled in the early 1990s by Douglas Biber (Northern Arizona University) and Edward Finegan (University of Southern California), it contained the seven written registers – journals/diaries, letters, fiction prose, news, legal opinion, medicine, and science

– and the three speech-based registers – fiction dialogue, drama, and sermons. The texts were arranged in ten fifty-year periods, and for each period ARCHER-1 contained ten files of about 2,000 words in each register. After the universe of texts was established, the sampling proceeded randomly for most registers. Special limitations held for the registers legal opinion, medicine and science. The samples for the latter two registers were taken from the journals mentioned above, and here only from special volumes. The samples of the first register were selected from decisions of the *Supreme Court of Pennsylvania*. British English samples for this register were missing.

In the meantime, ARCHER developed into a corpus in progress.[12] In the present context it is important to mention that the version ARCHER 3.2 will also include British English legal texts. Yet they will not enhance the comparability between the HC and ARCHER, because the legal texts in the corpora belong to different genres; those in the HC are legislative texts with a prescriptive function, whereas those prepared for ARCHER 3.2 are legal opinions with a descriptive function.[13] Comparability is also adversely affected by the different kinds of science and medicine texts in the two corpora. In HC the texts of these registers are passages from book-length publications, whereas the corrresponding ARCHER texts are self-contained articles. That different formats represent different aspects of language variation was shown by Moessner (2009) in a multidimensional analysis of the science texts of the second half of the seventeenth century in ARCHER and a parallel corpus of HC-like texts. Even if some other text categories in ARCHER and the HC can be matched (e.g. sermons, letters), the overall compilation principles of the two corpora are too different to consider them as comparable corpora.

For twentieth-century English, comparable corpora are available for the analysis of subjunctive use in British English. The time span which can be investigated is becoming bigger through work in progress on B-LOB,[14] a 1931 counterpart of LOB and FLOB, and it reaches into the twenty-first century with *The British English 2006 Corpus* (BE06). These corpora have recently been exploited in a diachronic study by Tim Waller (2017), who in his doctoral dissertation traces the development of the subjunctive in mandative constructions.

---

[12] The history of ARCHER is aptly documented in Yañez-Bouza (2011).

[13] López-Couso and Méndez-Naya (2012: 8) describe them as follows: 'Legal or judicial opinions . . . are accounts written by a judge or a group of judges which accompany an order or ruling in a case, explain the facts of the case, and clarify the rationale and the legal principles of the ruling.'

[14] Cf. Leech and Smith (2005), 'Extending the possibilities of corpus-based research in the twentieth century: A prequel to LOB and FLOB', *ICAME Journal*, 29, pp. 83–98.

Because of the present corpus situation, the development of the subjunctive can be approached from two ends with a gap in between. Comparable results can be achieved on the basis of the HC for the periods OE, ME and EModE. Comparable results can also be achieved on the basis of the corpora of the extended Brown family for the twentieth/twenty-first century. There are two ways of bridgeing the gap in between. Both require an additional corpus along the compilation principles of either the HC or those of the Brown family. There is one corpus which matches the earlier parts of the HC exactly and contains texts up to the First World War, namely *The Penn Parsed Corpus of Modern British English*. Unfortunately, this corpus is not accessible to me, and this is why the present book will be based on the HC only and therefore necessarily will stop at the end of the EModE period.

All three periods of the HC exist in traditional non-annotated form, but also as extended and annotated versions (*The York-Toronto-Helsinki Parsed Corpus of Old English Prose*, *The York-Helsinki Parsed Corpus of Old English Poetry*, *The Penn-Helsinki Parsed Corpus of Middle English*, *The Penn-Helsinki Parsed Corpus of Early Modern English*). The latter allow automatic searches for special morphological forms and special syntactic patterns. They would have been preferable tools for data collection, if only a quantitative analysis had been intended. Yet since each relevant verbal syntagm had to be analysed in its situational context to capture its modality, I decided to use the original form of the HC.

As a consequence of this decision the corpus to be established for this book had to be restricted to a subset of the files of the HC. It reflects the structure of the complete HC with respect to the parameters period, region, text category and format (prose vs. verse). The period specifications O1, O2, O3 and O4 for the OE subcorpora, M1, M1, M1 and M4 for the ME subcorpora, and E1, E2, E3 for the EModE subcorpora were taken over from the HC as well as the names for the seven text categories: STA (statutory), IS (instruction secular), IR (instruction religious), NI (narration imaginative), NN (narration non-imaginative), EX (expository) and XX (none of the others). It comprises thirty files of 128,200 words in its OE part, thirty-one files of 166,390 words in its ME part and thirty files of 193,140 words in its EModE part.

1.4 Research agenda and research method

So far only individual aspects of the history of the English subjunctive have been investigated, e.g. the subjunctive in a particular construction type, the subjunctive in a particular period, the subjunctive in a particular text type, etc. What is lacking is a combination of these (and perhaps other) aspects. Therefore, the first topic on my research agenda is to produce a comprehensive and consistent description of the English subjunctive in all construction types where it is attested across the periods OE, ME and EModE. It must include an answer to the question of which linguistic patterns competed with – and perhaps ultimately replaced – the subjunctive.

From the results presented in earlier studies it can be concluded that the simplification of the verbal paradigm lead to a long-term frequency decrease of the subjunctive. This cannot be the whole truth, because it is not compatible with the observation that in PDE the subjunctive is next to non-existent in relative clauses, is restricted to set phrases and 'formulaic frames' (Huddleston and Pullum 2002: 944) in main clauses, has been increasing in noun clauses since the beginning of the twentieth century, and enjoys different degrees of popularity in different types of adverbial clauses. It is not compatible either with the observation that in PDE adverbial clauses of reason the indicative prevails, whereas in concessive subclauses the subjunctive enjoys a healthy life. Therefore, the second topic on my research agenda is to find an answer to the question of which factors apart from the simplification of the verbal paradigm account for the frequency development of the English subjunctive. Here modality as the meaning component of the subjunctive and its communicative purpose will play an important role.

This agenda required close reading of all texts of my corpus so as to identify all relevant verbal syntagms, and only those. Since the verbal paradigm was simplified during the history of the English langue, it was to be expected that the number of relevant verbal syntagms would decrease from period to period. The verbal syntagms which had to be identified were those realised by the subjunctive and those competing with the subjunctive in the construction types main clause (*The devil take the hindmost*), adverbial clause (*If a water authority have not before the commencement of this Act made any such byelaws for a part of their area, the Minister may make such byelaws for that part of that area with or without a local inquiry*), noun clause (*It is important that the process be carried out accurately* or *he demanded that she be informed*) and adjectival relative clause (*A clause that exhibit subjunctive mood marking, P_{SUB}, is defined only if ... P_{SUB} is evaluated with respect to modal bases $f(w)$*[15]).[16]

The competitors of the subjunctive follow from its definition as realising the category mood and contributing to the expression of root modality. Modal and semi-modal constructions compete with the subjunctive in all periods. The imperative as a competitor of the subjunctive is restricted to the second person, and the indicative is excluded from the list of competitors of the subjunctive in main clauses.

---

[15] Panzeri (2006: 64).
[16] The terminology of clause types follows Quirk et al. (1985).

The formal marking of the subjunctive differs from period to period. In OE, the subjunctive was marked in the second and third person singular present and in all persons of plural present, and additionally in all persons of plural past and in the second person singular past of weak verbs and in the first and third person singular past of strong verbs. The inflectional paradigm of *beon/wesan* 'be' distinguished even more different forms. The verb *be* is a high-frequency verb in all periods of English, but the inclusion of its additional subjunctive forms would have biased the results of the quantitative analyses, because texts with an exceptionally big number of occurrences of *be* would stand a greater chance of scoring high for subjunctives; this is why *be* was treated on a par with all other verbs. The exclusion of the past forms of all verbs followed from a similar argument. If they were included in the counts, the results of the quantitative analyses would depend on the distribution of weak and strong verbs in the texts of my corpus and on the distribution of second vs. first and third person singular verbal syntagms. With these restrictions the relevant verbal syntagms in the ME part of my corpus were those of the second and third person singular present tense. In the second person singular the subjunctive was formally marked only after the subject *thou*. This counted as an additional restriction on the number of relevant verbal syntagms. This restriction was even more prominent in the EModE period, so that in most EModE texts of my corpus only third person singular present tense forms proved relevant.

Each relevant verbal syntagm was coded for its location in a particular text, so that it could be rediscovered after its analysis when one of its properties needed to be commented on. Then the parameters for the analysis were set up. Among those provided by the parameter coding of the HC the following were taken over: period (including the subperiods O1 = before 850, O2 = 850–950, O3 = 950–1050, O4 = 1050–1150 for OE, M1 = 1150–1250, M2 = 1250–1350, M3 = 1350–1420, M4 = 1420–1500 for ME, and E1 = 1500–1570, E2 = 1570–1640, E3 = 1640–1710 for EModE); region (with the variables Anglian, Kentish and West Saxon for OE, and Northern, East Midland, West Midland, Southern, Kentish for ME); text category (with the variables STA = statutory, IS = instruction secular, IR = instruction religious, NI = narration imaginative, NN = narration non-imaginative, EX = expository, XX = unclassified); and format (with the variable prose and poetry). They were supplemented by the morphosyntactic parameters person, number, mood, and construction type (with the variables main clause, adjectival relative clause, noun clause and adverbial clause). For each construction type a separate data sheet was prepared which contains additional construction type specific parameters. The construction type specific parameters for adjectival relative clauses are relative marker, antecedent and mood of the matrix verb. The data sheet for noun clauses contains the construction type specific parameters noun clause function, clause type (with the variables declarative, *wh*-interrogative, *yes/no*-interrogative, and (nominal) relative), and mood of the matrix verb. The construction type specific parameters for adverbial clauses are clause type (with the variables temporal clause, clause of place, clause of reason, concessive clause, conditional clause, clause of purpose/result, comparative clause), conjunction, mood of the matrix verb, and negation of the matrix clause. These data sheets were processed with the statistics program SPSS. The resulting quantitative analysis was used as the starting point for the derivation of a comprehensive and consistent picture of subjunctive use. Its features were then interpreted qualitatively with the aim of detecting the factors that apart from the simplification of the verbal paradigm in the history of English contributed to the frequency decrease during the periods investigated.

1.5 Structure of the book and mode of presentation

The structure of the book is geared towards the expectations of different types of readers, and its mode of presentation follows from its empirical focus and its corpus-linguistic approach.

Chapters 2–5 deal with subjunctive use in individual construction types. Chapter 2 describes subjunctive use in main clauses, Chapter 3 in adjectival relative clauses, Chapter 4 in noun clauses and Chapter 5 in adverbial clauses. Each chapter follows the chronological order from OE via ME to EModE, and each period starts with a survey of earlier studies and introduces the relevant research parameters, then follows the analysis of the data in the corresponding part of the corpus.

These chapters are self-contained so that the reader who is only interested in one construction type will find the information s/he is looking for in all detail but in condensed form in one chapter and not spread across the whole book. The picture of subjunctive use to be derived from these chapters is necessarily restricted because it is construction type specific.

Other readers may want to get a survey of subjunctive use in one special historical period. They are advised first of all to turn to the first three sections of Chapter 6, where the results of the analyses of subjunctive use in all construction types are joined together: in section 6.1 for OE, in section 6.2 for ME and in section 6.3 for EModE. This combination of pieces of information coming from two different points of view results in a more comprehensive – if you like two-dimensional – picture of subjunctive use. For readers who skipped Chapters 2–5 frequent cross-references are provided.

A multidimensional picture of subjunctive use is provided in the last section of Chapter 6, where the diachronic perspective is added. It contains the synthesis of the construction type specific and the period specific analyses and hopefully satisfies the expectations raised by the research agenda.

The last chapter (Epilogue: Summary and outlook) briefly summarises the main results of the study and discusses the parameters with a particularly noteworthy influence on the development of subjunctive use at particular points in time. They are identified as starting points for further rewarding research, among them the unexpected rising frequency trend of the subjunctive in main clauses in EModE, the special role played by the third person singular, by the text category statutory texts and by the parameter modality.

All issues addressed in the book are illustrated by examples from the corpus. Their source is given in the form used in the HC, so that they are easily recoverable in their bigger context. Yet the symbols '+a', '+d', etc. have been expanded for the sake of easier readability. Modern English translations are provided for OE and ME examples; the sources of those translations which were taken over from earlier editions of a text are indicated explicitly.

The quantitative results of the analysis are displayed in tables, usually as absolute numbers and as percentage values. Both figures are relevant for the interpretation of the tables: when a feature – say, the subjunctive – is attested five times in a population of ten items, this equals 50 per cent and seems quite remarkable. Yet the population is so small that the result of 50 per cent is hardly generalisable. It is also important that the distribution of the subjunctive and its competitors is measured in terms of the relevant verbal syntagms, not in terms of the size of the texts in which they are attested. The following example clarifies why this is a preferable measure for the distribution of frequencies. When a feature – say, the subjunctive – occurs fifty times in a text of 1,000 words containing 100 relevant verbal syntagms and also fifty times in another text of 1,000 words containing only fifty relevant verbal syntagms, the frequency calculation on the basis of text size yields the same result for both texts, namely a frequency of 50/1,000 words. The frequency calculation on the basis of the number of relevant verbal syntagms yields a frequency of 50 per cent in the first text, and of 100 per cent in the second text. This result is much more telling, since in the first text only every second verbal syntagm is realised by a subjunctive, whereas in the second text all verbal syntagms are realised by the subjunctive. This holds irrespective of the size of the two texts.

2

The subjunctive in main clauses

Grammars and handbooks of all periods of the English language agree that the subjunctive in main clauses expresses a special type of modality. The terminology varies: 'directives and exhortations' (Traugott 1992: 184); 'le souhait réalisable, le conseil, la prescription, le commandemant et, à la forme négative, l'interdiction' (Mossé 1945: 151); 'wishes and commands' (Burrow and Turville-Petre 1992: 48); 'contingency and supposition' (Fischer 1992: 246); 'wishes and exhortations' (Nevalainen 2006: 97); 'desire' (Görlach 1991: 113); 'doubt, unreality, wishes, commands' (Denison 1998: 160).[1]

These types of modality are captured in speech act theory by the notion of directive speech act. In directive speech acts, an agent commands, requests, recommends, desires, etc. that an action be performed (Searle 1976: 11). According to my descriptive model of the subjunctive directive speech acts express several kinds of root modality, in particular deontic and bouletic modality. Subjunctives are, however, only one realisation possibility of directive speech acts. The competitors of subjunctives are identified via their modality.

For PDE, several descriptive models of directive speech acts exist; they correlate communicative intentions and linguistic structures (Blum-Kulka et al. 1989: 18, Diani 2001: 78f., Ervin-Tripp 1976: 29, Trosborg 1995: 35). Basically, these models distinguish between direct and indirect directives, and within these categories between types of a higher or lower degree of directness or explicitness. The illocutionary force of these types is expressed by well-defined sets of linguistic patterns.

My treatment of the subjunctive in main clauses will progress along the periods OE, ME and EModE, and each period will start with a review of

---

[1] Although Mitchell (1985: §877) agrees that 'when the *subjunctive* is found, some mental attitude to what is being said is usually implied – condition, desire, obligation, supposition, perplexity, doubt, uncertainty, or unreality', he rejects the idea of a complementary distribution of the indicative as an expression of epistemic and the subjunctive as an expression of root modality.

relevant publications and will be followed by the analysis of my corpus of the respective period.

2.1 Old English main clauses: the subjunctive and its competitors in earlier publications

Models of the type described above have also been applied to the analysis of directives in texts of earlier periods (Culpeper and Archer 2008, Kohnen 2000, 2002, 2007, 2008a, 2008b, Moessner 2010b). Only Kohnen (2000, 2007, 2008a, 2008b) includes data from the OE period. The most complex model which he uses for the analysis of directives in prayers, sermons and letters (Kohnen 2008b) distinguishes the following seven types of directives:

1. Direct directives
    i.   Performatives
    ii.   Imperatives
    iii. Modal constructions
2. Indirect directives
    iv.   Hearer-based interrogatives
    v.   Speaker-based declaratives
    vi.   Hearer-based conditionals
    vii. Other manifestations

His label 'imperatives' is a cover term for proper imperatives, subjunctives and constructions with *uton* or *let*, and 'modal constructions' include 'impersonal or passive constructions which denote obligation' (Kohnen 2008b: 299). The linguistic patterns realising types ii and iii are also treated as equivalents of the OE subjunctive in grammars, handbooks and special studies. Therefore, they will be dealt with here in some detail in their function as competitors of the subjunctive in the second and third person singular and in all persons of the plural present.

2.1.1 *The imperative*

There is general agreement that in the second person singular and plural the strongest competitor of the subjunctive is the imperative. In his doctoral dissertation on *The Subjunctive in Old English Poetry* Frank Behre distinguishes a hortative and an optative subjunctive in main clauses. He attests the imperative a higher frequency than both subjunctive subclasses. Concerning the hortative subjunctive, he explains the rarity of examples by 'the fact that OE, like other languages, has a proper mood of command, i.e. the imperative' (Behre 1934: 16). Mitchell (1985: §896) considers the imperative singular the prevailing form, and it is only with some hesitation that he admits unambiguous forms of the subjunctive of the second person singular. For the second person plural he accepts the subjunctive, because otherwise there would be no unambiguous form for the expression of a wish or exhortation in main clauses with a subject (§§909–911). Traugott, who takes the functional equivalence of the two moods for granted, stresses the meaning difference between imperative and subjunctive: 'Because the imperative and subjunctive contrast morphologically, we must assume that there was a difference in meaning, at least in early OE times, between more or less directive, more or less wishful utterances' (Traugott 1992: 185). Frequency comparisons between subjunctives and imperatives cannot be derived from Kohnen's results, because both moods figure in the same type of directive.

2.1.2 *Modal constructions*

Modal constructions, i.e. patterns of the form 'modal auxiliary + infinitive', compete with subjunctives in all persons and numbers. The modal auxiliaries which are usually mentioned in the relevant publications are **sculan* (Behre 1934: 19f., Mitchell 1985: §918) and **þurfan* (Mitchell 1985: §918). These modal auxiliaries are classified as equivalents of the hortative subjunctive by Behre, whereas he identifies *motan*, *magan* and *willan* as equivalents of the optative subjunctive (1934: 30f.). Mitchell, who does not explicitly distinguish between a hortative and an optative subjunctive, describes the construction '*nelle þu* + infinitive' as 'an alternative in second person negative commands and wishes' (1985: §917; cf. Traugott 1992: 185). Taking up the debate 'whether or not OE had syntactic auxiliary verbs', Traugott (1992: 186) attributes auxiliary status to *willan*, **motan*, **sculan*, *magan* and *cunnan*. She calls them 'pre-modals' and attests them the possibility of expressing modal meanings, yet without explicitly discussing them in the context of the subjunctive.[2]

2.1.3 *'Semi-auxiliary (+ to) + infinitive'*

It is probably the expression of a modal meaning which motivated Traugott (1992: 194) to describe another construction, namely '*beon + to* + inflected infinitive', together with the pre-modal verbs; it will here be classified as one of the realisations of the pattern 'semi-auxiliary (+ to) + infinitive'. Mitchell (1985: §§934–944) extensively discusses it as an

---

[2] Denison (1993: 330) interprets Traugott's comment on her example (1992: 195) with **sculan* as proof that she considers the construction 'pre-verbal + infinitive' as an equivalent of the subjunctive.

equivalent of the Latin gerund. That the construction also serves as an equivalent of the subjunctive can be derived from its meaning 'expressing necessity or obligation' and from examples like *Bi þæm midlestan is nu to secgenne* . . . (Bede 334. 30; quot. Mitchell 1985: §937) as a translation of Latin *De medio nunc dicamus*. . . . The construction is impersonal with the person on whom the necessity or obligation falls, expressed by a substantival syntagm or a pronoun in dative. Pronouns like *hit* or *þæt* occur as optional grammatical subjects. Visser (1963–1973: §367) distinguishes three construction types with the surface form '*Beon* + *to* + infinitive', all of them expressing obligation, duty or necessity. In the first type, '*us is to donne hit*', the person whose duty or obligation it is to carry out the action denoted by the inflected infinitive is expressed by a noun or pronoun in dative. This impersonal construction type dies out after the OE period and is replaced by personal constructions of the type '*we are to* + infinitive'. In the second construction type, '*þæt þing is to donne*', the performer of the action is not expressed, but – as Visser says – is 'present in the mind of the speaker'. The construction type is personal, and 'the person or thing referred to by the subject functions as the object of the activity denoted by the infinitive' (Visser 1963–1973: §1384). In the ME period it was replaced by a construction with a passive infinitive. The third construction type, '*þonne is to arisenne*' is impersonal. It contains no subject, and its verb is intransitive. Visser (1963–1973: §368) claims that it became 'extinct before the Modern Period'. His last example dates from 1425.

2.1.4 '*Uton* + *infinitive*'

The subjunctive of the first person plural also competes with the construction '*Uton* +/- personal pronoun + infinitive' (Mitchell 1985: §916, Traugott 1992: 185). Since the construction expresses a mild request, it is only natural that Behre (1934: 19) mentions it only as an alternative of the hortative subjunctive.

2.2 The subjunctive and its competitors in the OE corpus

The relevant verbal syntagms of the OE part of my corpus are realised by subjunctives, imperatives, 'modal auxiliary + infinitive', 'semi-modal (+ *to*) + infinitive' and '*Uton* + infinitive'. The realisations for the individual persons and numbers are summarised in Table 2.1.[3]

---

[3] Non-self-explanatory abbreviations used in the tables are explained in individual footnotes.

Table 2.1 The subjunctive and its competitors in OE main clauses

	Subjunctive	Imperative	Modal	Semi-modal	*Uton*
2nd ps sg	✕	✕	✕		
3rd ps sg	✕		✕	✕	
1st ps pl	✕	✕	✕		✕
2nd ps pl	✕	✕	✕		
3rd ps pl	✕		✕	✕	

Examples of each realisation possibility are given below:

2nd person singular
Subjunctive:

[2.1]   *wite þu þæt Apollonius ariht arædde mynne rædels* (O3 NI FICT
        APOLL, p. 6) 'be aware that Appollonius knew the right answer to my
        riddle'

Imperative:

[2.2]   *adryg gate blod & gnid to duste* (O2/3 IS HANDM QUADR, p. 35)
        'dry goat's blood and rub it to powder'

Modal construction:

[2.3]   *þu sweltan scealt mid feo and mid feorme* (OX/3 XX XX GEN, p. 79)
        'you shall die with your riches and possessions'

3rd person singular
Subjunctive:

[2.4]   *hæbbe þone ylcan dom* (O3 STA LAW LAW11C, p. 315) '[he shall]
        have the same judgement'

Modal construction:

[2.5]   *Mid þam pater nostre man sceal to Gode gebiddan* (O3 IR HOM
        WULF8C, p. 176) 'with the Lord's Prayer man shall pray to God'

Semi-modal construction:

[2.6]   *Se is to lufianne & to weorðianne ofer ealle oðre ðing* (O3 IR HOM
        WULF8C, p. 207) 'He [= the Lord] is to be loved and to be praised
        beyond everything else'

1st person plural[4]
Subjunctive:[5]

[2.7]   *Bidden we nu men þa untodeledlican þrinnesse* (O2/4 NN BIL CHAD,
        p. 184) 'let us pray now, men, to the undivided trinity'

Modal construction:

[2.8]   *On ðisum wræcfullum life we sceolon earmra manna helpan* (O3 IR

---

[4] Dual forms are subsumed under plural.
[5] The postposition of the subject pronoun is optional; introductory particles tend to
     trigger it.

HOM AELFR2/8, p. 258) 'in this miserable life we shall help poor people'

Uton + infinitive:

[2.9]   *ac utan don swa us þearf is* (O3 IR HOM WULF8C, p. 181) 'but let us do as we should'

2nd person plural

Subjunctive:

[2.10]   *Ne swergen ge næfre under hæðne godas* (O2 STA LAW ALFLAWIN, p. 42) 'you shall never swear by heathen gods'

Imperative:

[2.11]   *singað him song neowne* (OX/2 XX OLDT VESP, p. 28) 'sing a new song to him'

Modal construction:

[2.12]   *Ne ðurfan ge on þa fore frætwe lædan, gold ne seolfor.* (OX/3 XX XX AND, p. 12) 'You will not need to carry with you on the journey ornate treasures, neither gold nor silver.' (Transl. Bradley 1982: 120.)

3rd person plural

Subjunctive:

[2.13]   *hie brucen londes hiora die* (O2 XX DOC HARM4, p. 10) 'they shall enjoy the land during their lifetime'

Modal construction:

[2.14]   *Lareowas sceolon læran and styran* (O3 IR HOM AELFR2/8, p. 538) 'preachers shall teach and guide'

Semi-modal construction:

[2.15]   *Soðlice ða þuneras þe Iohannes ne moste awritan on apocalipsin sind gastlice to understandenne* (O3 EX SCIA TEMP, p. 80) 'Truly the thunderstorms which John could not describe in the apocalypse are to be understood spiritually'

2.2.1 *The parameters 'person' and 'number'*

The analysis of the OE corpus yielded 2,753 relevant verbal syntagms; this corresponds to a normalised frequency of 21.47/1,000 words. Their distribution across the morphological categories person and number is shown in Table 2.2.[6]

Subjunctives are the most frequent realisation, and they occur most frequently in the third person singular, where they have a share of 83.11 per cent of all 1,255 subjunctives. Although some authors claim that second person subjunctives are 'extremely rare' (Rütten 2017: 202), but that it is 'difficult to dismiss [them] completely' (Mitchell 1985: 378), in my corpus they occur with a share of 6.14 per cent. Imperatives occupy

---

[6] Because of their small frequencies the patterns 'semi-modal + (*to*) + infinitive' and '*Uton* + infinitive' are subsumed under 'Modal' in the tables of this chapter.

Table 2.2 The distribution of the subjunctive and its competitors in the main clauses of the OE corpus

	Subjunctive		Imperative		Modal		Total	
2nd ps sg	60	5.36%	1,024	91.43%	36	3.21%	1,120	100%
3rd ps sg	1,043	85.07%			183	14.93%	1,226	100%
1st ps pl	15	14.71%	1	0.98%	86	84.31%	102	100%
2nd ps pl	17	10.83%	132	84.08%	8	5.09%	157	100%
3rd ps pl	120	81.08%			28	18.92%	148	100%
Total	1,255	45.59%	1,157	42.03%	341	12.38%	2,753	100%

the second rank on the frequency scale (42.03 per cent), and they occur nearly exclusively in the second person, where they have a share of 99.91 per cent. Modal constructions follow with a relative frequency of 12.38 per cent.

2.2.1.1 The first person plural
Although it was pointed out before that the imperative competes with the subjunctive only in the second person, I discovered one example of an imperative of the first person plural.

[2.16]   *micliað dryhten mid me & uphebbað we noman his betwinum* (OX/2 XX OLDT VESP, p. 29)
'magnify Lord with me and uplift we name his between'
'magnify the Lord with me and let us exalt his name in turns'

The first imperative (*micliað*) is addressed to the psalmist's hearers only, but the pronoun *we* that follows the imperative *uphebbað* clearly indicates that its addressees include the speaker as well. An analysis of *uphebbað* as an indicative would not render the meaning of the verse correctly. The subjunctive reading is supported by the Latin original from which the OE text is translated. It reads *Magnificate dominum mecum, et exaltemus nomen eius in inuicem*. The psalmist asks his hearers to perform two actions: the first is expressed by the imperative *magnificate*, the second by the subjunctive *exaltemus*. The addressees of the imperative are the hearers only, those of the subjunctive include the speaker. Visser (1963–1973: §844) claims to have detected the only instance of an imperative of the first person plural in Blickl. Hom. 19.19: *gehyrap we nu*. Mitchell (1985: §886) dismisses this form as an indicative with the comment: 'A reading of *BlHom* 17.9–25.36 will, I think, persuade readers that *gehyrap* can reasonably be taken as an unromantic indicative.' My reading of the whole homily has not persuaded me that the verb form in question is an indicative, unromantic or otherwise. The homily starts with the narration of Christ's healing of the blind man, then follows a series of admonitory interpretations of the story. They are addressed to the preacher's hearers and to himself, starting with '*Nu we sceolan, men þa leofestan, ða wundor gecyrran on soþfæstnesse geleafan ures Drihtnes Hælendes Cristes*' ('Now, dearest men, we must turn (apply) those marvels to the truth of (our) faith in our Lord Jesus Christ', Morris 1880: 16–17). The preacher's interpretation is given in several steps. The first three instances are introduced by a subjunctive plural + *we* (*Cleopian we nu, Smeagean we nu, Gehyran we nu*). They are followed by two stylistic variants, the first of which is the imperative in question (*Gehyraþ we nu*), the second realises the construction type 'Semi-modal + *to* + infinitive' (*Eac is to geþencenne*). For the rest of the homily the preacher follows the subjunctive pattern again (*Gehyran we eac, onhyrgean we, biddan we, biddon we, Gehyron we*, etc.). My analysis of *gehyraþ we nu* as an imperative is not only supported by the stylistic argument, but also by the word order. In this homily it is regularly subject plus indicative verb in statements, unless they are introduced by an adverb, whereas it is verb plus subject in requests.

The strongest competitors of the subjunctive in the first person plural are modal constructions and '*Uton* + infinitive'.[7] Kohnen (2008a: 35) found that the *uton*-construction was more frequent than modal constructions (and less frequent than performative verbs) in his OE corpus. At first sight this result is in conflict with the figures for 1st ps pl in Table 2.2. It should be pointed out, however, that Kohnen compares directives addressed to the first person plural to those addressed to the second person singular or plural (*þu scealt/ge sculon*), i.e. constructions with verbal syntagms with different realisation possibilities. In his context this is acceptable, because he is interested in the distribution of realisations of directives of different degrees of directness, and directives including the first person are less direct than directives addressed solely to the second person. But even a comparison of the figures for the *uton*-construction (37) and those for modal constructions in the first person plural (49) yields a different picture in my corpus. The different results may be due to the different corpora.[8] In my corpus, directive speech acts addressed to the first person plural modal constructions are most frequent, they are followed by the pattern '*Uton* + infinitive' and subjunctives. If we assume that modal constructions, especially those with **sculan*, express a more direct directive, i.e. a strong type of root modality, than subjunctives and '*Uton* + infinitive', my corpus contains slightly more verbal syntagms expressing a weak type of root modality in the first person plural. The ratio 52:49 must probably be even somewhat corrected in the direction

---

[7] Table 2.2 contains thirty-seven tokens of the pattern '*Uton* + infinitive' under 'Modal'.

[8] Kohnen used <u>all</u> texts of the OE part of the HC.

of weak root modality, because among the modal constructions only 27 are with **sculan*, and the modality of some examples with **sculan* shades off into futurity, i.e. a weak type of epistemic modality.

> [2.17] *to eorðan we sculan ealle geweorðan* (O3 IR HOM WULF8C, p. 225)
> 'to dust we shall all return'

In sum, we note that directives addressed to the first person plural stand out in that they are least frequent and tend to be realised by construction types expressing a weak type of root modality.

2.2.1.2 The second person
In the second person singular and plural the subjunctive competes with the imperative and modal constructions, with the latter of conspicuously low frequency. The formal coalescence of the imperative and the subjunctive in the singular as well as that of the second and third person singular present subjunctive caused some problems in the analysis of the corpus.

For the irregular verbs *don*, *gan* and *beon* there is no formal distinction between present subjunctive singular and imperative singular; they coincide under *do*, *ga* and *beo*. For the analysis of these forms the context was taken into consideration.

> [2.18] *Wið heafodwærce, betan wyrtruman, <u>cnuca</u> mid hunige, <u>awring</u>, <u>do</u> þæt seaw on þæt neb* (O2/3 IS HANDM LACN, p. 96) 'against headache beetroot, beat with honey, squeeze out, do that juice on the face'
> [2.19] *<u>hæbbe</u> him ær on muðe buteran oððe ele, <u>asitte</u> þonne uplang, <u>hnige</u> þonne forð, <u>læte</u> flowan of þæn nebbe þa gilstre, <u>do</u> þæt gelome oððæt hyt clæne sy.* (O2/3 IS HANDM LACN, p. 96) 'before [that], [let] him have butter or oil in his mouth, [let him] then sit up straight, lean forward, let flow the pus from the nose, [let him] do that often until it be clean'

In example [2.18] *do* follows a series of imperatives, it is therefore analysed as an imperative. In example [2.19], which occurs in the immediate neighbourhood of [2.18], *do* follows a series of subjunctives and is therefore analysed as a subjunctive.

In some cases, the decision was not between imperative and subjunctive but between subjunctive of the second or the third person singular. In these cases, clues were sought in the context as well.

> [2.20] *Drænc wið lungenadle, <u>wyl</u> marubian in wine oððe in ealað, <u>geswet</u> hwon mid hunige, <u>syle</u> drincan wearme on nihtnicstig, & þonne <u>licge</u> on ða swiðran sidan gode hwile æfter ðæm drænce & <u>þænne</u> þone*

> *swiðran earm swa he swiþast mæge.* (O2/3 IS HANDM LACN,
> p. 120) 'potion against lung-disease, boil common horehound in wine
> or in beer, sweeten a little with honey, give to drink warm after fasting
> for a night, and then lie on the right side a good while after the potion
> and stretch out the right arm so he most may [= as much as he can]'

[2.21] *Slæpdrænc, rædic, hymlic, wermod, belone, <u>cnuca</u> ealle þa wyrte,
<u>do</u> in ealað, <u>læt</u> standan ane niht, <u>drince</u> ðonne.* (O2/3 IS HANDM
LACN, p. 120) 'sleeping-potion, radish, hemlock, wormwood,
henbane, pound all these herbs, put in beer, let stand one night, drink
then'

In example [2.20] the imperatives <u>*wyl*</u>, <u>*geswet*</u> and <u>*syle*</u> are addressed to a
second person, but the subjunctives <u>*licge*</u> *and* <u>*þænne*</u>, which follow these
imperatives, are analysed as a third person, because it is the patient who
is asked to lie on his/her right side, whereas the instructions for the preparation of the medicine are addressed to the nursing person. In example
[2.21] the subjunctive <u>*drince*</u> also follows a list of imperatives (<u>*cnuca*</u>, <u>*do*</u>,
<u>*læt*</u>), but the context provides no clue concerning the addressee of the
actions to be performed. Is the person who prepares the sleeping-potion
supposed to drink it him-/herself, or is a third person involved? In the
absence of context clues pointing to a third person, <u>*drince*</u> and similar
forms in similar contexts were analysed as second person.

Imperatives express a stronger type of root modality than subjunctives: 'Because the imperative and subjunctive contrast morphologically,
we must assume that there was a difference in meaning, at least in early
OE times, between more and less directive, more and less wishful utterance' (Traugott 1992: 185). The ratio 1:15 in my corpus indicates that
imperatives expressing a strong type of root modality were the preferred
realisation of mood, whereas subjunctives played only a minor role in the
second person.

2.2.1.3 The third person

In my corpus the real domain of the subjunctive is the third person, especially the third person singular. Subjunctives of the third person singular
constitute 38 per cent of all relevant verbal syntagms of the corpus and
83 per cent of all subjunctives. Apart from modal constructions, which
have a share of 14 per cent in the third person singular and of 18 per cent
in the third person plural, the pattern 'Semi-modal + *to* + infinitive' is
attested.[9] Both examples of the third person plural occur in the same text
and represent Visser's construction type 'þæt þing is to donne'.

---

[9] In Table 2.2 nine examples of the pattern 'semi-modal + (*to*) + infinitive' of the
third person singular and two examples of this pattern of the third person plural
figure under 'Modal', cf. fn 6.

[2.22] *se winterlica, & seo hærfestlice emniht sind to emnettenne be ðyssere emnihte* (O3 EX SCIA TEMP, p. 46) 'the winter and the autumn equinox are to regulate by this equinox' = 'the winter equinox and the autumn equinox are to be calculated by this equinox'

Among semi-modal constructions of the third person singular there is one representative of Visser's type 'us is to donne hit':

[2.23] *Ac hwæt is þam men betere to þencenne þonne embe his sawle þearfe* (O3/4 IR HOM SUND6, p. 164) 'But what should man be more eager to think about than his soul's need?'

The only example in my corpus which represents his type 'þonne is to arisenne' is also quoted by himself (Visser 1963–1973: §367) and by Mitchell (1985: §936):

[2.24] *þonne is æfter eallum þisum mid rihtum geleafan to efstanne wið font-bæðes georne* (O3 IR HOM WULF8C, p. 179) 'then is after all this with right faith to hurry to baptismal bath eagerly' = 'then after all this one should hurry eagerly to the baptismal bath'

Four of the remaining seven examples are ordinary representatives of Visser's construction type 'þæt þing is to donne'; in three examples the subject is extraposed and follows the infinitive in the form of a *that*-clause:

[2.25] *Be ðam is to understandenne þæt se mona is ormæte brad* (O3 EX SCIA TEMP, p. 25) 'by this is to understand that the moon is excessively broad' = 'this means that the moon is extremely big'

From the distribution of the subjunctive and its competitors in the third person singular and plural it can be concluded that in these constellations subjunctives as expressions of a weak type of root modality are the default realisation of the category mood.

Considering all person/number constellations, we note a complementary distribution of strong and weak types of root modality. The former holds in the second person, where imperatives dominate, the latter holds in the third person, where subjunctives dominate, and also – and here less saliently – in the first person plural, where subjunctives together with *uton*-constructions are the most frequent forms of the verbal syntagm.

2.2.2 *The parameter date of composition*

Statements about the development of the frequency of the subjunctive and its competitors are usually of a global nature. Denison (1993: 330) reports a claim by Frans Plank 'that even during the OE period there was an increasing tendency to use a (subjunctive) modal + infinitive instead of subjunctive main verb'. The most comprehensive treatment of the share of modal constructions in OE is Ogawa (1989). The author describes the use of modal verb (not only modal auxiliary) constructions with *magan, *sculan, willan, *motan, agan, cunnan, *durran, þurfan, wuton* and compares their frequency to that of inflected lexical verb forms in the present and past, and he treats independent sentences and dependent clauses separately. His data consist of a poetry corpus, a prose corpus of texts dated before c. 900 and a prose corpus of texts dated after c. 900. In the diachronic part of his book he discusses the hypothesis that modal constructions replaced the subjunctive (Kellner 1892, Wilde 1939/1940), and he comes to the conclusion that this hypothesis is far too general and without sufficient empirical support. The share of modal constructions is bigger in his poetry corpus than in both prose corpora, but smaller in the later than in the earlier prose corpus. These relations hold for independent sentences and for subordinate clauses alike (Ogawa 1989: 231, table 41). Only in the subclass of dependent desires do his data show a slight increase in modal constructions between the earlier and the later prose corpus (Ogawa 1989: 232, table 42). Ogawa argues that modal constructions are not real equivalents of subjunctive forms, and that the choice of either pattern is a function of the subject matter and the genre of the text. He also notes a low frequency of modal constructions in texts which heavily rely on their Latin original. His final verdict is that if the replacement hypothesis can be supported at all this process took place only after the OE period.

From my OE corpus precise quantitative statements can be derived about the chronological frequency development of the subjunctive and its competitors in main clauses across the subperiods O1–O4 (cf. Table 2.3).

Table 2.3 The distribution of the subjunctive and its competitors in main clauses from O1 to O4

Subperiod	Subjunctive	Imperative	Modal	Total
O1	36 92.31%		3 7.69%	39 100%
O2	453 58.68%	271 35.10%	48 6.22%	772 100%
O3	703 41.95%	751 44.80%	222 12.25%	1,676 100%
O4	63 23.69%	135 50.75%	68 25.56%	266 100%
Total	1,255 45.59%	1,157 42.03%	341 12.38%	2,753 100%

Clear frequency developments are observable in all realisations. The share of the subjunctive decreases dramatically, whereas that of imperatives and modal constructions increases. Since the imperative competes with the subjunctive only in the second person, its frequency rise between O2 and O3 above that of the subjunctive – as well as the fact that in O4, too, imperative frequency is bigger than subjunctive frequency – must not be interpreted as a sign of subjunctive replacement by the imperative. The corpus data show that modal constructions are the only serious competitor of the subjunctive. This becomes obvious when the frequency development of all realisations is calculated separately for the second person and for the other two persons (see Table 2.4).

In O1, imperatives are not attested at all. As soon as they are attested, i.e. from subperiod O2 onwards, their share drops by nearly 5 per cent until the end of the OE period, whereas the frequency development of the subjunctive is not unidirectional. The same wave-like frequency development holds for modal constructions, although they show a general trend towards rising frequency.

In the environments where the imperative is not an option subjunctives and modal constructions show inverse developments, with the frequency of the former falling, and that of the latter rising (see Table 2.5). By the end of the OE period the share of modal constructions has nearly reached that of subjunctives. The discrepancy between Ogawa's results and mine

Table 2.4 The distribution of subjunctives, imperatives and modal constructions in the second person from O1 to O4

Subperiod	Subjunctive	Imperative	Modal		Total	
O1			1	100%	1	100%
O2	12 4.14%	270 93.10%	8	2.76%	290	100%
O3	62 6.80%	751 82.35%	99	10.85%	912	100%
O4	3 1.97%	135 88.82%	14	9.21%	152	100%
Total	77 5.68%	1,156 85.32%	122	9.00%	1,355	100%

Table 2.5 The distribution of subjunctives, imperatives and modal constructions in the first person plural and in the third person singular and plural from O1 to O4

Subperiod	Subjunctive	Imperative	Modal		Total	
O1	36 94.74%		2	5.26%	38	100%
O2	441 91.49%	1 0.21%	40	8.30%	482	100%
O3	641 83.90%		123	16.10%	764	100%
O4	60 52.63%		54	47.37%	114	100%
Total	1,178 84.26%	1 0.07%	219	15.67%	1,398	100%

probably stems from two sources, namely from the different corpus compositions and from the different research designs. Ogawa's corpus must be bigger than mine, judging from the nearly 5,000 tokens of modal constructions, and he compares the frequencies of all inflected verb forms on the one hand and of modal constructions on the other.

2.2.3 *The parameter text category*

Correlations between the use of the subjunctive and the parameter text category went largely unnoticed in earlier publications. Exceptions are Traugott (1992) and Ogawa (1989). Traugott (1992: 185) comments on the preference of the subjunctive to the imperative, whereas Ogawa presents percentage figures of modal constructions in different text categories.[10] He also mentions a higher incidence of modal constructions in poetry than in prose. Traugott does not specify on which corpus she bases her claims, and Ogawa contrasts modal constructions to all inflected verb forms in his corpus, not only to subjunctives. A more detailed and precise quantitative study of the share of the subjunctive and its competitors in a balanced corpus was therefore badly needed. The analysis of my OE corpus across the text categories distinguished in the HC yielded the distribution shown in Table 2.6.

Before interpreting Table 2.6 it should be taken into consideration that the relevant main clauses are not equally distributed across the text categories. Their relative frequency per 1,000 words is 21.47 across the whole corpus, but only in the categories STA, IS and IR do they occur with a greater than average frequency.[11] The distribution of the realisation possibilities of their verbal syntagms is therefore particularly revealing.

The clustering of directive speech acts in these text categories was to be expected, since law texts regulate societal behaviour, and instructions – in the secular or in the religious sphere – are given as commands, requests, prohibitions or wishes. Yet the individual text categories prefer different means for the expression of their directive speech acts; in the texts

---

[10] 'By the time of Alfredian OE . . . the subjunctive continued to be preferred [to the imperative] in monastic and legal regulations; charms, medical prescriptions and similar generalised instructions are normally in the subjunctive' (Traugott 1992: 185).
  '[T]he incidence of modal verbs in independent and subordinate clauses altogether is distinctly higher in argumentative (i.e. religious and philosophical) and homiletic prose than in narrative prose. The legal and scientific texts come somewhere between the two, the former being closer to the argumentative and homiletic, the latter to the narrative texts' (Ogawa 1989: 234).

[11] The relative frequencies in these text categories are: STA = 49.24, IS = 89.84, IR = 23.98, NI = 7.09, NN = 4.91, EX = 3.54, XX = 13.98.

Table 2.6 The distribution of the subjunctive and its competitors in main
clauses across text categories of the OE corpus

Category	Subjunctive	Imperative	Modal	Total
STA	720 85.31%	36 4.27%	88 10.42%	844 100%
IS	112 17.83%	508 80.90%	8 1.27%	628 100%
IR	169 42.89%	137 34.77%	88 22.34%	394 100%
NI	21 21.43%	68 69.39%	9 7.14%	98 100%
NN	14 13.86%	66 65.35%	21 20.79%	101 100%
EX	3 15.79%	3 15.79%	13 68.42%	19 100%
XX	216 32.29%	339 50.67%	114 17.04%	669 100%
Total	1,255 45.59%	1,157 42.03%	341 12.38%	2,753 100%

of the categories STA and IR the subjunctive is preferred, in those of IS
the imperative dominates. In terms of modality analysis this means that
secular instructive texts are characterised by verbal syntagms expressing a strong type of root modality, whereas statutory texts and religious
instructive texts prefer verbal syntagms expressing a weak type of root
modality.

The relatively large share of modal constructions in texts of the category IR is partly a consequence of the inclusion of thirty tokens of
the pattern '*Uton* + infinitive'.[12] Since it includes the speaker among its
addressees, it expresses only a weak type of root modality. The subjunctive as a weak type of root modality in IR is also prominent in the eight
examples in the first person plural:

[2.26]   *Don we þonne, men þa leofestan, soðe bote for urum synnum* (O3/4
IR HOM SUND6, p. 165) 'do we then men the dearest true penitence
for our sins' = 'let us then, dear people, make true amends for our sins'

In sum, we note that the three text categories with many directive
speech acts show a characteristic distribution of the realisations of their
verbal syntagms. In texts of the categories STA and IR subjunctives
occupy the first rank on the frequency scale, whereas in the text category
IS imperatives take the lead. Since the text category XX (= unclassified)
contains a mixed bag of text types, and since the number of verbal syntagms expressing root modality is not negligible, it will be looked at in
more detail below.

[12] This result is in line with what Kohnen found in a study based on all texts of the
OE part of the HC (2008a: 36, table 3).

2.2.4 *The subjunctive and its competitors in individual text files*

The files of the text category XX do not lend themselves easily to a uniform classification. On the basis of their format, seven of them are to be classified as prose, the remaining six as poetry. On the basis of their textual history, five are translations from Latin originals, the other eight are original OE compositions. On the basis of the dichotomy secular vs. religious, six files belong to the secular sphere, the remaining seven to the religious sphere. The distribution of the subjunctive and its competitors in the files of text category XX in the OE corpus is presented in Table 2.7.

The four document files CODOCU1–CODOCU4 differ from all other files of the category XX by their nearly exclusive use of the subjunctive. Their labels suggest that they contain a single text, but this is not the case. The document files contain between four and twenty different text passages. Their sizes range from seventy-seven words (Q O2 XX DOC ROB10) to a little more than 1,000 words (Q O3 XX DOC WHIT20). What is even more striking is their different contents. The first three of the four files combine wills and charters, the file CODOCU4 contains only extracts from three charters. Since wills are about a person's 'intention as to the disposal of his property or other matters to be performed after his death' (*OED*, s.v. *will*, 23.a), whereas charters are 'documents or deeds relating to conveyance of landed property' (*OED*, s.v. *charter*, 2b), different amounts of directive speech acts, i.e. different frequencies of verbal syntagms expressing root modality, were to be expected depending on the respective shares of wills and charters in the files. Their distribution is displayed in Table 2.8.

Table 2.7 The distribution of the subjunctive and its competitors in the files of text category XX in the main clauses of the OE corpus

Text	Subjunctive	Imperative	Modal	Total
COANDREA	2 4.45%	23 51.11%	20 44.44%	45 100%
COCHRIST	8 9.30%	35 40.70%	43 50.00%	86 100%
CODOCU1	36 100%			36 100%
CODOCU2	33 100%			33 100%
CODOCU3	52 96.30%	2 3.70%		54 100%
CODOCU4	6 100%			6 100%
COGENESI	2 5.26%	17 44.74%	19 50.00%	38 100%
COKENTIS		25 96.15%	1 3.85%	26 100%
COMETBOE	10 27.78%	2 5.55%	24 66.67%	36 100%
CONORTHU			3 100%	3 100%
COPREFCP	3 60.00%	1 20.00%	1 20.00%	5 100%
COPREFSO	3 75.00%		1 25.00%	4 100%
COVESPS	64 21.26%	234 77.74%	3 1.00%	301 100%

Table 2.8 The distribution of directive speech acts in wills and charters in the
main clauses of the files CODOCU1–CODOCU4

File name	Directive speech acts in will-part	Directive speech acts in charter-part	Directive speech acts total
CODOCU1	36 1,750 words	0 210 words	36 1,960 words
CODOCU2	32 1,470 words	1 890 words	33 2,360 words
CODOCU3	46 5,144 words	6 2,886 words	52 8,030 words
CODOCU4	0 0 words	6 2,440 words	6 2,440 words

All 127 directive speech acts of Table 2.8 are realised as subjunctives,
and of these 114 occur in the will-parts, whereas only thirteen occur in
charter-parts. The two imperatives in CODOCU3 occur also in charter-
parts (cf. Table 2.7). It follows that the large number of subjunctives in
the document files reflects a genre-specific feature of OE wills (cf. examples [2.27] and [2.28]).

[2.27] *Ond ðas forecuedenan suesenda all agefe mon ðem reogolwarde & he
brytnie swæ higum maest red sie & ðaem sawlum soelest.* (Q O1 XX
DOC HARM1, p. 2) 'And all the victuals mentioned above shall one
give to the abbot, and he shall distribute them as is most suitable for
the members of the monastery and best for their souls.'

[2.28] *Gief hwa buton gewyrhtum hit awendan wille God adilgie his noman
of lifes bocum & habbe him gemæne wið hine on þam ytemestan dæge
þysses lifes* (Q O3 XX DOC ROB46, p. 96) 'If anyone, without due
cause, attempts to change it, God shall blot out his name from the
books of life, and he shall have to account for it to him on the last day
of this life' (Robertson 1956: 97)

The frequencies of directive speech acts in the document files suggest that
after subperiod O2 a sharp decline of subjunctives in wills sets in.[13] The
question which immediately arises is: What replaced the subjunctive? A
verb form in the indicative? A modal construction?

Wills in O3 with a saliently low subjunctive frequency contain
sequences of parallel constructions starting with *ic gean* 'I bestow', e.g.:

[2.29] *ic geann Leofwynne minan wife ealles þæs þe ic læfe hire dæig . . .
& ic geann þæs landes æt Rægene be westan into sancte Paule þam
bisceope . . . & ic geann þarto twegra hida þe Eadric gafelaþ . . . & ic*

[13] The relative frequencies of directive speech acts per 1,000 words in the document
files are as follows: CODOCU1: 18.37, CODOCU2: 13.98, CODOCU3: 6.72,
CODOCU4: 2.46.

> *geann þæs landes æt Norðho healf into sancte Gregorie . . .* (Q O3XX
> DOC WHIT13, p. 32)

In this kind of will the focus is on the testator, whereas in the kind of wills illustrated earlier the focus is on the inheritance. Testator centred wills can also have the form '*ic* + *bidde*/*wille* + *that*-clause'. The verb in the *that*-clause is mostly in the subjunctive (cf. section 4.2.2). Testator centred wills are also attested in the earlier subperiods, but there they are less conspicuous. In sum, we note that subjunctive frequency in main clauses in documents, in particular in wills, decreases after subperiod O2. Yet it is not the case that subjunctives in main clauses are replaced by another form of the verbal syntagm, but that wills in O3 tend to be testator centred and more often than before rely on the construction types '*ic* + *gean* + the inheritance' and '*ic* + *bidde*/*wille* + *that*-clause'. This result makes us aware of the far more general issue of appropriate text classification (e.g. 'wills' and 'charters' instead of 'documents' in OE) and of the changing linguistic profiles of the same genre (e.g. wills in O1–O2 vs. wills in O3).

Different linguistic profiles of the texts of the same category can also be illustrated by the files of the text category STA, which is represented by law files of the subperiods O2–O4. The frequencies of the subjunctive and its competitors in these files are displayed in Table 2.9.

Table 2.9 The distribution of the subjunctive and its competitors in the main clauses of the law files of the OE corpus

File name	Subjunctive	Imperative	Modal	Total
COLAW2	353 82.67%	35 8.20%	39 9.13%	427 100%
COLAW3	334 95.16%	1 0.29%	16 4.55%	351 100%
COLAW4	33 50.00%		33 50.00%	66 100%

In contrast to the document files, in the law files subjunctive shares rise between O2 and O3, before they fall dramatically between O3 and O4. The large figures in the law files in O2 and O3 are easily explained by the nature of the texts. They enumerate unlawful actions and the corresponding punishments in the form '*if*-clause (verb in subjunctive) + main clause (verb in subjunctive)'. Here is an example:

[2.30]   *Gif mon cierliscne mon gebinde unsynnigne, gebete mid X scillingum.*
          Gif hine mon beswinge, mid XX scillingum gebete.
          Gif he hine on hengenne alecgge, mid XXX scillingum gebete.
          Gif he hine on bismor to homolan bescire, mid X scillingum gebete.
          Gif he hine to preoste bescire unbundenne, mid XXX scillingum gebete.
          Gif he ðone beard ofascire, mid XX scillingum gebete.

*Gif he hine gebinde & þonne to preoste bescire, mid LX scillingum
gebete.*
(Q O2 STA LAW ALFLAW, p. 68)
'If somebody binds a guiltless common man, he shall repair it with 10
shillings.
If he beats him, he shall repair it with 20 shillings.
If he puts him into prison, he shall repair it with 30 shillings.
If he shamefully shaves his hair off, he shall repair it with 10 shillings.
If he gives a tonsure to a lay person, he shall repair it with 30 shillings.
If he shaves his beard off, he shall repair it with 20 shillings.
If he binds him and then shaves him a tonsure, he shall repair it with
30 shillings.'

An alternative way of stating the unlawful action is by a relative clause
as in example [2.31]:

[2.31]   *And se ðe unlage rære oððe undom gedeme heonon forð, for lædðe
oððe for feohfange, beo se wið þone cingc CXX scyllinga scyldig on
Engla lage* (Q O3 STA LAW LAW11C, p. 318) 'And he who pro-
motes injustice or pronounces an unjust judgement henceforth, out of
malice or by taking a bribe, he shall be owing 120 shillings to the king
according to English law'

As in *if*-clauses which specify the unlawful action, the verb in the relative
clause is in subjunctive mood; the same holds for the verb in the main
clause.

The O4 law file with its notably smaller subjunctive share contains two
texts of unequal size, of 2,100 and 220 words respectively. The shorter
text is entitled 'King William's Law' and consists of eight parallel passages of the form 'if-clause (specifying a special type of law trespass) +
main clause (specifying the punishment)'. The only difference between
this text and the texts of the law files of the earlier periods is the form of
the verb in the *if*-clause; six out of eight verbal syntagms are indicatives.

The longer text differs from all other law texts in form and content. It
is not about unlawful actions and their legal consequences, but it specifies
the rights and the duties of several social classes. They are not expressed
as consequences which materialise if certain conditions are fulfilled. They
are introduced by nominal syntagms of the type *geneates riht* 'tenant's
right', *gebures gerihte* 'farmer's right', *cotsetlan riht* 'cottager's right', *be
oxanhyrde* 'about the oxherd', *by berebrytte* 'about the barnkeeper', *be
wuduwearde* 'about the forester', etc. The rights and duties are specified
in the form 'optional *if*-clause with a verb in indicative + main clause
with a verbal syntagm realised by either a subjunctive or by a modal construction'. The most frequent modal auxiliary is *sceal*.

[2.32] *sylle his cyricsceat to Martinus mæssan* (O3/4 STA LAW LAWLAT,
p. 446) 'he [= the cottager] shall pay his church tax at Martinmas'

[2.33] *gyf he wel gelend bið, he sceal beon gehorsad, þæt he mæge to
hlafordes seame þæt syllan oððe sylf lædan* (Q O3/4 STA LAW
LAWLAT, p. 448) 'if he is furnished with much land, he shall be given
a horse so that he may give it for carrying his lord's burden or lead it
himself'

The different linguistic profile of this text correlates with its different
purpose and contents; unlike the other law texts, which outline unlawful
actions and their punishment, it defines the rights and duties of particular
social classes.

2.2.5 Other extralinguistic parameters

The OE part of the corpus contains twenty-four prose texts and six verse
texts. The normalised frequency of directive speech acts is about twice
as high in prose as in verse texts (23.81/1,000 words vs. 10.45/1,000
words). In prose texts the most frequent realisation pattern is the subjunctive (48.95 per cent) followed by the imperative (41.88 per cent). In
verse texts, modal constructions are highest on the rank list (45.30 per
cent), followed by imperatives (43.59 per cent). These figures support
Ogawa's finding that modal constructions occur more often in verse than
in prose texts.

The corpus files are also coded for the dialect areas Anglian, Kentish
and West Saxon. Yet the distribution across these dialect areas is very
unbalanced in the HC. I included HC's only Kentish text file and five of
the eight Anglian text files. The remaining text files of my corpus come
from the West Saxon dialect area. Under these circumstances the only
noteworthy result of my analysis is the dominance of imperatives in the
Anglian text files (59.00 per cent), which contrasts with the dominance
of the subjunctive in the West Saxon text files (45.86 per cent) and the
subjunctive in the only Kentish file (100 per cent).

2.2.6 Summary

The verbal syntagms of directive speech acts have five realisation possibilities in OE: subjunctives, imperatives, modal constructions, semi-modal
constructions, and *Uton* + infinitive. Subjunctives occupy the top rank
on the frequency scale, followed by imperatives and modal constructions. The other realisation possibilities play only a minor role. During
the four OE subperiods subjunctive frequency steadily decreases, while
the frequency of modal constructions rises. The extralinguistic parameter
text category has a strong influence on the density of directive speech

acts as well as on the distribution of the subjunctive and its competitors. Directive speech acts are most frequent in the categories IS, IR and STA. Imperatives with their strong directive force dominate in texts of secular instruction, whereas subjunctives with their weaker directive force are the most frequent realisation in texts of religious instruction and in statutory texts. The relatively high density of directive speech acts in the mixed category XX was explained as a consequence of the large number of imperatives in two texts (COKENTIS, COVESPS), and the exceptionally large share of subjunctives in the OE documents was interpreted as a function of the communicative purpose of the wills contained in the respective files. Wills were shown to undergo a genre shift from bequest centred to testator centred with a concomitant decrease of subjunctive frequency. A correlation between the content and purpose of texts and their linguistic profile was also identified in the category STA after subperiod O3. Among the other extralinguistic parameters only the dichotomy prose vs. verse yielded noteworthy results: OE prose texts have a higher frequency of directive speech acts than verse texts. They are preferably realised as subjunctives, whereas the fewer directive speech acts in verse texts are mostly realised as modal constructions.

In terms of modality the distribution of the subjunctive and its competitors in the main clauses of my OE corpus revealed a dominance of deontic modality of different degrees of force. Strong deontic modality characterises directive speech acts addressed to the second person and directive speech acts in texts of the category secular instruction. Weak deontic modality characterises directive speech acts adressed to the third person and to the first person plural, as well as those in texts of the categories statutory and religious instruction. The rising frequency of directive speech acts expressing strong deontic modality is a consequence of the larger numbers of directive speech acts addressed to the second person in subperiods O3 and O4.

2.3 Middle English main clauses: the subjunctive and its competitors in earlier publications

In ME the indicative vs. subjunctive contrast in present tense is formally marked only for the second and third person singular (Lass 1992: 138), and through the gradual replacement of *th*-forms by *y*-forms of the personal pronoun of the second person singular – which started in the ME period and which went hand in hand with the loss of the verb ending for the second person singular – resulted in a further reduction of overtly marked subjunctive forms (Lass 1999: 148f.).

The imperative which in OE was a successful competitor of the subjunctive for the expression of a directive speech act in main clauses lost its distinctive endings as well, so that in ME the subjunctive vs.

imperative contrast in the second person singular was basically marked only by the presence (subjunctive) vs. absence (imperative) of a personal pronoun indicating the addressee of the directive speech act. The analysis of a given verb form in the second person singular as either subjunctive or imperative is difficult though, since the imperative could be accompanied by a subject pronoun (Mustanoja 1960: 475f.). This variant of the imperative was not very frequent, and the agent pronoun is sometimes interpreted as a sign of emotional colouring (Jespersen 1909–1949: vol. III. 11.8.41). Preposition of the agent pronoun is attested for OE (Mitchell 1985: §888 and Visser 1963–1973: §25), but there is some disagreement about the further development of this realisation possibility. Mustanoja (1960: 476), Visser (1963–1973: §25) and Fischer (1992: 249) claim that it continued to be used in ME, whereas Jespersen (1909–1949: vol. III. 11.8.42) found that the position of the pronoun was generally after the verb until around 1700, when the word order changed (cf. Franz 1939: 535). The imperative with a preceding agent pronoun must have steadily decreased in importance. It became restricted to the register of conversation, and even there its frequency amounts to less than 20 per cent of imperative constructions in PDE (Biber et al. 1999: 221).

The set of modal auxiliaries which, followed by an infinitive, competed in OE with the subjunctive for the expression of directive speech acts is preserved in ME and is used with the same function. Fischer (1992: 263) calls them the 'core modals' and lists the items *shal, wil, may, mot, can.* She claims that 'by the end of the Middle English period periphrastic constructions far outweighed subjunctive forms' (Fischer 1992: 262). Mustanoja (1960: 453) even claims that in the fifteenth century the ratio between subjunctives and modal constructions was 1:9.

According to Visser the OE periphrastic construction type '*us is to donne it*' 'becomes obsolete in later Middle English' (1963–1973: §367). It is replaced by the personal construction of the type 'we are to do', thus representing another instance of the more general trend of the development from impersonal to personal constructions (1963–1973: §1381). The ME equivalent of the OE type '*þæt þing is to donne*', i.e. 'that thing is to do', was very popular, but in the fourteenth century a new construction arose, in which the object function of the surface subject is made explicit by a passive infinitive: 'that thing is to be done' (1963–1973: §1384). The frequency of the new construction rose rapidly, it became the rule in the EModE period, and in PDE the older construction has virtually died out (1963–1973: §2151). The other OE impersonal construction type, '*þonne is to arisenne*', survived into ME. In the fifteenth century it was replaced by a construction with a dummy subject *it* and a following *that*-clause (1963–1973: §§1374–1376.). The set of semi-modal constructions realising a direct directive speech act in ME is not restricted to combinations with *be*, it also comprises constructions with *have*,[14] *ahte* ('ought') and *nede* ('need').

2.4 The subjunctive and its competitors in the ME corpus

In the analysis of my ME corpus I distinguish the following realisations of the relevant verbal syntagms: subjunctives, imperatives, modal constructions, and semi-modal constructions.[15] The possible realisations are summarised in Table 2.10:

Table 2.10 The realisation possibilities of ME verbal syntagms in main clauses

	Subjunctive	Imperative	Modal	Semi-modal
2nd ps sg	×	×	×	×
3rd ps sg	×		×	×

Examples of each realisation possibility are given below:

Subjunctive
2nd person singular:
[2.34] *kyng edward, honoured þou be* (M2 NN HIST HPOEM5, p. 23) 'King Edward, may you be honoured'
3rd person singular:
[2.35] *Vre lauerd þurh his grace halde ower earen feor hare attrie tungen.* (M1 IR RELT ANCR, p. 47) 'Our Lord through his grace may keep your ears far from their poisonous tongues.'
Imperative
2nd person singular:
[2.36] *send me sume sutelungæ* (MX/1 NN RELT HROOD, p. 10) 'send me some token'
Modal construction:
2nd person singular:
[2.37] *And thou also most nedes lese thyn heed* (M3 NI FICT CTSUMM, p. 133.C1) 'and you, too, must necessarily lose your head'
3rd person singular:
[2.38] *te fulitohe wif; mei beon wil ihaten* (M1 IR HOM SWARD, p. 165) 'the ill-disciplined wife may be called Will'
Semi-modal construction:
2nd person singular:
[2.39] *Ah þu queðen ha keiser ahest to cuðen for hwet icud þing þu hete*

---

[14] Mustanoja (1960: 599) and Fischer (1992: 263) date the beginnings of this construction back to OE.
[15] Semi-modal constructions are subsumed under 'Modal' in the tables.

> *us hider to cumene.* (M1 NN BIL KATH, p. 27) 'But you, said they,
> Emperor, ought to tell [us] for which notable thing you asked us to
> come here.'

3rd person singular:

> [2.40]   *a gode wille is moor to be commended than eny bodily yifte* (M4 IR
>   RULE AELR4, p. 17] 'a good will is more to be commended than any
>   bodily gift'

2.4.1 *The parameter 'person'*

My ME corpus contains 1,577 relevant verbal syntagms; this corresponds to a normalised frequency of 9.48/1,000 words. Compared to the
main clauses of the OE corpus (21.47/1,000 words), it is much lower in
the ME corpus. The distribution of the individual realisation possibilities
is shown in Table 2.11:

Table 2.11 The distribution of subjunctives and alternative constructions in
main clauses of the ME corpus

	Subjunctive	Imperative	Modal	Total
2nd ps sg	30 3.12%	781 81.10%	152 15.78%	963 100%
3rd ps sg	197 32.08%		417 67.92%	614 100%
Total	227 14.40%	781 49.52%	569 36.08%	1,577 100%

The most frequent realisation of ME directive speech acts is the imperative mood. Next on the frequency scale are modal constructions, subjunctives occupy the third place.

In the directive speech acts of my ME corpus which are addressed to
a second person singular the strongest competitor of the subjunctive is
the imperative. Second person non-indicative verb forms were analysed
as subjunctives when they were preceded by the pronoun *thu/thou* (e.g.
[2.41]) or when they were followed by this pronoun and the inversion
of subject and verb was triggered by a clause-initial adverb.[16] In most
cases this was the negative particle *ne* (e.g. [2.42]). They were analysed as
imperatives when the addressee was not expressed (eg. [2.43]), or when
they were followed by the pronoun *thu/thou* and this pronoun had an
emphatic function (e.g.[2.44]). Only very few examples of this last construction type are attested in my corpus.

> [2.41]   *þu me æfter folge* (MX/1 IR HOM VESPD42, p. 133) 'you shall
>   follow me'
> [2.42]   *Ne beo þu to ormod, þeh þe beo unriht gedemed.* (MX/1 IS PHILO

---

[16] Cf. Fischer (1992: 375) and Traugott (1992: 275).

VESPD3, p. 5] 'you shall not be too hopeless, even if a wrong judgement is passed on you'

[2.43] *To alle þyse opene þy brest, to þyse ȝif þyn almesse, to þyse departe þy bitere terys, for þyse sched out þy clene preyeres* (M2/3 IR RULE AELR3, p. 38) 'to these open your heart, to these give your alms, to these shed your tears, for these say your pure prayers'

[2.44] *Go þu yunder and sit þore, And Y shal yeue þe ful fair bred* (M2 NI ROM HAVEL, p. 30) 'go you thither and sit down there, and I will give you a nice meal'

In directive speech acts addressed to the third person singular modal constructions are the most frequent realisation. Semi-modal constructions are represented by ME equivalents of Visser's types II (example [2.45]) and III (examples [2.46] and [2.47]) and by constructions in which the first element is not *be*. In my corpus the following are attested: *ought, need, be about, have* (examples [2.48] and [2.49]).

[2.45] *a gode wille is moor to be commended than eny bodily yifte* (M4 IR RULE AELR4, p. 17] 'a good will is more to be commended than any bodily gift'

[2.46] *Now it is to say of sekenessis* (MX/4 EX SCIM CHAUL, p. 63) 'now it is to say of diseases' = 'now diseases are to be dealt with'

[2.47] *Wherfore it is not to beleue þat þei ben tombes or sepultures* (M3 NI TRAV MAND, p. 34) 'therefore it must not be believed that these are tombs or sepulchres'

[2.48] *he haueð to beten lease i pine of purgatoire* (M1 IR RELT ANCR, p. 168) 'he has to make amends for less in the pain of purgatory'

[2.49] *Wel oghte a preest ensample for to yive* (M3 NI FICT CTPROL, p. 31. C2) 'a priest ought to set an example'

A comparison with the OE corpus yields some interesting results. Subjunctives and modal constructions experienced the most prominent changes in relative frequency; the share of subjunctives dropped from 45.59 per cent to 14.40 per cent, whereas the share of modal constructions rose from 12.38 per cent to 36.08 per cent. Imperatives increased less conspicuously from 42.03 per cent in OE to 49.52 per cent in the ME corpus.

In the second person the imperative is the default option in ME; it expresses strong deontic modality. This is what Traugott (1992: 185) described for OE as 'more directive' than the subjunctive.

In the third person the majority of relevant verbal syntagms is realised by modal constructions. They also express deonticity, although with a weaker force than imperatives. This interpretation is in line with the scale of directness established by Blum-Kulka et al. (1989: 18), where imperatives also figure at the top end of the scale. The force of the deontic modality of modal constructions is strongest when the modal auxiliary *shall* is used; this is the case in 339 examples of modal constructions (= nearly 60 per cent).

> [2.50]   *Thus shalt thou arraye thyn autier of thyn oratorye* (M4 IR RULE
>   AELR4, p. 15) 'thus you shall arrange you altar of your chapel'

This directive speech act is addressed to a recluse, and she is given very specific instructions about how to set up the altar in the room where she says her prayers.

My interpretation of a shift from weaker to stronger deonticity between OE an ME is also supported by the growing number of semi-modal constructions, whose strength of deonctic modality is comparable to that of modal constructions.[17]

From the figures presented in Table 2.11 it is obvious that in ME main clauses fewer directive speech acts were used than in OE, but those which were preferably used, namely imperatives and modal constructions, especially those with the modal *shall*, expressed a stronger type of deontic modality than their OE predecessors with their greater share of subjunctives. In terms of politeness theory this means that ME directive speech acts in main clauses are more face-threatening, and this in turn offers a new explanation of the decreasing frequency of subjunctives between OE and ME.

2.4.2 *The parameter date of composition*

Following the periodisation of the HC, the subperiods M1–M4 are distinguished in my corpus. The distribution of subjunctives and alternative constructions across these subperiods is shown in Table 2.12.

The decrease of subjunctive shares which was noted in the OE corpus continues in M1. Then the frequency development is uneven, but the general tendency is towards a frequency decrease. Modal constructions tend towards bigger shares and imperatives towards smaller shares in the course of the ME period, but their relative frequencies do not follow a steady development. These changes support the hypothesis set up earlier that in main clauses the only serious competitor of the subjunctive is the modal construction (cf. section 2.2.2). Yet its frequency rise is not as great as Mustanoja claims.

---

[17] Kohnen (2007:155) suggests a similar interpretation: 'a decrease in directives does not necessarily imply that the directives become less "forceful" or more "polite"'.

Table 2.12 The distribution of subjunctives and alternative constructions in main clauses across the subperiods M1–M4

Subperiod	Subjunctive	Imperative	Modal	Total
M1	59 17.15%	189 54.94%	96 27.91%	344 100%
M2	34 19.54%	54 31.03%	86 49.43%	174 100%
M3	55 9.95%	312 56.42%	186 33.63%	553 100%
M4	79 15.61%	226 44.66%	201 39.73%	506 100%
Total	227 14.40%	781 49.52%	569 36.08%	1,577 100%

2.4.3 *The parameter text category*

In my ME corpus the same text categories are represented as in the OE corpus. The analysis of the corpus across text categories is presented in Table 2.13.

Table 2.13 The distribution of the subjunctive and its competitors across text categories in the main clauses of the ME corpus

Category	Subjunctive	Imperative	Modal	Total
STA	29 96.67%		1 3.33%	30 100%
IS	14 2.94%	313 65.76%	149 31.30%	476 100%
IR	92 14.89%	320 51.78%	206 33.33%	618 100%
NI	25 14.45%	48 27.75%	100 57.80%	173 100%
NN	18 17.48%	47 45.63%	38 36.89%	103 100%
EX	17 24.64%	28 40.58%	24 34.78%	69 100%
XX	32 29.63%	25 23.15%	51 47.22%	108 100%
Total	227 14.40%	781 49.52%	569 36.08%	1,577 100%

Main clauses with directive speech acts occur with an average frequency of 9.48/1,000 words in my ME corpus. This value is surpassed only in the text categories IS (32.05), IR (12.20) and EX (16.79). Since instructions are usually given in the form of commands, requests, prohibitions or wishes, the high density of main clauses with directive speech acts in the first two categories is a natural consequence of their communicative purpose. Their higher than average density in the text category EX is extraordinary, because expository texts are mainly informative, i.e. they present facts in a neutral way. Yet the only expository text of the ME part of the HC, which is also contained in my corpus, is an early medical handbook by Guy de Chauliac. In addition to a description of human anatomy it contains detailed instructions about the preparation of individual medicines.

The most frequent realisations of the verbal syntagms overall are imperatives and modal constructions, i.e. verbal syntagms that express a strong type of root modality. As in the OE corpus, the imperative has its biggest share in the category IS.

The individual modal auxiliaries are unevenly distributed in the corpus. With 60.79 per cent, *shall* is the most frequent auxiliary (324 tokens); it expresses a strong type of deontic modality.

> [2.51]   *And þan schalt þou latyn him blod a-boue on his necke* (M3 IS
> HANDM HORSES, p. 89) 'and then you shall bleed him on the upper
> side of his neck'

The distribution of subjunctives does not really fit into this picture. Although it is the purpose of statutory texts to impose rules on the members of society, category STA stands out from all others in that except for one instance all its verbal syntagms are realised by a subjunctive, i.e. a realisation expressing only a weak type of deonticity. Although subjunctives already played a prominent role in category STA of the OE corpus, the share of subjunctives increased by 11 per cent in STA between the two periods. This change of the linguistic structure of law texts must be seen against the background of changes in the field of legislation, where after the Norman Conquest tribal law was replaced by statutory law. The form of statutory law with its introductory formula of the form *be it enacted/ ordained* + *that*-clause explains the large number of subjunctives.

> [2.52]   *Also be it enacted that the Jugementis to be yeven from hensfourth*
> *... shall not be perjudiciall to eny of the seid persons so beyng in*
> *the servyce of our sovereign lord the kyng in Britayn* (M4 STA LAW
> STAT2, p. II, 529) 'may it also be enacted that the judgements pro-
> nounced from now on ... shall not be prejudicial to any of the said
> persons who are in the service of our sovereign lord, the king, in
> Britain'

2.4.4 *Other extralinguistic parameters*

My ME corpus contains twenty-six prose texts and five verse texts. Their analysis yielded no noteworthy influence of the format on the density of directive speech acts nor on the realisation patterns of their verbal syntagms. The density of directive speech acts is a little bigger in poetic texts (9.80/1,000 words) than in prose texts (9.41/1,000 words). In both text forms the share of subjunctives differs only minimally (prose texts: 14.13 per cent, verse texts: 15.63 per cent); in either form it is smaller than that of imperatives and modal constructions.[18]

---

[18] The shares of the other realisations are: modal constructions: 30.57 per cent in
prose texts, 49.09 per cent in verse texts; imperatives: 53.07 per cent in prose texts,

The texts are also coded for the traditional ME dialect regions: East Midland, West Midland, Northern, Southern, and Kentish. The density of main clauses with directive speech acts is conspicuously higher in the two southern dialect areas, and in both areas imperatives occur with remarkably large shares. By contrast, large shares of modal constructions are found in the Midlands and in the Northern dialect areas.[19]

2.4.5 *Summary and comparison with the OE corpus*

The relative frequency of main clauses with directive speech acts is lower in the ME corpus (9.48/1,000 words) than in the OE corpus (21.47/1,000 words).

Concerning the shares of the most frequent realisations, it is obvious that the subjunctive suffered the biggest loss (OE: 45.59 per cent > ME: 14.40 per cent), and that this loss was compensated for by an increase in the shares of imperatives (OE: 42.03 per cent > ME: 49.52 per cent) and modal constructions (OE: 12.38 per cent > ME: 36.08 per cent).

The steady decrease of subjunctive frequency which was observed in the OE corpus continued in M1. Then the frequency development is uneven, but the general tendency is towards a frequency decrease. The rising frequency of modal constructions continued during the ME period, but with uneven speed. The frequency rise of imperatives in OE continued in M1, then started to drop, but with the exception of M2 remained the most frequent realisation of the verbal syntagm in ME main clauses.

Text category proved the extralinguistic parameter with the biggest influence on the frequency of main clauses with directive speech acts and on the realisation of their verbal syntagms. In the OE corpus and in the ME corpus relevant main clauses cluster in the categories IS and IR, in the OE corpus additionally in the category STA, in the ME corpus additionally in the category EX. The high density of main clauses with directive speech acts in the categories IS and IR and in the category STA in the OE corpus was explained by the purpose of these texts: they aim at regulating human behaviour, which in the category EX in the ME corpus was interpreted as a consequence of the fact that the only text in this category, a medical handbook, contains not only a description of

---

32.73 per cent in verse texts; semi-modal constructions: 2.23 per cent in prose texts, 2.54 per cent in verse texts.

[19] The figures are density of main clauses with directive speech acts: in Southern texts: 22.61/1,000 words; in Kentish texts: 15.04/1,000 words; in East Midland texts: 6.57/1,000 words; in West Midland texts: 10.56/1,000 words; in Northern texts: 7.53/1,000 words. Percentage shares of imperatives: in Southern texts: 69.61 per cent; in Kentish texts: 74.10 per cent. Percentage shares of modal constructions: in East Midland texts: 40.47 per cent; in West Midland texts: 44.14 per cent; in Northern texts: 31.82 per cent.

human anatomy but also a number of instructions on how to prepare certain medicines.

The relevant verbal syntagms in the ME corpus are preferably realised by imperatives and modal constructicons with the auxiliary *shall*. They express a strong type of root modality. Category STA was identified as a stronghold of the subjunctive. Since subjunctives express a weak type of root modality, their rising share in texts of the category STA between OE and ME contrasts sharply with the general development, which is characterised by a frequency increase of verbal syntagms realising a strong type of root modality. This text type specific development was explained as a consequence of a change of the linguistic profile of legislative texts in the wake of the introduction of statutory law.

The other extralinguistic parameters which were analysed in the OE corpus and in the ME corpus for their influence on the density of main clauses with directive speech acts and on the distribution of the realisation of their verbal syntagms are format (prose vs. verse) and regional dialect. Concerning both features a levelling was observed in the ME corpus. The higher density of relevant main clauses in OE prose text fell in the ME corpus, and the large share of subjunctives in the OE prose texts dropped to the same level as in verse texts in ME.

The two southern dialect areas show a higher density of the relevant ME main clauses, and in both the imperative is the preferred realisation of the verbal syntagms.

The gist of all changes from OE to ME can be summarised as a decrease of the density of main clauses with directive speech acts and an increase in the strength of the type of root modality expressed by the most frequent realisations of their verbal syntagms.

2.5 Early Modern English main clauses: the subjunctive and its competitors in earlier publications

In EModE the subjunctive of lexical verbs is formally marked for the second and third person singular (Barber 1997: 172, Nevalainen 2006: 96, Rissanen 1999: 228). With reference to Franz (1939: 522), Görlach (1991: 113) notes subjunctive marking only in the third person singular. Both descriptions are correct, the first holds for the earlier texts in which the personal pronoun of the second person singular is realised by the form *thou*, the second for later texts with their extension of the original plural form *you* to the singular.

The imperative competes with the subjunctive in the second person only. Both forms have a zero ending, but the subjunctive follows its subject, whereas the imperative is either not accompanied by a subject, or its subject is postposed (Barber 1997: 202, Rissanen 1999: 277–278).

As in the earlier periods, modal constructions can be used instead of the subjunctive for the expression of root modality. Rissanen (1999: 231), who lists the same forms as Fischer (1992: 263) for ME, distinguishes two modal meanings of the modal auxiliaries: 'they indicate either "some kind of human control over events" ("permission", "obligation", "volition"), or "human judgement of what is or is not likely to happen" ("possibility", "necessity", "prediction")'. This dichotomy corresponds to Quirk et al.'s (1985: 219) terms intrinsic modality vs. extrinsic modality and to root modality vs. epistemic modality in my model.

Semi-modal constructions, which compete with the subjunctive, contain the elements *dare*, *need*, *ought* and *used*. They can be combined with *to* or can be directly followed by the infinitive of a lexical verb.

In EModE, *let*-constructions with a third person singular addressee are additional competitors of the subjunctive. Jespersen's morphological description of this construction (1909–1949: vol. V. 24.14) may have set Thomas Kohnen thinking again about its pragmatic value. Focusing on constructions with *let me*, he argues (Kohnen 2004: 160) that the analysis of *let*-constructions as periphrastic imperatives proposed in many handbooks needs to be revised. Based on data from the ME and EModE parts of the HC he found that the 'majority of the examples in Middle English and Early Modern English texts must be understood as constructions with the full verb *let* with the meaning "allow" or "cause"'. He comes to the conclusion that 'the "hortative" periphrastic imperative only plays a minor role, which . . . seems to be confined to the Early Modern period' (2004: 167). As competitors of EModE subjunctive constructions only *let*-constructions with a third person singular addressee need to be considered. Yet each example has to be carefully checked if *let* is used as an introductory particle or as a full verb.

2.6 The subjunctive and its competitors in the EModE corpus

In the analysis of my EModE corpus I distinguish the following realisations of the relevant verbal syntagms: subjunctives, imperatives, modal constructions, semi-modal constructions, and *let*-constructions. The modal auxiliaries involved are *may, can, shall, must* and *will*. The possible realisations in the second and third person singular are entered in Table 2.14.[20]

Table 2.14 The subjunctive and its competitors in EModE main clauses

	Subjunctive	Imperative	Modal	Semi-modal	*Let*
2nd ps sg	X	X	X	X	
3rd ps sg	X		X	X	X

[20] In the frequency tables, semi-modal constructions and *let*-constructions are entered under 'Modal'.

Examples of each realisation possibility are given below:

<u>Subjunctive</u>
2nd person:
This is only a theoretical possibility; my corpus attests only examples for the
3rd person.
3rd person:
[2.53] *the Lord pardon the sinne for which I was so punished* (E2 NN
DIARY HOBY, p. 71)
<u>Imperative</u>
2nd person:
[2.54] *folow not my example in yougth* (E1 IS/EX EDUC ASCH, p. 215)
<u>Modal construction</u>
2nd person:
[2.55] *there thou shalt see anone the same true and perfyt felicitie and bless-*
ednes (E1 XX PHILO BOETHCO, p. 70)
3rd person:
[2.56] *in the milking of a Cowe the woman must sit on the neare side of the*
Cowe (E2 IS HANDO MARKHAM, p. 108)
<u>Semi-modal construction</u>
2nd person:
[2.57] *Thou art to be a Father and a Mother to her, and a Brother* (E3 IR
SERM JETAYLOR, p. 20)
3rd person:
[2.58] *there needs not much to be said about it* (E3 IS EDUC LOCKE, p. 44)
<u>*Let*-construction</u>
3rd person:
[2.59] *but let it not be,' quoth she, 'before nine of the clocke at nyghte* (E1 NI
FICT HARMAN, p. 69)

2.6.1 *The parameter 'person'*

My EModE corpus contains 694 relevant verbal syntagms; this corresponds to a normalised frequency of 3.59/1,000 words. Compared
to the frequency of verbal syntagms expressing root modality in the
earlier periods, this is a steady decline. This is still the case when only
the frequencies of third person singular occurrences are considered
(OE: 9.56, ME: 3.69, EModE: 2.97). This frequency decrease may be
a chance effect of the composition of my corpora, but it can also indicate a more general tendency of the speakers to use verbal syntagms
expressing root modality less and less frequently. The distribution of
the different realisations of directive speech acts adressed to the second
and third person in main clauses of the EModE corpus is shown in
Table 2.15:

Table 2.15 The subjunctive and its competitors in the main clauses of the EModE corpus

	Subjunctive	Imperative	Modal	Total
2nd ps sg		77 64.17%	43 35.83%	120 100%
3rd ps sg	119 20.73%		455 79.27%	574 100%
Total	119 17.15%	77 11.10%	498 71.75%	694 100%

Modal constructions are the preferred realisation, followed by subjunctives and imperatives. The most striking changes between ME and EModE are the dramatic increase of modal constructions and the equally dramatic decrease of imperatives. In terms of the strength of root modality expressed by these realisations, this indicates that EModE speakers preferred realisations of directive speech acts expressing weaker types of root modality. This interpretation is also supported when only the relative shares of the different realisation possibilities in the second person singular are compared (ME: 81.10 per cent imperatives, EModE: 64.17 per cent imperatives; ME: 15.78 per cent modal constructions, EModE: 35.83 per cent modal constructions).

2.6.2 *The parameter date of composition*

Following the HC, the subperiods E1–E3 are distinguished for the texts of my EModE corpus. Table 2.16 shows the distribution of the subjunctive and its competitors across these subperiods.

Table 2.16 The distribution of the subjunctive and its competitors in main clauses across subperiods E1–E3

Subperiod	Subjunctive	Imperative	Modal	Total
E1	31 14.49%	44 20.56%	139 64.95%	214 100%
E2	44 18.11%	24 9.88%	175 72.01%	243 100%
E3	44 18.57%	9 3.80%	184 66.67%	237 100%
Total	119 17.15%	77 11.10%	498 71.75%	694 100%

The share of subjunctives shows a steady rise through the whole period, whereas that of the imperatives follows an inverse development. There is also a rising frequency trend in modal constructions, but it is less steady than in subjunctives. For the subjunctive this is a new and unexpected trend, whereas frequency decrease in imperatives and frequency increase in modal constructions were observed already in ME.

2.6.3 *The parameter text category*

The text categories of my EModE corpus are the same as in the corpora of the earlier periods. The distribution of the subjunctive and its competitors across these text categories is shown in Table 2.17.

Table 2.17 The distribution of subjunctives and alternative constructions in main clauses across text categories in the EModE corpus

Category	Subjunctive	Imperative	Modal	Total
STA	99 69.72%		43 30.28%	142 100%
IS	3 2.19%	8 5.84%	126 91.97%	13 100%
IR	2 2.15%	19 20.43%	72 77.42%	93 100%
NI	5 10.00%	18 36.00%	27 54.00%	50 100%
NN	5 0.00%	4 16.00%	16 64.00%	25 100%
EX	2 2.94%		66 97.06%	68 100%
XX	3 1.68%	28 15.64%	148 82.68%	179 100%
Total	119 17.15%	77 11.10%	498 71.75%	694 100%

Main clauses with directive speech acts occur in my EModE corpus with the largest relative frequencies in the text categories STA, IS, IR, and in the unspecified category XX.[21] Concerning the first three text categories, this result was to be expected because of their highly prescriptive nature. The more interesting result is that statutory texts stand out for their preference of subjunctives for the expression of directives. The other text categories with a large relative frequency of directive speech acts prefer modal constructions.

The category STA is represented by three law texts, one from each subperiod, and subjunctives are used with a relative frequency of about 70 per cent in all subperiods. It is one of the genre conventions of legislative texts in EModE that they start with a promulgation formula of the pattern *be it . . . enacted/ordained/established . . . that* (Moessner 2010b: 235). It expresses a weak type of deontic modality. Out of the ninety-nine subjunctives in the statutory texts of my EModE corpus, ninety-four are realisations of the promulgation formula.

[2.60]   *Be it ordeyned by the Auctoritie of this present Parliament that no*
persone of whate estate condicion or degre that he be use in his
apparell eny Cloth of golde of Purpoure Coloure or Sylke of Purpoure
Coloure but onely the Kyng the Qwene the Kyngs Moder the Kyngs
Chylder the Kings Brethers and Susters, upon payne to forfett the seid

---

[21] The values of the relative frequency of relevant main clauses per 1,000 words are: STA: 3.86; IS: 5.19; IR: 6.02; NI: 3.17; NN: 0.50; EX: 2.91; XX: 6.99.

> *Apparell wherwyth so ever yt be myxte, and for usying the same to forfaite xx pounde* (E1 STA LAW STAT3, p. III, 8)

[2.61] *And bee it alsoe enacted by the Authority aforesaid That if any Prisoner who hath been or shall bee discharged by virtue of any of the Acts before mentioned or by virtue of this Act shall att any time here-after be arrested or sued for any Debt contracted before such his or her Discharge hee or she may plead the General Issue and give this Act and the said Two first mentioned Acts and the Proceedings thereon had in Evidence* (E3 STA LAW STAT7, p. VII, 77)

This type of promulgation formula is first attested in subperiod M4 of my ME corpus (cf. section 2.4.3 and example [2.52]). The corresponding text contains twenty-nine examples of directive speech acts. The verbal syntagms of these are realised by subjunctives (twenty-eight examples) and by modal constructions (one example). Out of the twenty-eight sub-junctives, twenty-one figure in a promulgation formula. This is a relative share of 75 per cent.

The modal constructions in the category IS are noteworthy because of their large share of the auxiliary *will*. The pattern *will* + infinitive has a share of 20.89 per cent in the directive speech acts in main clauses of the whole EModE corpus, a share of 34.31 per cent in the texts of category IS. This category is represented by five handbooks/treatises, and in two of them the pattern in question is not attested at all. It clusters in the texts of the later subperiods E2 and E3. Very often the construction occurs in the apodosis of conditional constructions, where it expresses the weak epistemic modality prediction.

[2.62] *if it be ouer heated, it will looke white, crumble, and be bitter in tast* (E2 IS HANDO MARKHAM, p. 111)

[2.63] *If the awe I spoke of be once got, a looke will be sufficient in most cases* (E3 IS EDUC LOCKE, p. 57)

The most frequent modal auxiliary in the texts of category IR is *can*, with a share of 24.61 per cent as against 15.96 per cent in the relevant main clauses of the whole EModE corpus. All texts of category IR are sermons, and their *can*-constructions, which cluster in the subperiod E3 in the apodosis of conditional constructions, express the weak epistemic modality possibility.

[2.64] *And if the man cannot endure her talking, how can she endure his striking?* (E3 IR SERM JETAYLOR, p. 26)

Modal constructions have the biggest share in category XX, which is represented by three EModE translations of Boethius's *De consolatione philosophiae.* In these philosophical dialogues, *can* reaches an even bigger share than in text category IR, namely 27.54 per cent. Here, too, it expresses the weak epistemic modality possibility.

> [2.65]   *He then who considers this cannot deny that Good and Happiness*
> *are of one and the same Substance* (E3 XX PHILO BOETHPR,
> p. 139)

As in the previous periods, category STA occupies a special position in that the verbal syntagm of directive speech acts in main clauses is preferably realised by the subjunctive. In the other text categories, modal constructions prevail in main clauses. EModE is the first period in which the modal auxiliaries *will* and *can* occur unusually frequently. It remains to be seen how many of them express epistemic modality. Those which do are strictly speaking not competitors of the subjunctive, which in main clauses expresses only root modality.

2.6.4 *Other extralinguistic parameters*

EModE was a period of growing standardisation. This is why the EModE texts of the HC are not coded for the parameter region. Accordingly, an influence of this parameter on the distribution of the subjunctive and its competitors could not be investigated in my EModE corpus.

Among the eighty-one text files of the HC there are only two verse texts. They do not figure in my corpus. So the parameter format proved irrelevant for the EModE period.

2.6.5 *Summary and comparison with the ME part of the corpus*

In EModE the subjunctive is formally marked for the third person singular, and for the second person singular only when the subject is realised by *thou.* Its competitors are modal and semi-modal constructions; in the 2nd person additionally the imperative, in the 3rd person singular additionally the *let*-construction.

With 3.59/1,000 words the relative frequency of relevant main clauses is lower than in the ME corpus. Modal constructions have the biggest share of the realisation possibilities of the verbal syntagm, followed far behind by subjunctives and imperatives. The most striking changes between ME and EModE are the dramatic increase of modal constructions and the equally dramatic decrease of imperatives. During the EModE period the shares of subjunctives and modal constructions rise, whereas the share of imperatives falls. Taken together these developments indicate a change between ME and EModE towards realisations that express root modality with a weaker force. The steadily rising shares of subjunctives are particularly noteworthy because they disprove the claim of a steadily decreasing subjunctive frequency.

The EModE text categories with the largest relative frequencies of main clauses with directive speech acts are STA, IS, IR and XX. As XX is represented by translations of passages from Boethius's didactic dialogue *De consolatione philosophiae*, the density of directive speech acts in all four categories is a consequence of their highly prescriptive character. Concerning the categories IS and IR, this distribution is similar to that in the ME corpus.

The prevalence of the subjunctive in the texts of category STA was explained as a consequence of a change of genre conventions in legislative texts. Beginning in subperiod M4 in ME, English laws were introduced by a promulgation formula with a fixed linguistic pattern of the form '*be + it + enacted/ordained/established*', and this obligatory formula created a new niche for the subjunctive. It expresses deontic modality.

The preferred realisations of the other text categories containing many relevant verbal syntagms in main clauses are modal constructions with the auxiliaries *will* in the texts of the category IS and *can* in the categories IR and XX. Modal constructions with these auxiliaries in the apodosis of conditional constructions express the weak types prediction and possibility of epistemic modality. Modal constructions were frequent in the ME corpus as well, but their preferred auxiliary was *shall*, expressing deontic root modality.

In sum, the EModE period is characterised by a dramatic frequency drop of imperatives and an equally dramatic frequency rise of modal constructions in main clauses. Very surprisingly, subjunctives also experienced a frequency rise, though of a less conspicuous kind. In terms of modality, the strong types of deontic root modality, which prevailed in ME, gave way to weaker types of deontic root modality. Further research including a careful analysis of the conversational background of modal constructions with the auxiliaries *will* and *can* is needed to account for the observation that they (together with *may*) challenged *shall*'s leading position on the frequency scale of modal auxiliaries.

3

The subjunctive in adjectival relative clauses

Relative clauses exist on the sentence, the clause and the phrase levels. They are referred to as sentential, nominal and adnominal or adjectival relative clauses. Only adjectival relative clauses will be discussed in this chapter. In their prototypical realisation they expand the nucleus of a substantival syntagm, their antecedent. The clause containing the antecedent is the matrix clause of the relative clause. If adjectival relative clauses delimit the range of the referents of the antecedent, they realise the subtype restrictive, if they contain additional information, they realise the subtype non-restrictive.

3.1 Old English adjectival relative clauses: descriptive parameters

3.1.1 Mood

In PDE grammars the subjunctive is not mentioned at all in the context of adjectival relative clauses. In the examples which illustrate the properties of this clause type the indicative or a modally ambiguous verb form is used (cf. Quirk et al. 1985: 1245–1260).

In Harsh's diachronic study of the English subjunctive (1969) adjectival relative clauses constitute one of the thirteen syntactic patterns which he found relevant. The pattern 'relative clause' is characterised as 'describing a person or persons who fulfill(s) hypothetical conditions. The clause is usually introduced by an indefinite pronoun, e.g., *all*, *each*, or by a personal pronoun used to express an indefinite reference' (1969: 117–118). In the *Rushworth Gospels*, the only OE text which Harsh analysed, he identified fifty-nine subjunctives, of which twelve occurred in relative clauses.

A very thorough treatment of the subjunctive in OE relative clauses is provided by Frank Behre in his doctoral dissertation (1934). He devotes two chapters to this topic. In chapter VI (pp. 181–195) he deals with ordinary relative clauses, and chapter XI (pp. 292–312) is about relative clauses that can be replaced by consecutive clauses. He identifies the following six environments in which the subjunctive is used in his data, i.e. in OE poetry, and he illustrates them by examples:

1. The verbal syntagm of the matrix clause is a volitional expression realised by an imperative, a subjunctive, or by *sceal* plus infinitive.
    [3.1]   *Syle þam ðe þe bidde* (Matth. 5:42) 'give to those who ask you' (imperative in matrix clause)
    [3.2]   *Se ðe earan hæbbe to gehyrynne, gehyre* (Matth. 11:15) 'he who has ears to hear shall listen' (subjunctive in matrix clause)
    [3.3]   *Þu hine secan scealt, leofne alysan of laðra hete ond eal þæt mancynn, þe him mid wunige elþeodriga inwitwrasnum bealuwe gebundene* (Andr. 945) 'you are to seek him out and free the cherished man from the hatred of his enemies, and all the humankind that languishes with him evilly shackled with the foreigners' spiteful bonds' (transl. Bradley 1982) (modal construction with *sceal* in the matrix clause)
2. The antecedent of the relative clause is an indefinite pronoun, e.g. *eall*, *gehwylc*, *æghwylc*, *ælc*, etc.
    [3.4]   *gebletsade bearna æghwylc, þe on innan þe ahwær wæren* (PPs. 147:2) 'he blessed each of the children who were somewhere in you [= Jerusalem]' (indefinite pronoun *æghwylc* in matrix clause)
3. The antecedent of the relative clause is a genitive dependent on a superlative.
    [3.5]   *Þa gieng to Adame idesa scenost, wifa wlitegost, þe on woruld come* (Gen. B 627)
    'To Adam then she went, the most lovely of women, the most beautiful of wives that might come into the world' (transl. Bradley 1982) (genitive *wifa* depending on *wlitegost*)
4. The matrix clause of the relative clause contains a negative expression.
    [3.6]   *Næni eft cymeð hider under hrofas, þe þæt her forsoð mannum secge, hwylc sy meotodes gesceaft* (Cott. Gn. 65) [= *Maxims II*] 'nobody ever comes hither below the skies who may for certain tell people what the Lord's creation is like' (negative expression *næni*)
5. The matrix clause of the relative clause is a rhetorical question.
    [3.7]   *Hwa is on eorðan nu unlæredra þe ne wundrige wolcna færeldes* (Met. 28:2) 'who is now on earth among the unlearned who does not wonder at the movement of the clouds?'
6. The matrix clause of the relative clause is an indirect question.
    [3.8]   *Dryhten sceawað, hwær þa eardien, þe his æ healden* (Guth. A 26) 'the Lord shows where they live who respect his law'

Relative clauses of the types 4–6 alternate with consecutive clauses. Concerning clause type 1, Behre admits that the volitional expression can also be realised by a different form, and he quotes the following example:

[3.9]   *Secgas mine to þam guðplegan gearwe sindon, þa þe æninga ellenwe-orcum unfyrn faca feorh ætþringan* (Andr. 1371) 'My men are ready for the sport of battle, who in a short while will quickly crush the life out of you by their valiant deeds.' (Transl. Bradley 1982.)

Comments on Behre's subjunctive conditioning environments are the major issue of Mitchell's treatment of mood in OE relative clauses (1985: §§2386–2415). They are flanked by his general statement that the indicative is the prevailing mood in OE relative clauses: 'Understandably (I hope), I do not have full figures for the prose. But in the poetry, the indicative occurs in almost sixty per cent of the examples. Less than five per cent have the subjunctive. The remainder have a form which is ambiguous for mood.'

Mitchell's criticism is most pronounced concerning Behre's clause types 2 and 6. He excludes indefinite pronouns as subjunctive conditioning elements in prose completely, and the only example from OE poetry that he considers a potential candidate is rejected on the grounds that the subjunctive is a scribal error. For indirect questions Mitchell presents the following distribution in OE poetry: indicative 42 per cent, subjunctive 8 per cent, ambiguous forms 50 per cent. It remains unclear, however, on which data these figures are based.

Behre's clause type 3 is on the whole favourably reviewed by Mitchell, but he adds that it is not the superlative that conditions the subjunctive, but the fact that relative clauses in this environment are restrictive.

Mitchell's verdict on Behre's remaining three clause types, i.e. 1, 4 and 5, can best be described as 'Yes, but'.[1] It is the speaker's attitude towards the facts or the situation presented which determines the choice of the mood. This is the recurring argument in many descriptions of OE relative clauses. Behre claims a 'volitional attitude on the part of the speaker towards the content of the dependent clause' (1934: 183), for Visser (1963–1973: §876) the subjunctive 'expresses the speaker's reserve as to the possibility of the fulfilment of the condition in the clause', and Mitchell first suggests to find out the speaker's attitude by translating the examples (1985: §2388) but in the end admits the futility of all attempts at detecting the speaker's attitude: 'I have to confess that I become almost schizophrenic when I try to apply these explanations to the examples . . .' (1985: §2398). He also envisages individual mood preferences of specific authors.

---

[1] For Behre's type 1 he postulates the following approximate distribution in OE poetry: subjunctive 20 per cent, indicative 40 per cent, ambiguous forms 20 per cent (Mitchell 1985: §2395).

3.1.2 *The relative marker*

OE relative clauses are introduced by a relative marker, which relates to an antecedent on which the relative clause depends. The inventory of relative markers contains the pronouns *se, seo, þæt*, optionally followed by the invariant particle *þe*, and the invariant particles *þe, þæt* and *þær*. Very rarely the relative marker is zero. Relative pronouns agree in number and gender with their antecedents, their case indicates their syntactic function in the relative clause. The form *þæt* is to be interpreted as a relative pronoun, when there is number and gender agreement with the antecedent, otherwise it is an invariant particle. The invariant marker *þær* is used with antecedents with a locative function (Traugott 1992: 223–233).[2]

Mitchell (1985: §2105, §§2109–2121) points out that the identification of relative clauses introduced by the pronouns *se, seo, þæt* and of those introduced by the combination of the pronouns *se, seo, þæt* and the invariant particle *þe* present a problem, because *se, seo, þæt* cannot only function as relative pronouns but also as demonstrative pronouns (cf. examples [3.10] and [3.11]):

[3.10]   *He his aras þonan, halig of heahðu, hider onsendeð, þa us gescildaþ
         wið sceþþendra [[eglum[] earhfarum* (OX/3 XX XX CHRI, p. 24)
         'He sends thence his holy messengers here from the heights who/these
         shield us against the dreadful arrow-attacks of adversaries'

The element *þa* can be analysed as a demonstrative or as a relative pronoun. In the first case the sequence *þa us gescildaþ wið sceþþendra [[eglum[] earhfarum* is an independent sentence with *þa* anaphorically referring to *aras* in the preceding sentence. Otherwise the sequence *þa us gescildaþ wið sceþþendra [[eglum[] earhfarum* is an adjectival relative clause depending on the antecedent *aras*.

[3.11]   <u>*Se ðe*</u> *him bringe þin heafod, onfo se hundteontig punda goldes* (O3
         NI FICT APOLL, p. 12) 'Who/he who brings him your head, he shall
         receive one hundred pounds of gold'

The sequence *se ðe* can be analysed as the complex relative marker or as the antecedent *se* followed by the invariant relative particle *þe*. In the first case the clause *Se ðe him bringe þin heafod* is a nominal relative clause which functions as the subject of the whole sentence. Otherwise the adjectival relative clause *ðe him bringe þin heafod* expands the subject

---

[2] Mitchell (1985: §§2104, 2154, but §2338) claims different agreement rules for the pronominal relative marker. I follow Traugott in my analysis.

se of the whole sentence. Irrespective of the analysis chosen, the second
element *se* takes up the preceding subject.

Unambiguous instances of the complex relative marker are given,
when the antecedent realises a different function from the relative
marker:

> [3.12]   *Maria geceas þone selestan dæl. se ðe ne bið hire næfre ætbroden* (O3
> IR HOM AELFR2/29, p. 25) 'Mary chose the best part, which will
> never be taken away from her'

The sequence *se ðe* can only be analysed as a relative marker, since its
antecendent *þone selestan dæl* functions as the direct object in the matrix
clause and is therefore marked as accusative, whereas *se ðe* functions as
subject in the relative clause and is therefore marked as nominative.

Mitchell (1985: §2283) notes that the complex relative marker and
invariant *þe* are preferred in restrictive relative clauses in poetry, whereas
there is a slight preference for *se, seo, þæt* in non-restrictive relative
clauses.

3.1.3 *The antecedent and the relative marker*

Mitchell (1985: §2249) points out that OE relative clauses may have
the same antecedents as PDE relative clauses, namely 'nouns of any
sort (including proper nouns), either alone or qualified by a demonstrative and/or adjective(s); personal pronouns; demonstratives; possessives;
indefinites; numerals; superlatives; and sentences or clauses'. He rejects
Anklam's (1908) claim that there is a regular correspondence between
the form of the antecedent and that of the relative marker, but he notes
the following tendencies (Mitchell 1985: §2253–2270):

- when the antecedent is a substantive modified by a demonstrative or
  a possessive or an indefinite pronoun, the preferred relative marker is
  þe (cf. also Traugott 1992: 226–227 and Traugott 1972: 103–104);[3]
- when the antecedent is a noun which is not modified at all or only
  by an adjective, the preferred relative marker is *se, seo, þæt* when the
  noun is singular, and the combination of *se, seo, þæt* plus invariant *þe*
  when the noun is plural;[4]
- when the antecedent is a third person personal pronoun, the relative
  pronoun *se, seo, þæt* or the complex relative marker are preferred;
- when the antecedent is a demonstrative pronoun, the preferred relative
  marker is invariant *þe*;

---

[3] In these environments the relative clauses are restrictive.
[4] In these environments the relative clauses are non-restrictive.

- when the antecedent is an indefinite pronoun, the preferred relative markers are invariant *þe* and the complex relative marker;
- when the antecedent is a numeral, the relative pronoun *se, seo, þæt* is preferred;
- when the antecedent is a superlative in a restrictive relative clause, invariant *þe* and the complex relative marker are preferred, in non-restrictive relative clauses the relative pronoun *se, seo, þæt* is preferred.

3.1.4 *The verbal syntagm in the matrix clause*

An influence of the verbal syntagm in the matrix clause on the form of the verbal syntagm in the relative clause was not only postulated by Behre, but before him by Glunz (1929), and after him by Wilde (1939/1940). Although these authors use different terms for the matrix clause (Behre: 'main clause', Glunz: 'Hauptsatz', Wilde: 'Vordersatz', 'Hauptsatz', 'übergeordneter Satz'), they all denote the clause that contains the antecedent of the relative clause. This is illustrated in the following example, where the relative clause is embedded in the object clause depending on the verb form *bæd* of the main clause.

> [3.13] *Ða bæd he Oswio ðone cyning, þæt he him hwylcehugu lareowas sealde, ða ðe his ðeode to Cristes geleafan gecyrde, and mid þa halwendan wyllan fulluhtbæþes aþwoge* Be.552,35 (quot. Glunz 1929: 26–27) 'then he asked King Oswio to send him some teachers, who should convert his people to the Christian faith and baptise them with the sanctifying fountain of the baptismal bath'

For Wilde, the relation between the matrix clause and relative clause is the most important factor that determines the form of the verbal syntagm in the relative clause: 'Als maßgebender Grund für das Vorkommen des Konjunktivs im Relativsatz ist allein der gesamte modale Zusammenhang des Satzgefüges anzusetzen' (Wilde 1939/1940: 376).[5] The overall modality required for the occurrence of the subjunctive is request, wish or possibility (the title of Wilde's study is *Auffforderung, Wunsch und Möglichkeit*). Yet even if this modality is given, the subjunctive, or alternatively a modal construction, is not the rule. Glunz (1929: 19) explicitly states that the subjunctive is one of the stylistic choices available to the OE writer: '. . . daß ein so dehnbares, schmiegsames und anpassungsfähiges Stilmittel, wie der Konjunktiv es im Altenglischen noch ist, nicht in Regeln gezwungen werden kann. Er ist noch Stil und noch nicht

---

[5] 'The sole factor which determines the use of the subjunctive in the relative clause is to be seen in the overall modal meaning of the complex sentence.'

Grammatik.'[6] Both Glunz and Wilde are more interested in the modality expressed by the subjunctive in OE relative clauses. This is why they neglect the formal parameters which influence the distribution of the realisation possibilities of the verbal syntagm in relative clauses.

3.2 The subjunctive and its competitors in the OE corpus

Relevant adjectival relative clauses are those with a verbal syntagm in the second or third person singular present or in any person plural present. In my OE corpus I identified 836 relevant adjectival relative clauses. This equals a relative frequency of 6.52/1,000 words. In 210 of them (= 1.64/1,000 words, 25.12 per cent) the verbal syntagm is realised by a subjunctive, in 540 (= 4.21/1,000 words, 64.59 per cent) by an indicative, and in the remaining 86 (= 0.67/1,000 words, 10.29 per cent) by a modal construction.[7] The modal auxiliary is a subjunctive in thirty-six examples, an indicative in thirty-three examples and an ambiguous form in the remaining seventeen examples. The modal auxiliaries involved are *willan*, *sceal*, *can*, *mot* and *mæg*. Subjunctive frequency is greatest in verbal syntagms of the third person singular. The following sections will deal with the influence of linguistic and extralinguistic parameters on the distribution of the realisation possibilities of the verbal syntagm in the relative clauses of my OE corpus.

3.2.1 The parameter date of composition

Table 3.1 shows the distribution of subjunctives, indicatives and modal constructions in the relative clauses of the OE corpus across the subperiods O1–O4.

Table 3.1 The distribution of subjunctives, indicatives and modal constructions in the relative clauses of the OE corpus across the subperiods O1–O4

Subperiod	Subjunctive	Indicative	Modal	Total
O1	12 54.55%	9 40.91%	1 4.54%	22 100%
O2	49 30.63%	100 62.50%	11 6.87%	160 100%
O3	134 25.38%	343 64.96%	51 9.66%	528 100%
O4	15 11.90%	88 69.84%	23 18.26%	126 100%
Total	210 25.12%	540 64.59%	86 10.29%	836 100%

---

[6] '. . . that such a flexible, subtle, and adaptable stylistic device that the subjunctive still is in Old English cannot be pressed into rules. It is still a stylistic device and not a feature of grammar.'

[7] The share of 25.12 per cent for subjunctives is five times greater than the 5 per cent claimed by Mitchell (1985: §2386) for OE poetry.

The share of subjunctives decreases from the first to the last sub-period, whereas that of indicatives and modal constructions rises. The greatest frequency change of subjunctives and of indicatives took place between O1 and O2. Modal constructions increased most conspicuously between O3 and O4. The decrease of subjunctive frequency is in line with handbook wisdom, the increase of modal constructions requires a separate treatment, because the modal auxiliaries themselves occur as subjunctives, as indicatives, or as ambiguous forms. The distribution of subjunctives, indicatives and ambiguous forms in relative clauses with a modal construction across the OE subperiods is shown in Table 3.2.

Table 3.2 The distribution of subjunctives, indicatives and ambiguous forms in relative clauses with modal constructions in subperiods O1–O4

Subperiod	Subjunctive	Indicative	Ambiguous	Total
O1		1 100%		1 100%
O2	8 72.73%	1 9.09%	2 18.18%	11 100%
O3	23 45.10%	18 35.29%	10 19.61%	51 100%
O4	5 21.74%	13 56.52%	5 21.74%	23 100%
Total	36 1.86%	33 38.37%	17 19.77%	86 100%

It is obvious that apart from subperiod O1, when modal constructions play a minor role anyway, the share of subjunctives of modal auxiliaries is higher than that of indicatives up to subperiod O4. This indicates that after O3 the subjunctive as a marker of root modality lost its role as the preferred realisation of the verbal syntagm in relative clauses in modal constructions and in finite verbs.

3.2.2 The parameter dialect

In the coding of the parameter dialect in the HC the following varieties are distinguished: Anglian, Anglian Mercian, Anglian Northumbrian, Kentish and West Saxon (Kytö 1996: 50). In my dialect analysis I conflated the first three varieties under Anglian. The distribution of subjunctives, indicatives and modal constructions in the different dialects is displayed in Table 3.3.

Table 3.3 The distribution of subjunctives, indicatives and modal constructions in relative clauses across the OE dialect areas

Dialect	Subjunctive	Indicative	Modal	Total
Anglian	35 21.88%	115 71.87%	10 6.25%	160 100%
Kentish	6 42.86%	7 50.00%	1 7.14%	14 100%
West Saxon	169 25.53%	418 63.14%	75 11.33%	662 100%
Total	210 25.12%	540 64.59%	86 10.29%	836 100%

Read horizontally, the table shows that the indicative is the preferred realisation in the whole corpus and also in all individual dialect areas. The columns show that indicatives have the biggest share in Anglian texts, whereas subjunctives prevail in Kentish texts and modal constructions in West Saxon texts. Since these two realisations express root modality, the conclusion is that root modality in OE adjectival relative clauses plays the biggest role in the southern dialect areas.

3.2.3 The parameter text category

Before looking at the distribution of the realisation possibilities of the verbal syntagm in the seven text categories of the HC, the frequency of adjectival relative clauses across the text categories will be established. It is shown in Table 3.4.

Table 3.4 Relative frequency of relative clauses across the text categories of the OE corpus

Text category	Size/words	Relative clauses/ absolute numbers	Relative clauses/ 1,000 words
STA	17,140	172	10.04
IS	6,990	49	7.01
IR	16,430	153	9.31
NI	13,820	28	2.03
NN	20,590	69	3.35
EX	5,360	75	13.99
XX	47,870	290	6.06
Total	128,200	836	6.52

Relative clauses have a bigger than average frequency (= 6.52 relative clauses/1,000 words) in the text categories EX, STA, IR and IS. However, it does not follow that in these text categories subjunctives are particularly frequent. The distribution of the realisation possibilities of the verbal syntagm can be gleaned from Table 3.5.

Subjunctives stand out as particularly frequent in the category STA, which consists of law texts. Here are some typical examples:

[3.14] *Se mon se ðe his gewealdes monnan ofslea, swelte se deaðe* (O2 STA LAW ALFLAWIN, p. 30) 'the person who intentionally kills a man, shall suffer death'

[3.15] *se munuc, þe mynster næbbe, cume scirebiscope* (O3 STA LAW LAW11C, p. 238) 'the monk who has no monastery shall come to the bishop of the diocese'

[3.16] *Forðige ofer þæt gear ealle gerihtu, ðe him to gebyrigean* (O3/4 STA

Table 3.5 Subjunctives, indicatives and modal constructions in relative clauses in the text categories of the OE corpus

Text category	Subjunctive	Indicative	Modal	Total
STA	107 62.21%	42 24.42%	23 13.37%	172 100%
IS	19 38.78%	26 53.06%	4 8.16%	49 100%
IR	17 11.11%	120 78.43%	16 10.46%	153 100%
NI	6 21.43%	20 71.43%	2 7.14%	28 100%
NN	2 2.90%	56 81.16%	11 15.94%	69 100%
EX	1 1.33%	71 94.67%	3 4.00%	75 100%
XX	58 20.00%	205 70.69%	27 9.31%	290 100%
Total	210 25.12%	540 64.59%	86 10.29%	836 100%

LAW LAWLAT, p. 447) '[he] shall accomplish after that year all legal actions which pertain to him'

In all of these the antecedent is a substantival syntagm whose nucleus is expanded by a form of the *se, seo, þæt* paradigm or by an indefinite pronoun (cf. section 3.2.6).

The second biggest share of subjunctives in OE relative clauses is found in the text category IS. There are two texts in my corpus which belong to this category, and both are medical handbooks. Like the texts in the category STA, medical handbooks are prescriptive in nature and written in a formal style. Typical examples of subjunctives in relative clauses of the medical handbooks in my corpus are [3.17] and [3.18]:

[3.17] *smyre his heafod mid, þær hit acy* (O2/3 IS HANDM LACN, p. 102) 'anoint his head with it where it aches'
[3.18] *him þonne of cwicum þa teþ ado þa þe he mæste hæbbe* (O2/3 IS HANDM QUADR, p. 3) 'then take those teeth away from the live [animal] of which it has most'

It is noteworthy in these examples, too, that their antecedent is a substantival syntagm, whose nucleus is expanded. In both examples the premodifiers together with the relative clause restrict the potential referents of the nucleus (cf. section 3.2.6).

3.2.4 The parameter format

Although only six out of the thirty files of my OE corpus consist of verse texts, I tested the influence of the parameter format on the realisation of the verbal syntagm in adjectival relative clauses (cf. Table 3.6).

The indicative is the preferred realisation of the verbal syntagm in prose and in verse texts. Yet the share of subjunctives is greater in prose texts than in verse texts. It is difficult to compare Mitchell's figures

Table 3.6 The distribution of the subjunctive and its competitors in relative clauses of OE prose and verse texts

Format	Subjunctive	Indicative	Modal	Total
Prose	196 26.81%	462 63.20%	73 9.99%	731 100%
Verse	14 13.33%	78 74.29%	13 12.38%	105 100%
Total	210 25.12%	540 64.59%	86 10.29%	836 100%

(1985: §2386) of his verse corpus with mine because he distinguishes the realisations subjunctive, indicative and ambiguous form. In my corpus the percentage shares of subjunctives and of indicatives in verse texts are greater than in his.

3.2.5 The relative marker

The relative markers to be expected are the pronouns *se*, *seo*, *þæt*, optionally followed by *þe*, and the invariable relative marker *þe* on its own. Additionally, there are some minor options (cf. section 3.1.2). The distribution of subjunctives, indicatives and modal constructions in relative clauses with these relative markers is shown in Table 3.7; the minor options are entered under 'Others'.[8]

Table 3.7 The distribution of subjunctives, indicatives and modal constructions in OE relative clauses with different relative markers

Relative marker	Subjunctive	Indicative	Modal	Total
Þe	156 26.44%	372 63.05%	62 10.51%	590 100%
Se þe	30 32.97%	53 58.24%	8 8.79%	91 100%
Se	18 13.53%	104 78.20%	11 8.27%	133 100%
Others	6 27.27%	11 50.00%	5 22.73%	22 100%
Total	210 25.12%	540 64.59%	86 10.29%	836 100%

Irrespective of the realisation of their verbal syntagm, the relative clauses of the OE corpus prefer the invariant relative marker *þe*. Yet the share of subjunctives is greatest after the complex relative marker *se þe* (cf. examples [3.11] and [3.19]).

[3.19]   *Mid his gelynde smyre þa hors þa þe syn on feofre oþe on ænigre adle* (O2/3 IS HANDM QUADR, p. 5) 'with his [the badger's] fat smear the horses that are in a fever or in another illness'

---

[8] The relative markers involved are *þær* (sixteen examples), *þætte* and zero (two examples each), *hwilc* and *swa* (one example each). On *þætte* as a relative marker cf. Mitchell (1985: §§2129, 2139–2144), on *whilc* as a relative marker cf. Mitchell (1985: §2385), on *swa* as a relative marker cf. Mitchell (1985: §§2379–2382).

Note that in these examples the matrix clause contains a volitional expression, i.e. a verbal syntagm realised by an imperative, a subjunctive or a modal construction with the auxiliary *shall*, which according to Behre (cf. sections 3.1.1 and 3.1.4) favours the use of the subjunctive. This is an environment which licenses subjunctives in relative clauses in the Romance languages as well (Kampers-Manhe 1991, Panzeri 2006). Since the percentage shares of the subjunctive after the different markers do not differ much, it is doubtful if the complex relative marker alone has a big influence on the choice of the realisation of the verbal syntagm in the relative clause.

3.2.6 *The antecedent*

Among the antecedents envisaged by Mitchell (1985: §2249), sentences and clauses are irrelevant in the context of adjectival relative clauses. Table 3.8 gives an overview of the distribution of subjunctives, indicatives and modal constructions after different antecedents; indefinite pronouns and some minor realisations are included under 'Others'.

Table 3.8 The distribution of subjunctives, indicatives and modal constructions in OE relative clauses with different antecedents

Antecedent	Subjunctive	Indicative	Modal	Total
Substantival syntagm	85 18.36%	335 72.35%	43 9.29%	463 100%
Personal pronoun	7 21.21%	20 60.61%	6 18.18%	33 100%
Se, seo, þæt	97 38.65%	133 52.98%	21 8.37%	251 100%
Possessive pronoun	2 28.57%	4 57.14%	1 14.29%	7 100%
Others	19 23.17%	48 58.54%	15 18.29%	82 100%
Total	210 25.12%	540 64.59%	86 10.29%	836 100%

All antecedents favour the indicative in the following relative clause. This tendency is strongest when the antecedent is realised by a substantival syntagm, and weakest after an antecedent of the *se, seo, þæt* paradigm. The salient co-occurrence frequency of the subjunctive and antecedents of the *se, seo, þæt* paradigm is noteworthy, because these antecedents are not mentioned by Behre as subjunctive favouring environments. After these antecedents realisations that express root modality, i.e. subjunctives and modal constructions, are nearly as probable as indicatives (cf. examples [3.20] and [3.21]).

[3.20]   *Se þe secge þæt he on Crist gelyfe, fare se þæs rihtweges þe Crist sylf ferde* (O3 IR HOM WULF10C, p. 200) 'The one who says that he believes in Christ shall go on the right way on which Christ himself went'

[3.21]   Nu cweðað sume men þe ðis gescead ne cunnon þæt se mona hine wende be ðan ðe hit wedrian sceall on ðam monðe (O3 EX SCIA

> TEMP, p. 62) 'Now some people who do not know this distinction say
> that the moon turns according to what the weather will be in the month'

Another noteworthy result is the large share of modal constructions after indefinite pronouns figuring under 'Others'.[9]

> [3.22]   *Gyf he ðonne eal wel gefriðað, <u>he healdan sceal</u>, ðonne bið he godes*
> *leanes ful wel wyrðe* (O3/4 STA LAW LAWLAT, p. 452) 'if he then
> observes everything well [that] he shall hold, then is he really worthy
> of God's reward'

I also tested Behre's claim that subjunctives are favoured by antecedents realised by a genitive dependent on a superlative. Genitives depending on superlatives are realised as substantival syntagms or as genitive forms of the *se, seo, þæt* paradigm. Examples of the first type do not occur in my corpus. Most of Behre's examples are of the second type:

> [3.23]   *Eala! Þu mære middangeardes seo clæneste cwen ofer eorþan, þara*
> *<u>þe gewurde to widan feore</u>* (Crist I: 277; quot. Behre 1934: 194) 'O
> splendour of the world, the purest woman on earth of those that have
> ever been' (transl. Bradley 1982)

There is just one example of this type in my OE corpus:

> [3.24]   *Wæs he under hiofenum hearpera mærost ðara <u>we an folcum gefrigen</u>*
> *<u>hæbben</u>* (OX/3 XX XX KHYMN, p. 88) 'He was the greatest harper
> under the sky of those [that] we have known among people'

Although example [3.24] confirms Behre's observation that in this environment the subjunctive is found, it is not sufficient to claim that in my corpus genitives depending on superlatives favour the subjunctive in the following relative clause.

Concerning the influence of the antecedent on the form of the verbal syntagm in the relative clause, it is to be noted that irrespective of the type of antecedent the indicative is the preferred realisation of the verbal syntagm in OE adjectival relative clauses. Antecedents of the *se, seo, þæt* paradigm show the greatest share of subjunctives, and indefinite pronouns attest a large share of modal constructions. Since relative clauses after these two types of antecedents are restrictive, it can be assumed that the feature restrictiveness licenses OE relative clauses with verbal syntagms expressing root modality.

---

[9] The percentage figures are: 22.58 per cent subjunctives, 56.45 per cent indicatives, 20.97 per cent modal constructions.

3.2.7 *The matrix clause*

In my analysis of a potential influence of the verbal syntagm in the matrix clause on the form of the verbal syntagm in the relative clause I first checked the feature volitional expression mentioned by Behre, i.e. a subjunctive, an imperative, or a modal construction with *sceal*. Table 3.9 shows the distribution of subjunctives, indicatives and modal constructions in OE relative clauses depending on matrix clauses with and without volitional expressions.

Table 3.9 Subjunctives, indicatives and modal constructions in OE relative clauses depending on matrix clauses with and without a volitional expression

Matrix \ Relative	Subjunctive	Indicative	Modal	Total
+ Volitional expression	168 51.37%	115 35.17%	44 13.46%	327 100%
– Volitional expression	42 8.25%	425 83.50%	42 8.25%	509 100%
Total	210 25.12%	540 64.59%	86 10.29%	836 100%

In the texts of my corpus there is a clear correlation between the form of the verbal syntagm in the matrix clause and that of the dependent relative clause. The shares of subjunctives and modal constructions are saliently larger in relative clauses depending on matrix clauses containing a volitional expression. The subjunctive is even the prevailing mood in this environment. The figures also indicate that the subjunctive stands only a very small chance in relative clauses depending on matrix clauses without a volitional expression. This result is a first suggestion of a tendency towards the use of forms of the verbal syntagm expressing the same modality in a superordinate and a subordinate clause. This property is referred to as modal harmony in *The Cambridge Grammar* (Huddleston and Pullum 2002: 179).[10] So far it has not been applied in studies on the subjunctive in English relative clauses.

Although subjunctives, imperatives and *sceal*-constructions are subsumed under volitional expressions, their influence on the form of the verbal syntagm in the adjectival relative clause is not equally strong (cf. Table 3.10).[11]

---

[10] The original notion of vowel harmony was first transferred from phonology to lexicology as 'semantic prosody' by Louw (1993: 157) and from there to semantics in *The Cambridge Grammar*.

[11] Tables 3.9 and 3.10 contain all modal constructions irrespective of the modal auxiliary.

Table 3.10 Subjunctives, indicatives and modal constructions in OE relative clauses depending on antecedents in clauses with different volitional expressions

Matrix \ Relative	Subjunctive	Indicative	Modal	Total
Subjunctive	147 59.04%	64 25.70%	38 15.26%	249 100%
Imperative	18 33.33%	34 62.97%	2 3.70%	54 100%
Modal	3 12.50%	17 70.83%	4 16.67%	24 100%
Total	168 51.37%	115 35.17%	44 13.46%	327 100%

The most favourable environment for a subjunctive in a dependent relative clause is a subjunctive in the matrix clause (cf. also example [3.15]):

[3.25] *swælc monn se ðe to minum ærfe foe, ðonne gedele he ælcum messepreoste binnan Cent mancus goldes* (O1 XX DOC HARM2, p. 4) 'whosoever may succeed to my property is to distribute to every priest in Kent a mancus of gold' (transl. Harmer 1914)

Another subjunctive favouring feature, mentioned by Behre and by Wilde, is negation in the matrix clause. This environment is difficult to check in the data because it is defined in terms of form <u>and</u> content ('nach Form oder Inhalt verneint').[12] This vague description corresponds to Mitchell's (1985: §2405) 'virtual negatives such as *feawa*'. The example referred to here by Mitchell is also discussed by Behre (1934: 294), and he justifies the following subjunctive by the 'negative purport' of the superordinate clause. Since the criterion of negativity of the superordinate clause is so elusive, it was neglected in my analysis.

Similarly problematic is the environment rhetorical question of the superordinate clause. The close resemblance between rhetorical questions and statements containing a negative expression is hinted at by Behre (1934: 296) when he states that 'the questioning form is used as a stylistic device for paraphrasing a negative idea'. Whether a negative idea is involved can be a matter of dispute. Among the passages which Mitchell (1985: §2408) quotes as instances of rhetorical questions with embedded relative clauses with indicative is the following:

---

[12] Cf. also Vogt (1930: 70): 'Die Verneinung der Nebensatzaussage braucht nicht durch eine Negation zu erfolgen; sie kann auch durch eine rhetorische Frage mit negativem Sinn oder durch Wörter negativer Bedeutung wie insbesondere *fea* geschehen.' [The negation of the denotation of the subordinate clause need not be expressed by a negation particle; it can also be brought about by a rhetorical question with negative purport or by words with negative denotation like especially *fea*.]

[3.26]   *Se ðe ne lufað his broðor, <u>ðone ðe he gesihð</u>, hu mæg he lufian God,*
   <u>þone he ne gesihð lichamlice</u>? (ÆCHom i.326.8) 'How can he who
   does not love his brother, whom he sees, love God, whom he does not
   see in the flesh?'

According to Mitchell the implication here is that a person who does
not love his brother, although he can see him as a living creature, will
certainly not love God, who is invisible. Whether this interpretation is
correct cannot be decided on linguistic grounds. Mitchell also challenges
the interpretation of one of Behre's examples:

[3.27]   *Hwær is eac se wisa and se weorðgeorna and se fæstræda folces hyrde,*
   <u>se wæs uðwita ælces ðinges</u> cene and cræftig, <u>þæm wæs Caton nama</u>?
   Met. 10:50 (quot. Behre 1934: 296) 'Where is also the wise and the
   studious of glory and the inflexible guardian of the people, who was
   a philosopher in every respect, brave and virtuous, whose name was
   Cato?'

For Behre this question is not rhetorical, and this is how he justifies the
indicative in both relative clauses. For Mitchell the main clause is a rhetorical question, and the indicative in the relative clauses supports his
observation that rhetorical questions do not necessarily favour the subjunctive in dependent relative clauses. Since neither Behre nor Mitchell
provide linguistic arguments to support their respective interpretations
of individual examples concerning the feature rhetorical question, I dis-
regarded this feature in the analysis of my corpus.

The last environment to be tested as potentially subjunctive favouring
was the presence of an indirect question in the matrix clause (Behre's
clause type 6.). Yet Behre himself cannot have found many examples of
this type in his data; he quotes only four, and all of them are beside the
point. In one example the relative clause has no antecedent, it functions
as a noun clause. The adjectival relative clauses in the three remaining
examples expand an antecedent that is realised by a form of the *se,
seo, þæt* paradigm or a substantival syntagm containing one of these
forms, and the former environment was found to occur with the greatest share of subjunctives in the dependent relative clauses of my OE
corpus (cf. section 3.2.6). The subjunctive favouring feature in these
examples is therefore not the type of matrix clause, but the form of the
antecedent.

3.2.8 Summary

The OE corpus contains 836 adjectival relative clauses. Their verbal syntagms are realised by subjunctives (25.12 per cent), by indicatives (64.59

per cent) and by modal constructions (10.29 per cent). The occurrence probability of subjunctives is influenced by several factors.

Only in period O1 are subjunctives more frequent than the other realisation possibilities. The relative share of subjunctives decreases between O1 and O4, whereas that of indicatives and modal constructions increases. The frequency of modal constructions increases most conspicuously between O3 and O4.

The Kentish texts of the corpus contain the largest share of subjunctives. Yet this result is to be interpreted with caution, since the overall number of relevant relative clauses in these texts is very low. On a more general plane it was noted that adjectival relative clauses with verbal syntagms expressing root modality play the largest role in the southern dialect areas.

Among the text categories favouring the subjunctive, law texts (= category STA) proved the category with the biggest share of subjunctives, followed by texts of secular instruction (= category IS).

The analysis of the parameter format revealed that the share of subjunctives in prose texts is twice as large as in verse texts.

Although *þe* is by far the most frequent relative marker in the whole corpus, the biggest share of subjunctives is attested after the complex relative marker *se þe*.

Substantival syntagms are the most frequent antecedents of the relative clauses in the corpus, but antecedents of the *se, seo, þæt* paradigm co-occur most frequently with subjunctives in relative clauses. This co-occurrence, together with the large share of modal constructions after indefinite pronouns as antecedents, prompted my hypothesis that the feature restrictiveness licenses OE relative clauses with verbal syntagms expressing root modality.

The most telling result was achieved through the analysis of the matrix clauses of the relative clauses. If they contain a volitional expression – i.e. a subjunctive, an imperative or a modal construction – a subjunctive in the relative clause is more frequent than any other realisation of the verbal syntagm. This was interpreted as an instance of modal harmony. Among the volitional expressions it is the subjunctive in the matrix clause which shows the highest probability of being combined with a subjunctive in the relative clause.

A combination of the strongest subjunctive favouring parameters – i.e. the text categories STA or IS, antecedents of the *se, seo, þæt* paradigm, and a subjunctive, imperative or modal construction in the matrix clause – is found in seventy-two examples, and in fifty-nine of them (= 81.94 per cent) the verbal syntagm of the relative clause is realised by a subjunctive, in ten (= 13.89 per cent) by an indicative, and in three (= 4.17 per cent) by a modal construction.

3.3 Middle English adjectival relative clauses: descriptive parameters

3.3.1 *The verbal syntagm*

When descriptions of ME relative clauses contain statements about the realisation possibilities of the verbal syntagm at all, they agree that the indicative is the rule (Mustanoja 1960: 462, Fischer 1992: 311). The use of the subjunctive in ME relative clauses is interpreted as a relic of OE, where the subjunctive was preferred 'after an imperative, or when the principal clause contained a negative or a subjunctive expressing a wish' (Fischer 1992: 311).[13] Hypothetical or potential situations are also mentioned as optionally triggering the subjunctive in ME relative clauses.

Modal constructions are not often explicitly mentioned, but they are generally considered as replacing the subjunctive as a consequence of the erosion of the inflectional system starting in Late OE (Fischer 1992: 262). Consequently, they must also be expected in relative clauses. Mustanoja (1960: 462) notes that modal constructions occur only occasionally in ME relative clauses, and they express 'an activity which is merely contemplated or in prospect'. Harsh's analysis of the relative clauses in ten ME texts yielded a mere seven unambiguous subjunctives and three modal constructions (1968: table 7, pp. 160–161).

The realisations of verbal syntagms to be expected in ME adjectival relative clauses are illustrated in examples [3.28]–[3.30]:

[3.28] *How myghte a man han any adversitee / That hath a wyf?* (M3 NI FICT CTMERCH, p. 155.C2) 'How might a man meet with any adversity, who has a wife?' (indicative)

[3.29] *he shal neuer vexe ne inquiete þexecutours of þe testament of his last predecessour / þat was our Confessour þe whiche god assoille* (M3 XX CORO HENRY5C, p. 94f.) 'he shall never vex nor trouble the executors of the testament of his last predecessor, who was our confessor, whom God may absolve' (subjunctive)

[3.30] *it seemeþ þat þere is no more dignyte ne worþines þat a man mai come to, þan for to haue tribulacioun for Cristis loue* (M3/4 IR RELT HILTON, p. 10) 'it seems that there is no greater dignity or worthiness that a person may attain than to undergo tribulation for Christ's love' (modal construction)

---

[13] Cf. sections 3.1.4 and 3.2.7.

3.3.2 *The relative marker*

Handbooks on ME agree on *þe* as a relic of OE as a relative marker in early ME texts and on *that* as the most frequent ME relative marker (Burrow/Turville-Petre 1992, Moessner and Schaefer 1987, Mossé 1952, Mustanoja 1960: 188–191). The most detailed account of ME relative markers is to be found in the treatment of relative clauses by Fischer (1992: 295–310). Fischer's list additionally contains 'remnants of the *se, seo, þæt* system', the elements *whom, whose, what, (the) which (that), there, where (that/as)*, and the zero relative marker. Statements about correlations between relative markers and the form of the verbal syntagm in the relative clause are lacking.

3.3.3 *The antecedent*

Fischer (1992: 295f.) points out that the straightforward relation between the type of antecedent and the type of relative marker, which holds in PDE, is not given in ME. In ME the same relative marker can be used with animate and non-animate antecedents, in restrictive and non-restrictive relative clauses. On the other hand, Mustanoja (1960: 197) notes that in later ME texts the relative marker *that* was preferred in restrictive relative clauses.

Restrictive relative clauses specify the reference of the antecedent, and they preferably modify substantival syntagms expanded by a demonstrative, possessive or indefinite pronoun. A potential influence of the antecedent on the form of the verbal syntagm in the ME relative clauses of my corpus will be investigated in section 3.4.6.

3.3.4 *The verbal syntagm in the matrix clause*

The influence of the verb form of the matrix clause on that of the relative clause is claimed by Fischer and interpreted as a relic of OE (1992: 311). It was confirmed in the analysis of my OE corpus, which revealed that a subjunctive in the relative clause strongly correlated with a subjunctive, an imperative or a modal construction in the matrix clause (cf. section 3.2.7). The strength of this influence will also be investigated in the ME corpus.

3.4 The subjunctive and its competitors in the ME corpus

Relevant adjectival relative clauses are those with a verbal syntagm in the second or third person singular present, because the subjunctive is overtly marked only for these forms. In my ME corpus I identified 885 instances. This corresponds to a relative frequency of 5.32/1,000 words.

The verbal syntagm of these clauses is realised by an indicative (721 tokens, 4.33/1,000 words), a subjunctive (thirty-six tokens, 0.22/1,000 words), a modal construction (122 tokens, 0.73/1,000 words) or a semi-modal construction (six tokens, 0.04/1,000 words).[14] The first elements of the modal constructions are *shall* (fifty-five tokens), *may* (thirty-five tokens), *will* (twenty-three tokens) and *can* (nine tokens). They express root modality of the types deontic and bouletic. The semi-modal constructions are realised by *ought* (four tokens) or *is + to* (two tokens) + infinitive. They express deontic modality (cf. examples [3.31] and [3.32]).

> [3.31] *Ðe hertes hauen anoðer kinde, ðat us og alle to ben minde* (M2 IR RELT BEST, p. 11) 'the harts have another property, which ought to be remembered by all of us'
>
> [3.32] *foure wardeynes . . . don alle þing þat is for to done toucheng her offys* (M3 XX DOC RET, p. 54f.) 'four wardens shall do everything that is to be done concerning their office'

Compared to the OE corpus, the density of relative clauses is smaller in the ME corpus. This also holds for the share of subjunctives, whereas that of indicatives and modal constructions is larger in the ME than in the OE corpus. The frequency rise of indicatives between OE and ME is more pronounced than that of modal constructions.

In the following sections the influence of linguistic and extralinguistic parameters on the distribution of the realisation possibilities of the verbal syntagm in the relative clauses of the ME corpus will be tested and compared to the corresponding values of the OE corpus.

3.4.1 *The parameter date of composition*

In the HC the ME period is divided into the four subperiods M1, M2, M3 and M4. The data of my ME corpus are coded accordingly. Table 3.11 shows the distribution of subjunctives, indicatives and modal constructions in the four subperiods.

The share of subjunctives is smaller in the later subperiods than in M1, but a steady movement towards a smaller share cannot be observed. There is even a continuous increase of subjunctives after M2. The frequency changes of indicatives and modal constructions, by contrast, show a steady development; the share of indicatives decreases, whereas that of modal constructions increases.

---

[14] This realisation possibility is not mentioned in ME reference works. Since there are only a few tokens in my corpus, they will be subsumed under 'Modal' in the tables.

Table 3.11 The distribution of subjunctives, indicatives and modal constructions in the relative clauses of the ME corpus

Subperiod	Subjunctive		Indicative		Modal		Total	
M1	14	6.19%	197	87.17%	15	6.64%	226	100%
M2	1	0.95%	90	85.72%	14	13.33%	105	100%
M3	8	3.36%	191	80.25%	39	16.39%	238	100%
M4	13	11%	243	76.90%	60	18.99%	316	100%
Total	36	4.07%	721	81.47%	128	14.46%	885	100%

3.4.2 *The parameter dialect*

In the HC coding of the parameter dialect thirteen dialect specifications are distinguished; two codes are used for mixed dialects and one indicates that the dialect is unknown (Kytö 1996: 50). My corpus contains only texts of the well-known dialect areas East Midland, West Midland, Northern, Southern and Kentish. The distribution of subjunctives, indicatives and modal constructions across these is shown in Table 3.12:

Table 3.12 The distribution of subjunctives, indicatives and modal constructions in relative clauses of the different ME dialect regions

Dialect	Subjunctive		Indicative		Modal		Total	
East Midland	19	3.89%	393	80.37%	77	15.74%	489	100%
West Midland	6	2.94%	175	85.78%	23	11.28%	204	100%
Northern			15	93.75%	1	6.25%	16	100%
Southern	3	2.80%	85	79.44%	19	17.76%	107	100%
Kentish	8	11.59%	53	76.82%	8	11.59%	69	100%
Total	36	4.07%	721	81.47%	128	14.46%	885	100%

In all dialect areas the indicative is the preferred realisation of the verbal syntagm, its share is biggest in the Northern dialect and in the Midland dialect areas.[15] The realisations expressing root modality are favoured in the more southern dialect areas, the subjunctive in the Kentish dialect and modal constructions in the Southern dialect. A similar distribution was already observed in the OE corpus.

---

[15] Although the indicative is nearly exclusively used in the Northern dialect, it should be borne in mind that my corpus contains only a very few texts from this dialect area.

3.4.3 *The parameter text category*

The categories distinguished in my ME corpus are the same as in the OE corpus. Relevant relative clauses are unequally distributed across them. Table 3.13 shows their absolute numbers and their frequencies per 1,000 words in the respective text category.

Table 3.13 Relative frequencies of ME relative clauses across text categories

Text category	Size	Relative clauses absolute numbers	Relative clauses/ 1,000 words
STA	11,600	33	2.84
IS	14,850	83	5.59
IR	50,650	388	7.66
NI	22,520	90	4.00
NN	17,450	83	4.76
EX	6,430	44	6.84
XX	42,890	164	3.82
Total	166,390	885	5.32

The text categories IR, EX and IS show the largest relative frequencies of relative clauses, the categories STA and XX range at the lower end of the frequency scale. Yet a low density of relevant relative clauses in a text category does not entail a small share of subjunctives. This can be derived from Table 3.14, which displays the distribution of subjunctives, indicatives and modal constructions.

Table 3.14 The distribution of subjunctives, indicatives and modal constructions across the text categories of the ME corpus

Text category	Subjunctive	Indicative	Modal	Total
STA	3 9.09%	13 39.39%	17 51.52%	33 100%
IS	3 3.61%	68 81.93%	12 14.46%	83 100%
IR	16 4.12%	326 84.02%	46 11.86%	388 100%
NI		81 90.00%	9 10.00%	90 100%
NN	1 1.20%	76 91.57%	6 7.23%	83 100%
EX		41 93.18%	3 6.82%	44 100%
XX	13 7.93%	116 70.73%	35 21.34%	164 100%
Total	36 4.07%	721 81.47%	128 14.46%	885 100%

Since indicatives are the preferred realisation in the whole corpus, it was to be expected that this distribution would be mirrored in the individual text categories. Yet this is not the case. Categories STA and XX with their notably low density of relevant relative clauses contain the largest shares of subjunctives and modal constructions. The prominence of realisations expressing root modality in category STA was observed already in the OE corpus.

The category XX contains the files CAXPRO with prologues and epilogues, DIGBY, a religious play, DOCU3 and DOCU4 with petitions, proclamations, wills and excerpts from gild-books, and OFFIC3, a selection of official letters. The realisation possibilities of the verbal syntagm in these files are not equally distributed. Their analysis showed that the linguistic profile of official letters differs from all other files in this category: verbal syntagms realised by subjunctives and modal constructions occur in official letters with the same frequency as indicatives.

Compared to the OE corpus there are similarities concerning the density of relative clauses and concerning the realisations of verbal syntagms in individual text categories. The text categories IR and EX have a high density of relative clauses in both corpora, and the texts of category STA contain a saliently large share of verbal syntagms expressing root modality.

3.4.4 *The parameter format*

There are only five verse files among the thirty-one files of my ME corpus. Since the analysis of the OE corpus proved that the parameter format influenced subjunctive use, I tested if the same influence also held in the ME corpus (cf. Table 3.15).

Table 3.15 The distribution of the subjunctive and its competitors in ME prose and verse texts

Format	Subjunctive	Indicative	Modal	Total
Prose	35 4.52%	629 81.16%	111 14.32%	775 100%
Verse	1 0.91%	92 83.64%	17 15.45%	110 100%
Total	36 4.07%	721 81.47%	128 14.64%	885 100%

Subjunctive frequency is low in both prose and verse texts. Nevertheless, the share of subjunctives is larger in prose than in verse texts. This result coincides with that in the OE corpus.

3.4.5 *The relative marker*

My ME corpus is coded for the relative markers *the*, *the which*, *which*, *that*, *whom* and zero. All other relative markers are coded as 'Others'. The distribution of subjunctives, indicatives and modal constructions in relative clauses introduced by these markers is shown in Table 3.16.

In general there is not much variation in the percentage shares of the realisation possibilities of the verbal syntagm after the different relative

Table 3.16 The combination of subjunctives, indicatives and modal
constructions with different relative markers in the ME corpus

Relative marker	Subjunctive		Indicative		Modal		Total	
The	6	5.31%	99	87.61%	8	7.08%	113	100%
The which	5	8.33%	46	76.67%	9	15.00%	60	100%
Which	3	5.45%	39	70.91%	13	23.64%	55	100%
That	13	2.28%	475	83.19%	83	14.53%	571	100%
Whom	5	26.31%	12	63.16%	2	10.53%	19	100%
Zero			5	83.33%	1	16.67%	6	100%
Others	4	6.56%	45	73.77%	12	19.67%	61	100%
Total	36	4.07%	721	81.47%	128	14.46%	885	100%

markers. The only exception is the saliently high frequency of subjunctives
after the relative marker *whom*, which is a late addition to the system of
ME relative markers (Fischer 1992: 296f.). All of these noteworthy combinations occur in texts of subperiod M4 (cf. example [3.33]).

[3.33] *J thanke Almyghty God To whome be gyuen Honour/laude/and glorye*
(M4 XX PREF CAXTON, p. 67) 'I thank almighty God to whom be
given honour, praise, and glory'

Given the small overall number of subjunctives in the relative clauses of
the ME corpus, the hypothesis that the relative marker *whom* contributed to the preservation of the subjunctive in relative clauses would have
to be tested in a larger corpus, before it can be seriously maintained.

3.4.6 *The antecedent*

In the coding of antecedents I distinguished the elements substantival
syntagm, personal pronoun, possessive pronoun, and a category 'Others'
that contains mainly deictic and indefinite pronouns. The frequency of
subjunctives, indicatives and modal constructions after these antecedents
is shown in Table 3.17.

Table 3.17 The frequency of subjunctives, indicatives and modal constructions
in ME relative clauses after different antecedents

Antecedent	Subjunctive		Indicative		Modal		Total	
Substantival syntagm	26	3.78%	554	80.52%	108	15.70%	688	100%
Personal pronoun	1	1.21%	71	85.54%	11	13.25%	83	100%
Possessive pronoun			3	100%			3	100%
Others	9	8.11%	93	83.78%	9	8.11%	111	100%
Total	36	4.07%	721	81.47%	128	14.46%	885	100%

The number of possessive pronouns is too small to allow any generalisations, and the percentage figures of the realisations of the verbal
syntagm in the relative clauses after substantival syntagms and personal
pronouns do not deviate much from each other. The only noteworthy
finding is the relatively large amount of subjunctives after antecedents of
the category 'Others'. In seven out of the nine examples of subjunctives
the antecedent is a deictic pronoun, and in the remaining two it is an
indefinite pronoun. In all nine examples the verb in the matrix clause is
an imperative or a subjunctive (cf. examples [3.34] and [3.35]).

[3.34]   *forlæt þonne eall, þt þu age* (MX/1 IS PHILO VESPD3, p. 7) 'give then
         up all that you possess'
[3.35]   *aþet he cume o swuch; þt me on ende underuo* (M1 IR RELT ANCR,
         p. 117) 'until he comes to such [a one] that one finally accepts'

Relative clauses modifying deictic or indefinite pronouns specify the reference of their antecedents; they belong to the type restrictive relative clause.

A large share of subjunctives after deictic pronouns was observed
already in the OE corpus (cf. Table 3.8 in section 3.2.6).

3.4.7 *The verbal syntagm in the matrix clause*

In a first analysis I separated relative clauses with a volitional expression in the matrix clause (= a verbal syntagm realised by a subjunctive,
an imperative or a modal construction) from those without a volitional
expression. This procedure yielded the results in Table 3.18.

Table 3.18 The distribution of subjunctives, indicatives and modal
constructions in ME relative clauses after matrix clauses with and without
volitional expressions

Matrix \ Relative	Subjunctive	Indicative	Modal	Total
+ Volitional expression	15 9.15%	114 69.51%	35 21.34%	164 100%
− Volitional expression	21 2.91%	607 84.19%	93 12.90%	721 100%
Total	36 4.07%	721 81.47%	128 14.46%	885 100%

After it was clear that irrespective of the form of the verbal syntagm in
the matrix clause the indicative was the preferred realisation of the verbal
syntagm in the relative clause, but that subjunctives and modal constructions had a larger share after volitional expressions in the matrix clause,
I checked which type of volitional expression had the strongest influence

on the form of the verbal syntagm in the relative clause. The results of this analysis are shown in Table 3.19.

Table 3.19 The distribution of subjunctives, indicatives and modal constructions after matrix clauses with different volitional expressions

Matrix \ Relative	Subjunctive	Indicative	Modal	Total
Subjunctive	5 7.58%	44 66.67%	17 25.75%	66 100%
Imperative	9 19.15%	32 68.09%	6 12.76%	47 100%
Modal construction	1 1.96%	38 74.51%	12 23.53%	51 100%
Total	15 9.15%	114 69.51%	35 21.34%	164 100%

The share of subjunctives in the relative clauses of the ME corpus is largest when the verb in the matrix clause is an imperative; it is smaller when the verb in the matrix clause is a subjunctive (cf. examples [3.34] and [3.35]). Modal constructions in the main clause have next to no influence on the subjunctive share in the relative clause.

OE and ME relative clauses share the feature modal harmony between the verbal syntagm in the matrix clause and the verbal syntagm in the subordinate relative clause. The verbal syntagms of both clauses express the same type of modality, either epistemic or root modality. In OE a subjunctive in the matrix clause triggers a subjunctive in the relative clause more strongly than an imperative, in ME an imperative in the matrix clause has a stronger subjunctive triggering force in the relative clause than a subjunctive.

3.4.8 Summary and comparison with the OE corpus

The analysis of the ME corpus yielded 885 occurrences of relevant relative clauses. Only those with verbal syntagms of the second and third person singular present were considered relevant, because the subjunctive is overtly marked only for these forms. In ME relative clauses the subjunctive competes with the indicative and with modal and semi-modal constructions.

The indicative proved by far the most frequent verb form (81.47 per cent or 4.33 tokens per 1,000 words), followed by modal and semi-modal constructions (14.46 per cent or 0.77 tokens per 1,000 words), with the share of subjunctives taking the bottom place on the frequency scale (4.07 per cent or 0.22 tokens per 1,000 words). The distribution of these realisations of the verbal syntagm was tested for their dependence on several linguistic and extralinguistic factors.

The test of the influence of the parameter date of composition revealed a steady decrease of indicative frequency paired with a steady increase of modal constructions. Subjunctives could not be shown to follow a continuous movement, an initial frequency drop was followed by a frequency rise, yet without surpassing the value of the first subperiod.

The dialect of the texts also influences the occurrence frequency of the realisation patterns. The biggest share of subjunctives was found in the Kentish texts, of indicatives in West Midland and Northern texts, and of modal constructions in East Midland and Southern texts. From this distribution the conclusion was drawn that realisations expressing root modality are a feature of Southern, realisations expressing epistemic modality a feature of Northern texts. This distribution is similar to that in the OE corpus.

The analysis of the parameter text category showed first of all that relative clauses are unequally distributed across text categories, with the categories IR, IS and EX containing particularly many relevant relative clauses and the categories STA and XX particularly few relevant relative clauses. As indicatives are the preferred realisation of the verbal syntagm in the corpus as a whole, it came as a surprise that category STA stands out as the only one with modal constructions more frequent that the other realisations. Another surprise was the relatively large number of subjunctives in the heterogeneous category XX. It turned out that this was an effect of the file containing official letters.

The analysis of the parameter format revealed that ME prose texts contain a greater share of subjunctives than verse texts.

An influence of the relative marker on the form of the verbal syntagm in ME relative clauses could not be observed.

The analysis of the parameter antecedent suggested the hypothesis that antecedents of restrictive relative clauses favoured the subjunctive.

The verb form of the matrix clause was identified as the linguistic feature with the strongest influence on the form of the verbal syntagm in the relative clause. The share of subjunctives in the relative clauses of the ME corpus is largest when the verb in the matrix clause is an imperative. It is less than half as big when the verb in the matrix clause is a subjunctive. Modal constructions in the matrix clause have next to no influence on the share of subjunctives in the relative clause. These correlations were interpreted as instances of modal harmony.

The frequency of relative clauses is lower in the ME than in the OE corpus (5.32/1,000 vs. 6.52/1,000 words). The share of subjunctives is also smaller in the ME than in the OE corpus, whereas that of indicatives and modal constructions is bigger in the ME corpus. The frequency rise of indicatives between OE and ME is more pronounced than that of modal constructions. This result is in conflict with the development within the ME period; here the frequency of indicatives steadily decreases, whereas that of modal constructions increases.

In both periods Kentish texts show the biggest share of subjunctives, and in both periods verbal syntagms expressing root modality are more prominent in southern dialect areas.

The distribution of relative clauses across text categories was found to be similar in the OE and in the ME corpus. The text categories IS, IR and EX have a high density of relative clauses in both corpora. Category STA is the category with the biggest share of verbal syntagms expressing root modality in both periods.

A comparison of the influence of the relative marker on the distribution of the realisations of the verbal syntagm in OE and ME relative clauses is impossible because the sets of relative markers are different.

Among the antecedents of relative clauses, deictic pronouns were identified as favouring subjunctives in the dependent relative clauses of both periods.

The influence of the form of the verb in the matrix clause on that of the verb in the relative clause is similar in both periods. A verbal syntagm expressing root modality in the matrix clause stands a significant chance of being followed by a corresponding verbal syntagm in the relative clause. Yet the influence of the modality of the verbal syntagm of the matrix clause on that of the relative clause is weaker in ME than it was in OE.

3.5 Early Modern English adjectival relative clauses: descriptive parameters

3.5.1 *The verbal syntagm*

Reference works on the EModE period agree that the subjunctive occurred in main clauses, in noun clauses and in some types of adverbial clauses (Barber 1997: 171–173, Franz 1986: 521–535, Görlach 1991: 113, Nevalainen 2006: 96–97). Statements about its use in adjectival relative clauses are missing. The topics dealt with in the sections about relative clauses in these publications are the relative marker, the antecedent and the distinction between restrictive and non-restrictive relative clauses. It is only Rissanen (1999: 293) who mentions the possibility of a subjunctive or a modal construction, if 'hypotheticity, unreality, etc. is involved'.

3.5.2 *The relative marker*

The lists of EModE relative markers vary in size, Rissanen's (1999: 293–299) is probably the most comprehensive one. It contains the elements *that, which, the which, who, whose, whom, as, but* and zero. *Where* and combinations with *where* plus particles like *in, on*, etc., also occur; they figure as adverbial relative links in Rissanen's description of relative clauses (1999: 301).

3.5.3 The antecedent

The usual antecedents of EModE relative clauses are the nuclei of substantival or pronominal syntagms. More noteworthy are relative clauses whose antecedent is realised by a premodifier of a substantival syntagm (Barber 1997: 216) or by an adjectival syntagm (Rissanen 1999: 200).

3.6 The subjunctive and its competitors in the EModE corpus

In the EModE period the ending *-(e)st* for the second person indicative present disappeared from the inflectional system of the verb together with the ongoing replacement of the personal pronoun *thou* by *you* (Moessner 2017: 174). Therefore verb forms of the second person singular present were only taken into consideration in those texts of my corpus which contain the personal pronoun *thou* or its oblique forms and only in their immediate neighbourhood.

> [3.36]   *if sinne was so greuously punished in him that neuer did sinne, how bytterly shall it be punished in thee O sinfull creature, <u>the which haste done so many great outragious sinnes</u>* (E1 IR SERM FISHER, p. 1399)

The only verb form in which the subjunctive is overtly marked in all texts of my corpus is the third person singular. The overall number of relevant verbal syntagms in my EModE corpus amounts to 948 instances. This corresponds to a relative frequency of 4.91/1,000 words.[16] Their verbal syntagms are realised by an indicative (720 tokens, 3.73/1,000 words, 75.95 per cent), a subjunctive (16 tokens, 0.08/1,000 words, 1.69 per cent), a modal construction (200 tokens, 1.04/1,000 words, 21.10 per cent), or a semi-modal construction (12 tokens, 0.06/1,000 words, 1.26 per cent).[17] The first elements of the modal constructions are *may* (29 tokens), *can* (38 tokens), *shall* (100 tokens), *must* (7 tokens) and *will* (26 tokens).

The auxiliaries *shall* and *will* can express epistemic and root modality. When they denote future, they express weak epistemic modality. When *shall* denotes obligation, it expresses deonticity, when *will* denotes volition, it expresses bouletic modality.

> [3.37]   *And must I (quoth he) be the Man <u>that shall overthrow my Howse,</u> which hath continued soe longe?* (E2 NN BIO PERROTT, p. 232) [*shall* expressing deontic modality]

---

[16] Johansson (2017: 270) reports a frequency of 0.876 relative clauses per 1,000 words in her EModE corpus of spoken data.

[17] In the tables this realisation possibility is subsumed under 'Modal'.

[3.38]   *I will fil a freshe pot of ale shall make you mery agayne* (E1 NI FICT
         HARMAN, p. 41) [*shall* expressing weak epistemic modality]
[3.39]   *But hee that will not sorrowe and lament wyth Christ heere in thys
         lyfe, hee shall come fynallye to the place where is euerlasting woe* (E1
         IR SERM FISHER, p. 1397) [*will* expressing bouletic modality]
[3.40]   *Another thing that will require punishment is stubbornesse and an
         obstinate disobedience* (E3 IS EDUC LOCKE, p. 57) [*will* expressing
         epistemic modality]

The first elements of the semi-modal constructions are *be to, need to,
have to, be about to, be able to* and *be wont to*; the first three express
root modality, the last three espistemic modality.

[3.41]   *And whatsoeuer hath beene said here touching the order that is to be
         obserued in the first tables of (^Monte Regio^), whose totall Sine is
         6/ooo/ooo. The like in all points is to be obserued in the last tables,
         whose totall Sine is 10/ooo/ooo.* (E2 EX SCIO BLUNDEV, p. 51R)
[3.42]   *To the foregoing Experiments, whose success is wont to be uniform
         enough, I shall adde the Recital of a surprising (^Phaenomenon^)* (E3
         EX SCIO BOYLE, p. 26)

The figures presented above show that the relative frequency of relevant relative clauses continually decreased from OE via ME to EModE.
Compared to the ME corpus, the distribution of the realisation possibilities of the verbal syntagm changed such that the share of subjunctives
and indicatives dropped, while that of modal constructions increased.
The following sections will explore which linguistic and/or extralinguistic parameters influenced these changes.

3.6.1 The parameter date of composition

The coding of the parameter date of composition in my EModE corpus
follows the pattern of the HC, distinguishing the subperiods E1 (1500–
1570), E2 (1570–1640) and E3 (1640–1710). The distribution of the realisation possibilities of the relevant verbal syntagms is shown in Table 3.20.

Table 3.20 The distribution of subjunctives, indicatives and modal
constructions in the relative clauses of the EModE corpus

Subperiod	Subjunctive	Indicative	Modal	Total
E1	15 4.64%	257 79.57%	51 15.79%	323 100%
E2		252 76.60%	77 23.40%	329 100%
E3	1 0.34%	211 71.28%	84 28.38%	296 100%
Total	16 1.69%	720 75.95%	212 22.36%	948 100%

If we set aside the only example of a subjunctive in the last subperiod, it seems that the subjunctive in relative clauses died out in the second half of the sixteenth century. Indicatives and modal constructions show steady developments, with the share of indicatives decreasing and that of modal constructions increasing.

3.6.2 *The parameter text category*

The coding of my EModE corpus for the parameter text category follows that of the HC. Before checking the distribution of the realisation possibilities of the verbal syntagm in relative clauses, I established the occurrence frequency of the relevant relative clauses in the individual text categories. This is displayed in Table 3.21.

Table 3.21 Relative frequencies of relevant relative clauses across text categories in the EModE corpus

Text category	Size in words	Relative clauses absolute numbers	Relative clauses/ 1,000 words
STA	36,750	150	4.08
IS	26,420	149	5.64
IR	15,440	95	6.15
NI	15,770	25	1.59
NN	49,810	49	0.98
EX	23,360	191	8.18
XX	25,590	289	11.29
Total	193,140	948	4.91

The narrative text categories NN and NI turned out to be those with the lowest density of relevant relative clauses; the other end of the density scale is occupied by the categories EX and XX. The relative frequeny values of the categories IS and IR are also above average (= 4.91). If the realisation possibilities of the verbal syntagm were equally distributed among the text categories, most occurrences of the subjunctive would have to be expected in the categories EX and XX. The result of my analysis of the distribution of the realisation possibilities of the verbal syntagm in the relative clauses in Table 3.22 does not fulfil such an expectation.

Text category STA stands out for having the largest share of subjunctives and of modal constructions. It is represented in my corpus by law texts from all three subperiods, yet all twelve occurrences of the subjunctive cluster in subperiod E1. The earlier hypothesis (cf. section 3.6.1) that the subjunctive in relative clauses died out in the second half of the sixteenth century can now be refined by the observation that the subjunctive in relative clauses kept its ground longest in the text category

Table 3.22 The distribution of subjunctives, indicatives and modal constructions across the text categories of the EModE corpus

Text category	Subjunctive	Indicative	Modal	Total
STA	12 8.00%	34 22.67%	104 69.33%	150 100%
IS		117 78.52%	32 21.48%	149 100%
IR		82 86.32%	13 13.68%	95 100%
NI		20 80.20%	5 20.00%	25 100%
NN	1 2.04%	38 77.55%	10 20.41%	49 100%
EX		176 92.15%	15 7.85%	191 100%
XX	3 1.04%	253 87.54%	33 11.42%	289 100%
Total	16 1.69%	720 75.95%	212 2.36%	948 100%

STA. Root modality marking by modal constructions can be found in the statutory texts of all subperiods, but in subperiods E2 and E3 it is more frequent than in subperiod E1 (E1: 25 tokens = 55.55 per cent, E2: 40 tokens = 69.97 per cent, E3: 39 tokens = 92.98 per cent). This supports the generally held opinion that the subjunctive (as a root modality marker) was replaced by modal constructions in the history of English (Fischer 1992: 262).

The texts in my corpus which represent the categories IS and IR are educational treatises, handbooks and sermons. The prescriptive character of these texts is expressed by large shares of modal constructions in main clauses (cf. section 2.6.3), but most of their relative clauses are descriptive and this explains their exceptionally large shares of the indicative.

3.6.3 The relative marker

My EModE corpus is coded for the relative markers *that*, *which*, *the which*, *who*, *whose*, *whom*, zero, *where*, combinations of *where* + particle, and zero. Other relative markers are subsumed under 'Others'. The distribution of the realisation possibilities of the verbal syntagm in relative clauses introduced by these markers is shown in Table 3.23.

The distribution of relative markers in my corpus resembles that of earlier studies based on EModE written corpora (Dekeyser 1984, Rydén 1966) and differs from that in Johansson's spoken data (2017: 269). Taken together the *wh*-markers introduce 561 relative clauses, which amounts to 59.17 per cent. At the same time these are the relative clauses with the greatest share of subjunctives; 62.5 per cent of all subjunctives occur in *wh*-introduced relative clauses. Against the background of Nevalainen's general statement that '[f]ormal registers typically employ *wh*-relatives in all syntactic functions' (2006: 107) the significant share of subjunctives in *wh*-introduced relative clauses in my EModE corpus invites the hypothesis that here lies one of the starting points of the

Table 3.23 The combination of subjunctives, indicatives and modal constructions with different relative markers in the EModE corpus

Relative marker	Subjunctive	Indicative	Modal	Total
That	2 0.56%	287 80.85%	66 18.59%	355 100%
Which	1 0.30%	256 76.42%	78 23.28%	335 100%
The which		16 100%		16 100%
Who		42 73.68%	15 26.32%	57 100%
Whose	1 3.23%	26 83.87%	4 12.90%	31 100%
Whom	1 2.00%	37 74.00%	12 24.00%	50 100%
Where		9 36.00%	16 64.00%	25 100%
Where +	7 14.89%	28 59.58%	12 25.53%	47 100%
Zero		15 75.00%	5 25.00%	20 100%
Others	4 33.33%	4 33.34%	4 33.33%	12 100%
Total	16 1.69%	720 75.95%	212 22.36%	948 100%

association of the subjunctive with formal style in PDE (Quirk et al. 1985: 157–158, 1012, Rissanen 1999: 228).

3.6.4 *The antecedent*

The following antecedents are attested in my EModE corpus: substantival syntagm, personal pronoun, possessive pronoun, demonstrative pronoun, indefinite pronoun, and interrogative pronoun. Table 3.24 contains the distribution of subjunctives, indicatives and modal constructions after these antecedents.

Table 3.24 The distribution of subjunctives, indicatives and modal constructions after different antecedents in the relative clauses of the EModE corpus

Antecedent	Subjunctive	Indicative	Modal	Total
Substantival syntagm	14 1.98%	516 73.09%	176 24.93%	706 100%
Personal pronoun	1 0.85%	98 83.76%	18 15.39%	117 100%
Possessive pronoun		2 100%		2 100%
Demonstrative pronoun		75 92.59%	6 7.41%	81 100%
Indefinite pronoun		29 70.73%	12 29.27%	41 100%
Interrogative pronoun	1 100%			1 100%
Total	16 1.69%	720 75.95%	212 22.36%	948 100%

The largest number of subjunctives is attested in relative clauses depending on substantival syntagms, but these fourteen relative clauses account only for 1.98 per cent of the relative clauses depending on substantival syntagms. The only really interesting token of a subjunctive depends on an interrogative pronoun (cf. example [3.43]).

> [3.43] *Whereby it happeth that hatred hath no place emongeste wise men.*
> *For who hateth good folk but he be a very fole?* (E1 XX PHILO
> BOETHCO, p. 103) 'thus it happens that hatred has no place among
> wise men; for who hates good people who is not an outright fool?'

This relative clause is one of the few which are introduced by the relative marker *but*, and one of the few in which the relative marker does not function additionally as a nominal constituent in the relative clause (cf. Moessner 1992, 1999).

3.6.5 *The verbal syntagm in the matrix clause*

The following realisations of the verbal syntagm of the matrix clause were interpreted as expressions of volition: subjunctives, imperatives and modal constructions. Indicatives, ambiguous and non-finite forms were counted as not marked for the feature volition. The distribution of the realisation possibilities of the verbal syntagms in the relative clauses after matrix clauses with and without the feature volition are shown in Table 3.25.

Table 3.25 The distribution of subjunctives, indicatives and modal constructions in EModE relative clauses depending on matrix clauses with and without the feature volition

Matrix \ Relative	Subjunctive	Indicative	Modal	Total
Subjunctive	7 14.90%	24 51.06%	16 34.04%	47 100%
Imperative		6 54.55%	5 45.45%	11 100%
Modal construction	2 1.09%	106 57.61%	76 41.30%	184 100%
Non-volition	7 0.99%	584 82.72%	115 16.29%	706 100%
Total	16 1.69%	720 75.95%	212 22.36%	948 100%

The share of subjunctives in relative clauses is greatest after matrix clauses whose verbal syntagm is also realised by a subjunctive, and the share of modal constructions in the relative clause is greatest after matrix clauses whose verbal syntagm is realised by an imperative. The general tendency to be derived from Table 3.25 is that relative clauses with verbal syntagms expressing root modality correlate with matrix clauses with verbal syntagms that express the same modality. As in the OE corpus and the ME corpus this correlation is an instance of modal harmony. The expression of root modality is most impressive in relative clauses that are embedded in matrix clauses whose verbal syntagms are realised by subjunctives. In these relative clauses the share of verbal syntagms expressing root modality amounts to 48.94 per cent.

3.6.6 *Summary and comparison with the OE and the ME corpus*

In the EModE corpus I identified 948 relevant relative clauses. Verb forms of the third person singular were considered relevant in all texts; those of the second person singular only in those texts where the personal pronoun is realised by a *th*-form. Subjunctives in these clauses alternate with indicatives, modal constructions and semi-modal constructions.

The indicative turned out as the prevailing verb form (75.95 per cent or 3.73 tokens per 1,000 words), followed by modal constructions (21.10 per cent or 1.04 tokens per 1,000 words), subjunctives (1.69 per cent or 0.08 tokens per 1,000 words) and semi-modal constructions (1.26 per cent or 0.06 tokens per 1,000 words). Due to the very small number of tokens of this last form they were grouped together with modal constructions in the frequency tables.

It was assumed that the distribution of the realisation possibilities of the verbal syntagm was not random but was influenced by linguistic and extralinguistic parameters. The parameter coding of the HC allowed tests of the influence of the composition date of the texts and of their text category. Earlier publications on relative constructions suggested tests of the influence of the linguistic parameters relative marker, antecedent, and form of the verb in the matrix clause.

The parameter date of composition was established as crucial in the development of the subjunctive in relative clauses. Apart from a single example in subperiod E3 all occurrences of the subjunctive date from subperiod E1. This finding suggested the hypothesis that the subjunctive in relative clauses died out in the second half of the sixteenth century. The overall dominance of the indicative is mirrored in all subperiods.

The test of the parameter text category revealed that relative clauses are very frequent in the categories EX and XX in the EModE corpus, whereas they are nearly absent from the narrative categories NI and NN. Although the relative frequency of relative clauses is below average in category STA, this proved to be the category with the most subjunctives, and all of them are attested in subperiod E1. This result prompted a refinement of the hypothesis about the loss of the subjunctive in relative clauses in such a way that it kept its ground longest in legal texts. Category STA was also identified as the one with the largest share of modal constructions. Their frequency development across the subperiods supports the generally held opinion that the subjunctive as a root modality marker was replaced by modal constructions in the history of the English language.

The absence of subjunctives from the texts of the categories IS and IR came as a surprise. An explanation of this extraordinary distribution was found in the observation that the prescriptive character of these text categories was reflected in their verbal syntagms in main clauses. Their relative clauses are mainly descriptive and this explains the dominance of the indicative here.

The tests of the influence of the linguistic parameters yielded interesting results for relative markers and for the form of the verbal syntagm in the matrix clause.

Wh-relative markers were not only established as the preferred type of introductory elements but also as those with the biggest share of subjunctives. Since it was found in earlier studies that *wh*-relative markers are preferred in EModE texts with a formal style, the hypothesis was established that the frequent combination of *wh*-relative markers with the subjunctive in EModE relative clauses was one of the starting points of the association of the subjunctive with formal style.

The form of the verbal syntagm of the matrix clause influences the form of the verbal syntagm in the relative clause in such a way that verbal syntagms expressing root modality in the main clause favour the same type of verbal syntagms in the relative clause.

A diachronic overview of the developments from OE to EModE reveals a steady decline of the density of relevant relative clauses as a consequence of the decrease of the number of verb forms that are unambiguously marked for the category mood. The similarly steady decline of subjunctive frequency requires an additional explanation. The most convincing explanation comes from the steady increase of modal constructions which, like subjunctives, express root modality. Within the individual periods only two noteworthy developments can be observed; these are: the loss of the subjunctive after the first EModE subperiod, and the steady increase of modal constructions in ME and in EModE.

The parameter dialect is relevant only in OE and ME due to the growing standardisation in the EModE period. The form of the verbal syntagm shows the same regional distribution in OE and in ME: verbal syntagms expressing root modality are more frequent in the Southern dialect areas, verbal syntagms expressing epistemic modality dominate in the Northern dialect areas.

The instructive text categories IS and IR are in all periods among those with the highest density of relevant relative clauses. Yet in all three periods they favour the indicative.

The text category with the biggest share of subjunctives in all three periods is STA, the category which contains legal texts. It is at the same time the category which preserves the subjunctive longest in relative clauses.

The choice of the relative marker does not greatly influence the form of the verbal syntagm on the relative clause in the first two periods. Despite the small absolute number of relative clauses in the EModE corpus a salient correspondence was observed between *wh*-relative markers and the subjunctive in the relative clause. This was interpreted as a beginning of the association of the subjunctive with formal style.

Modal harmony between the verbal syntagm in the matrix clause and that in the relative clause is a pervasive feature in all three periods. Verbal syntagms of the matrix clause which express root modality favour similar verbal syntagms in the relative clause. Three realisation types of the verbal syntagm in the matrix clause are at issue: subjunctives, imperatives and modal constructions. In OE and in EModE a subjunctive in the matrix clause has the strongest influence on subjunctive frequency in the relative clause; in ME this is the imperative. Verbal syntagms of the matrix clause which express epistemic modality strongly favour indicative verb forms in the relative clause.

4

The subjunctive in noun clauses

The syntactic patterns dealt with in this chapter are called content clauses (Huddleston and Pullum 2002: 949–1030), sentential complements (Traugott 1992: 233–249), nominal clauses (Quirk et al. 1985: 1048–1068, Rissanen 1999: 282–292) or noun clauses (Mitchell 1985: §§1935–2102). They are a subclass of dependent clauses, and they have functions similar to noun phrases. Studies on subjunctives in noun clauses usually focus on object clauses; the relevant constructions are called mandative or subjunctive constructions. They will receive special attention in this chapter, too.

4.1 Old English noun clauses: descriptive parameters

4.1.1 Function

The simplest and most straightforward functional classification of OE noun clauses is applied in the subjunctive treatments by Vogt (1930) and Wilde (1939/1940). Both authors study the use of the subjunctive in object clauses and subject clauses. The same classification is also adopted by Visser (1963–1973: §§863–875).

The functions which Traugott (1992: 234–235) distinguishes are 'complements of NPs or predicates, and . . . objects, or oblique NPs'. She rejects the notion of OE subject clauses, because 'noun clauses cannot occur in sentence-initial position, i.e. there is no equivalent of *That they arrived so late is a problem*'. She prefers to analyse noun clauses which on the basis of their equivalents in PDE could be interpreted as subject clauses as 'oblique NPs in impersonal constructions, as complements of NPs or predicates'. She also considers the possibility that the function of some of these noun clauses is 'undecidable'. The cases she has in mind are constructions with impersonal verbs and constructions with *beon/wesan* or similar verbs and an adjectival subject complement.

[4.1]   *him þingð, <u>þæt he hine eað awerian mæge</u>* (O3 STA LAW LAW11C, p. 322) 'it seems to him that he can easily defend him'

[4.2]   *wærlic bið, þæt man æghwilce geare sona æfter eastron fyrdscipa*
         gearwige (O3 STA LAW LAW11C, p. 254) '[it] is circumspect that
         one makes the battle-ships ready every year right after Easter'

In examples [4.1] and [4.2] Traugott would prefer to analyse the *that*-
clause as an oblique NP and as a predicate complement respectively,
although she adds: 'On the other hand, it could be the subject' (Traugott
1992: 235). Visser (1963–1973: §§863–866) singles out exactly these
constructions plus constructions with *beon/wesan* or similar verbs and a
substantival subject complement and describes them as subject clauses.
   Mitchell (1985: §§1962–1964) states that apart from subject and
object a noun clause 'may be in apposition with, or dependent on, another
element in the principal clause; or that it may appear alone with no principle clause expressed'. He is aware of the problem involved in the analysis
of noun clauses as subject clauses in constructions with an impersonal
verb and in combinations of *beon/wesan* with an adjectival or substantival
subject complement. Therefore, he prefers to speak of noun clauses which
'can be described as the equivalent of a nominative'. He additionally
draws attention to the fact that these noun clauses can be accompanied
by a formal subject *hit*. They are then 'in apposition with the pronoun
subject *hit*'. The following example illustrates a noun clause of this type.

[4.3]   *Gif hit þonne geberige ðæt æðelwyrd læng libbe ðone Eadric* (O3 XX
         DOC ROB32, p. 60) 'If it then happens that Æthelwyrd lives longer
         than Eadric'

Mitchell's description is reminiscent of Traugott's 'complement of NPs',
but this analysis is only suggested for noun clauses in constructions with
combinations of *beon/wesan* with a substantival complement. For noun
clauses in constructions with impersonal verbs and those with an adjectival subject complement she suggests the analysis 'oblique NP'.
   A similar situation is given when the noun clause functions as object
in addition to a substantival syntagm. Mitchell (1985: §1968) acknowledges that these constructions 'present certain problems'. He distinguishes examples where 'the noun is essential to sense and syntax', and
others where the noun is 'syntactically superfluous'. Unfortunately, he
does not offer an adequate description of these cases.

[4.4]   *Ac we wyllað, þæt ælc man ofer XII wintre sylle þone að, þæt he nelle*
         þeof beon ne þeofes gewita (O3 STA LAW LAW11C, p. 324) 'And we
         wish that every man above the age of twelve years take an oath that he
         does not wish to be a thief or a thief's accessory'
[4.5]   *þæt oft doð to manege þe dreogað þa yrmþe, þæt sceotað togædere &*
         ane cwenan gemænum ceape bicgað gemæne (O3 IR HOM WULF20,

p. 270) 'what many too often do, who practise that wretchedness that they club together and buy one woman in common as a joint purchase' (transl. Swanton 1993)

In [4.4], the *þæt*-clause cannot be governed by the verb form *sylle*; it complements the noun *að*, which is syntactically and semantically necessary. In [4.5], the *þæt*-clause complements the noun *yrmþe*; at least semantically the noun is not obligatory.

For Behre (1934: 69) function is not an appropriate classification parameter of noun clauses, because 'such a classification is irrelevant from a modal point of view'. Instead he groups his material according to the meaning of the governing expression.

This is also the approach adopted in studies of the mandative subjunctive/mandative constructions in later periods (ME: Moessner 2007, 2010a; EModE: Fillbrandt 2006; PDE: Collins 2015, Crawford 2009, Hoffmann 1997, Hundt 1998a, 1998b, 2018, 2019, Ruohonen 2017, Serpollet 2001, Waller 2017). Quirk et al. (1985: §3.59) state that:

> [t]he mandative subjunctive is productive in that it can be used with any verb in a *that*-clause when the superordinate clause satisfies the requisite semantic condition, *viz* that the *that*-clause be introduced by an expression of demand, recommendation, proposal, resolution, intention, etc. This expression takes the form of a verb, an adjective, or a noun.

Övergaard (1995: 14) distinguishes mandative subjunctives after nouns and verbs on the one hand and after adjectives on the other hand, attributing a suasive meaning to the former and an emotive meaning to the latter. The syntactic function of clauses with mandative subjunctives is only mentioned in the context of noun clauses after emotive adjectives: 'the noun clause is invariably the subject of the whole structure' (Övergaard 1995: 31). It is only in Övergaard's Appendix 1.2 that we learn that noun clauses can also function as objects, subject complements and post-modifiers of nouns. The examples which illustrate these functions suggest that the subject function is not available for noun clauses after suasive verbs and nouns.

4.1.2 *Form*

For Mitchell (1985: §1937) the main classification parameter of noun clauses is their form. He distinguishes two types, namely noun clauses beginning with *þæt* or another conjunction on the one hand,[1] and noun

---

[1] Conjunctions which can be used instead of *þæt* are *gif* and *þeah*; combinations with *for* – e.g. *forðon, for ðam* – also occur.

clauses beginning with an interrogative or exclamatory word on the other hand. Each type is subclassified: the first into dependent statements and dependent desires, the second into dependent questions and dependent exclamations.

Yes/no-questions are introduced by *gif* and *hwæðer*, after governing verbs like *reccan* and *nytan* and verbs with similar meanings by *þeah*. Their analysis is without problems.

> [4.6] *axiað hire, gif hi seo frig* (O3/4 NN BIL MARGOE, p. 171) 'ask her if she is free'

Wh-questions are introduced by the pronouns *hwa* and *hwæt*, by *hwylc* as a pronoun or as a modifier of a noun, and by the adverbs *hwær*, *hwider*, *hwanon*, *hwonne*, *hu*, *humeta*, *forhwy* and *hwi*. Their analysis causes some problems, because they are difficult to distinguish from dependent exclamations on the one hand and from nominal relative clauses on the other. The first problem arises with noun clauses introduced by *hwæt* or *hu* (Mitchell 1985: §2063; cf. Quirk et al. 1985: 15.7).

> [4.7] *weorðe se carfull hu he swyþast mæge gecweman his Drihtne* (O3 IR HOM WULF8C, p. 207) 'he ought to be mindful how he may best please his Lord'
>
> [4.8] *Ga and gewite hwæt se iunga man sy þe me todæg swa wel gehirsumode* (O3 NI FICT APOLL, p. 20) 'Go and find out who the young man is who served me so well today'

The other problem concerns noun clauses which are introduced by elements that can also introduce nominal relative clauses.[2]

> [4.9] *Eala hu manful man þu eart, ðu þe wast þæt þu æfter axsast.* (O3 NI FICT APOLL, p. 10) 'Alas, what a wicked man you are, you who know what you ask about.' (Transl. Swanton 1993.)

The boy who speaks these words was asked why his city was in grief: *sege me for hwilcum intingum þeos ceaster wunige on swa micclum heafe and*

---

2 'Another problem is that of deciding whether the OE interrogatives *hwa*, *hwæt*, and *hwelc*, or *hwær*, *hwonne*, and the like ever introduce adjective or adverb clauses as opposed to dependent questions. Whether we answer "Yes" or "No" largely depends on how we define the terms and how we interpret the examples' (Mitchell 1985: §2049). Quirk et al. (1985: 15.8) note a similar ambiguity for PDE noun clauses. It can be illustrated with the sentence *I know what you asked me.* A paraphrase of the nominal relative clause reading of the noun clause is *I know the answer to your question*; a paraphrase of the dependent question clause reading of the noun clause is *You need not repeat your question (but give me another minute to think about it).*

wope 'tell me for which reason this city abides in such great grief and woe'. The implication of the boy's answer is that the person who asks the question knows the reason already. With this reading the noun clause *þæt þu æfter axsast* is to be analysed as a nominal relative clause. Yet as a kind of afterthought the boy seems to consider the possibility that a stranger might not know the reason for the city's grief, and he adds:

[4.9a]   *Oððe hwæt is manna þe nyte <u>þæt þeos ceasterwaru on heafe wunað</u>, forðam ðe [{Apollonius{] se ealdorman færinga nahwar ne ætywde siððan he ongean com fram [{Antiocho{] þam cyninge?* 'Now what man is there who does not know that these citizens live in grief because since Apollonius the prince returned from Antiochus the king he has suddenly disappeared' (transl. Swanton 1993)

With this reading the noun clause is to be analysed as a dependent interrogative clause.

These difficulties are neither commented on by Traugott nor by Behre. The former deals with the realisation of noun clauses rather cursorily, mentioning only the two complementisers *þæt* and *hwæþer* (Traugott 1992: 234).[3] Behre explicitly excludes indirect questions from his treatment of noun clauses, 'which although they may be regarded as object clauses, are best defined as question clauses in complex sentences' (Behre 1934: 69). Unfortunately, he does not give any reason for his idiosyncratic approach (cf. also section 4.1.3). In Wilde's study (1939/1940: 298–327) noun clauses figure under subordinate clauses under the influence of the verb in the principal clause ('Nebensätze mit Einfluß des Verbums des Vordersatzes'). The realisation types distinguished are statements and questions. This rather crude classification is also adopted by Vogt (1930).

4.1.3   Governing elements

The governing element is Behre's main classification parameter of noun clauses. He has separate chapters for noun clauses after expressions of volition, after expressions of thinking and saying, and after expressions of mental affection. In his chapter on indirect questions a slightly modified classification is used: indirect questions after '1) verbs of asking (. . .), 2) verbs of saying (. . .), 3) verbs of thinking, deliberating, knowing, etc.' (Behre 1934: 238). The chapter headings contain the neutral term

---

[3]   In a separate section, where she deals with interrogative clauses, we find the remark that *hwæþer*-clauses (= *yes/no*-questions) and content questions (= dependent *wh*-questions) can function as 'complements of NPs, and objects or oblique NPs of verbs and adjectival predicates', and the corresponding introductory elements are listed (Traugott 1992: 267).

'expressions of . . .', and Behre mainly describes noun clauses after verbs of these meanings. But his examples show that he is aware that noun clauses can also depend on other word classes (e.g. *sel*, p. 72, *wen*, p. 200, *gielp*, p. 224, *hyhtlic*, p. 226, *wundor*, p. 236). Since he considers the syntactic function of noun clauses as irrelevant in his descriptive model, he treats noun clauses after verbs like *þyncan* on a par with those after verbs like *wenan*; both are expressions of thinking. Some of Behre's examples fit his descriptive model only when the classification according to semantic properties of the governing expression is combined with the 'nature of the subjunctive' in the noun clauses governed by these expressions. This is how he explains the inclusion of impersonal verbs like *dafenian* 'to befit' among the expressions of volition; in these cases, the subjunctive has a 'preceptive . . . nature' (Behre 1934: 71).

The semantic feature of volition is singled out by Visser (1963–1973: §869) as the common denominator of verbs of 'wishing, desiring, commanding, exhorting, wanting, preferring, advising, urging, suggesting, proposing, intending, providing, promising, striving, teaching, warning, disapproving, asking, requiring, granting, allowing, omitting, etc.', which favour the subjunctive in object clauses. He provides a list of 107 expressions, for which he quotes OE examples. He follows Behre in that he also includes 'expressions of emotion (. . .) and other mental activities' and 'verbs of saying, declaring, lying and denying' (§§872–875) among the elements governing object clauses that favour the subjunctive.

The governing elements of noun clauses are described by Traugott (1992: 234) as 'terms for speech events, e.g. *wedd* "pledge", *að* "oath", *andettan* "think", mental states and activities, desires, obligations, and so forth, e.g. *leaf* "permission", *hycgan* "think", *unnan* "wish, grant", *gedafenian* "oblige" and *gemyndig* "mindful".'

Mitchell's description of the governing elements is very detailed, following his classification of noun clauses into dependent statements, desires and questions. Dependent statements and desires are governed by a verb, a noun, an adjective or a proposition. The elements governing dependent statements 'can imply the idea of saying; . . . of thinking; . . . of asking or knowing; . . . of giving or granting; . . . of obligation; . . . of forgetting and remembering; . . . and of feeling . . .' (1985: §1952). This description overlaps to a certain extent with that of dependent desires. They are governed by elements expressing 'commands, requests or entreaties, and wishes ... promises, precepts, or permissions' (§2001). The semantic properties of the elements governing dependent questions are not specified, but in addition to transitive verbs impersonal verbs are mentioned.

Semantic features of the governing elements, which determine the nature of the noun clause, are also listed in Wilde's and Vogt's studies. They include request ('Aufforderung'), saying and thinking ('Sagen und

Glauben'), wish and command ('Wünschen und Befehlen') and happening ('Geschehen').

4.1.4 *The verbal syntagm*

All descriptions of OE noun clauses agree that their verbal syntagm can be realised as an indicative, a subjunctive or as a modal construction. Some authors (Behre 1934: 72–73, López-Couso and Méndez-Naya 2006, Los 2005: 179–189, Mitchell 1985: §1992, Traugott 1992: 241–248, Visser 1963–1973: §2078, Vogt 1930: 37) additionally mention the possibility of infinitive constructions. These realisations are illustrated in the following examples:

[4.10]   *Soð ic eow secge, þæt ge sylfe ne becumað into heofonan rice* (O3 IR HOM AELFR15, p. 531) 'Indeed I tell you that you do not get into the kingdom of heaven' [indicative]

[4.11]   *Nu bidde we þe þæt þu geceose þe ænne of us þrym* (O3 NI FICT APOLL, p. 30) 'now we ask you that you choose one of us three' [subjunctive]

[4.12]   *we secgað eow þæt nan man hine ne sceal beladian þæt he godes cyrcan ne gesece* (O3 IR HOM AELFR2/29, p. 258f.) 'we tell you that nobody shall excuse him that he does not seek God's church' [modal auxiliary construction]

[4.13]   *gif ðu wel þencest wið þinne waldend wære gehealdan* (OX/3 XX XX AND, p. 9) 'if you honestly mean to keep faith with your ruler' [infinitive construction]

Statements about the distribution of these realisation possibilities and the factors which determine the choice of one or the other are rather vague. Mitchell notes that in dependent desires the subjunctive is the prevailing mood, but he does not exclude the indicative or modal constructions either (1985: §2003). Traugott (1992: 239) observes that the subjunctive is favoured in noun clauses governed by verbs of thinking, ordering and requesting, as well as by verbs and adjectives of being appropriate; Behre (1934: 225–233) adds verbs of mental affection. The other authors, too, consider the semantic features of the governing elements as the main factors that determine the form of the verbal syntagm in noun clauses. But since the same element can govern noun clauses with different forms of the verbal syntagm (cf. [4.10], [4.12]), several other factors are identified. Among them are the mental attitude of the text producer (Mitchell, Behre), the personal preferences of the writer (Mitchell), the form of the verbal syntagm in the corresponding Latin original (Mitchell), the person, tense and mood of the verb in the matrix clause (Mitchell, Vogt, Wilde, Behre), the presence of a negation or of a modal auxiliary in the matrix clause (Mitchell 1985, Traugott 1992), and non-factivity (Behre 1934, Traugott 1972).

The distribution of subjunctives vs. modal constructions was investigated by Gorrell (1895: 117). On the basis of four Early and four Late OE prose texts, he observed a growing frequency of modal constructions and a corresponding decrease of subjunctives: 'the relative proportion of the subjunctive to the auxiliary forms in the former period ["Alfredian prose"] is as 3 to 1, while at the time of Ælfric the proportion is as 2 to 1'. In his poetic texts the share of modal constructions is even greater than in the late prose texts. The influence of the Latin original is most conspicuous in his Gospel texts, where subjunctives are ten times as frequent as modal constructions.

It may be due to the choice of a different corpus that Yerkes achieved a different result. He contrasted the distribution of inflected verb forms and modal constructions in two versions of Wærferth's translation of Gregory's *Dialogues*. In the relevant forty-four verbal syntagms he found thirty-five modal constructions and nine finite verb forms in Wærferth's original and the reverse distribution in the revision. He explains the decreasing frequency of modal constructions by the tendency of the reviser to follow the Latin original as closely as possible (Yerkes 1976: §§189–195).

A more recent study (López-Couso and Méndez-Naya 2006) is based on data from the HC, thus avoiding a genre bias. A comparison of the figures of the authors for the subperiods shows that subjunctive frequency decreases from the second subperiod onwards.[4] It must be borne in mind, however, that López-Couso and Méndez-Naya counted only the occurrences of noun clauses depending on the verbs *biddan* and *beodan* and their derivatives. Their results also reveal a remarkable influence of the meaning of the governing verb on the realisation of the verbal syntagm in the noun clause. The share of subjunctives after commands reflects the overall tendency of a frequency decrease after O2; in requests the subjunctive frequency is more or less stable.[5]

Although it is a fact that some OE verbs can govern noun clauses with verbal syntagms realised by subjunctives or by infinitives, the latter must not be interpreted as competitors of the former. The competing constructions are finite (*þæt*-) clauses and non-finite infinitive clauses. The growing popularity of non-finite clauses in the history of English will,

---

[4] In O1 the percentage of subjunctives amounts to 93 per cent, in O2 to 95 per cent, in O3 to 87 per cent and in O4 to 66 per cent. These subjunctive figures include unambiguous subjunctives <u>and</u> ambiguous forms.

[5] In O1 and O2 the percentage of subjunctives in commands is 100 per cent, in O3 85 per cent and in O4 46 per cent. The percentage share of subjunctives in requests in O1 is 90 per cent, in O2 93 per cent, in O3 88 per cent and in O4 90 per cent. Differences in the use of modal constructions in commands and requests were also demonstrated in López-Couso and Méndez-Naya (1996).

however, be interpreted as one of the reasons for the decrease of subjunctive frequency (cf. section 6.4.5).

4.2 Noun clauses in the OE corpus

My OE corpus contains 738 relevant noun clauses (= 5.76/1,000 words). Their verbal syntagms are realised as subjunctives (450 = 3.51/1,000 words), indicatives (203 = 1.58/1,000 words), modal constructions (83 = 0.64/1,000 words) or as semi-modal constructions (2 = 0.02/1,000 words).[6] Subjunctive frequency is greatest in noun clauses with verbal syntagms of the third person singular. The following sections will show how the realisation patterns correlate with several linguistic and non-linguistic parameters.

4.2.1 *The parameter date of composition*

Table 4.1 shows the distribution of the realisation possibilities of the verbal syntagm in noun clauses across the four subperiods in the OE corpus.[7]

Table 4.1 The distribution of the realisation possibilities of the verbal syntagm in noun clauses across subperiods O1–O4

Subperiod	Subjunctive	Indicative	Modal	Total
O1	22 88.00%	1 4.00%	2 8.00%	25 100%
O2	63 61.76%	34 33.33%	5 4.91%	102 100%
O3	293 64.68%	100 22.07%	60 13.25%	453 100%
O4	72 45.57%	68 43.04%	18 11.39%	158 100%
Total	450 60.98%	203 27.51%	85 11.51%	738 100%

On the whole, subjunctives show a decreasing trend and indicatives and modal constructions an increasing trend.

This result is interesting when compared with Gorrell's and Yerkes's findings, because it supports neither. Both authors observed changes between subperiods O2 and O3. Gorrell noticed a decreasing frequency of subjunctives and an accompanying increase of modal constructions, whereas Yerkes found that many modal constructions of his earlier corpus were replaced by finite verb forms (subjunctive or indicative or ambiguous) in his later corpus. In my corpus the share of subjunctives

---

[6] Semi-modal constructions are reaslised by *be* + *to* + infinitive. They will be subsumed under 'Modal' in the tables.

[7] The first figure in every cell contains the absolute frequency, the second the percentage share. This kind of presentation is adopted in all of the tables in this chapter.

remains nearly constant between O2 and O3, and that of finite forms (= subjunctives and indicatives) decreases by about 8 per cent. The frequency changes of modal constructions in my corpus are more similar to Gorrell's than to Yerkes's, although the share of subjunctives is much higher than Gorrell's in both subperiods (cf. section 4.1.4). Yet, the increase of modal constructions in my corpus is not a consequence of the decrease of subjunctives, but of indicatives.

4.2.2 *The parameter text category*

The noun clauses of my corpus are unevenly distributed across the seven prototypical text categories of the HC. The unspecified text category XX occupies the top rank with 240 attestations (= 1.87/1,000 words), followed by IR with 189 attestations (= 1.48/1,000 words) and STA with 156 attestations (= 1.22/1,000 words). In the remaining four text categories noun clauses are less frequently attested. The distribution of the realisation possibilities across the text categories is displayed in Table 4.2.[8]

Table 4.2 The distribution of the realisation possibilities of the verbal syntagm in OE noun clauses across prototypical text categories

Text category	Subjunctive	Indicative	Modal	Total
STA	133 85.26%	7 4.49%	16 10.25%	156 100%
IS	11 73.33%	4 26.67%		15 100%
IR	96 50.79%	76 40.21%	17 9.00%	189 100%
NI	31 67.39%	10 21.74%	5 10.87%	46 100%
NN	38 55.07%	22 31.89%	9 13.04%	69 100%
EX	7 30.43%	15 65.22%	1 4.35%	23 100%
XX	134 55.83%	69 28.75%	37 15.42%	240 100%
Total	450 60.98%	203 27.51%	85 11.51%	738 100%

With the exception of category EX, subjunctives realise the verbal syntagm in at least 50 per cent of all noun clauses. Indicatives occupy the second rank on the relative frequency scale, and modal constructions the third. The category STA, which has the largest share of subjunctives, is represented only by law texts from the subperiods O2–O4 (cf. examples [4.14]–[4.16]).

[4.14] *æfter þam we bebeodað, þætte ealles folces æw & domas ðus sien gehealdene* (OX/2 STA LAW INE, p. 88) 'after that we command that each people's right and laws be kept in this way'

---

[8] The last line contains the distribution of the realisation possibilities of the verbal syntagms in the whole corpus.

[4.15] *beorge man georne, þæt man þa sawla ne forfare, þe Crist mid his agenum life gebohte* (O3 STA LAW LAW11C, p. 238) 'one should take heed assiduously that one does not ruin the souls which Christ bought with his own life'

[4.16] *On manegum landum stent, þæt he sylle ælce geare XV swyn to sticunge* (O3/4 STA LAW LAWLAT, p. 449) 'in many districts it is the rule that each year he gives away fifteen pigs to be killed'

Although the absolute frequency of noun clauses is very small in the category IS, the share of subjunctives as realisation of their verbal syntagms occupies the second rank. This rank order is similar to that in the relative clauses of my OE corpus (cf. section 3.2.3).

Among the eleven files of category XX which contain noun clauses, four belong to the subclass documents, five are verse texts, one belongs to the discipline history and one is an OE translation of the Psalms. The document texts stand out in showing a marked preference for subjunctives in noun clauses. The distribution of subjunctives, indicatives and modal constructions is entered in Table 4.3.

Table 4.3 The distribution of subjunctives, indicatives and modal constructions in the noun clauses of the OE document files

Text	Subjunctive	Indicative	Modal	Total
CODOCU1	21 84.00%	1 4.00%	3 12.00%	25 100%
CODOCU2	13 86.67%		2 13.33%	15 100%
CODOCU3	33 84.62%		6 15.38%	39 100%
CODOCU4		1 100.00%		1 100%
Total	67 83.75%	2 2.50%	11 13.75%	80 100%

It is noteworthy that the subjunctive frequency remains nearly constant on a very high level during the first three subperiods and then drops suddenly to zero. The same observation was made in main clauses, where it was explained as a consequence of the smaller share of wills in the document files of the last subperiod (cf. section 2.2.4). The same explanation holds here as well. The continuing prominence of the subjunctive in OE wills is a new finding, which was not noticed before in other publications (Moessner 2018: section 4.2.5). This may be a consequence of the lack of attention this text category has received so far. The only competitor of subjunctives is modal constructions in all subperiods.

4.2.3 *The parameter prose vs. poetry*

Since Gorrell found that the proportion of subjunctives to modal constructions decreased from 3:1 to 2:1 in his prose corpora, whereas in his poetry corpus the share of modal constructions was even larger than that in his late prose corpus (cf. section 4.1.4), I checked the distribution of the realisation possibilities of the verbal syntagm in the noun clauses of my prose and verse subcorpora as well. Table 4.4 summarises the results.

Table 4.4 The distribution of the realisation possibilities of the verbal syntagm in the OE noun clauses of the early prose subcorpus, the late prose subcorpus and the verse subcorpus

Format	Subjunctive	Indicative	Modal	Total
Early prose	84 66.67%	35 27.78%	7 5.55%	126 100%
Late prose	314 63.69%	128 25.97%	51 10.34%	493 100%
Verse	52 43.70%	40 33.61%	27 22.69%	119 100%
Total	450 60.98%	203 27.51%	85 11.51%	738 100%

The figures of my corpus support Gorrell's overall statements, although the proportion of subjunctives to modal constructions changes from 14.0:1 in the early prose texts to 6.2:1 in the late prose texts and is 1.9:1 in the verse texts. The share of subjunctives is larger in both of my prose subcorpora as well as in the verse subcorpus than in Gorrell's corpora.[9]

4.2.4 *The parameter noun clause function*

The noun clauses in my corpus are coded for the functions subject, object, subject complement, NP complement and adjectival complement.

Although the noun clauses of my corpus do not precede the verbal syntagm, I analyse them as <u>subject clauses</u> when the verbal syntagm requires no object or when all other nominal constituents of the sentence cannot realise the subject function. This is the case in the following construction types:

1. BE + adjectival/prepositional syntagm + noun clause (= *þæt*-clause, *wh*-question)
2. passive verbal syntagm + noun clause (= *þæt*-clause)
3. (NPdat.) + impersonal verb + noun clause (= *þæt*-clause)[10]
4. personal verb + (object) + noun clause (= relative clause)

The realisation possibilities of noun clauses with subject function are illustrated by examples [4.17]–[4.21]:

> [4.17] *Nis na god <u>þæt man nime his bearna hlaf, and wurpe hundum</u>* (O3 IR HOM AELFR2/8, p. 69f.) 'it is not right that someone takes his children's bread and gives it to the dogs' [type 1]

---

[9] Gorrell's proportion in his poetry corpus is 1.7:1.
[10] NPdat. stands for the affected person.

[4.18]　*Her is on sio swutelung hu Ælfhelm his are & his æhta geuadod hæfð for Gode & for wurulde* (O3 XX DOC WHIT13, p. 30) 'here is in the written testimony how Ælfhelm has disposed of his property and his goods with regard to God and to the world' [type 1]

[4.19]　*Nu is gesyne ðæt þe soð meotud, cyning eallwihta, cræftum wealdeð* (OX/3 XX XX AND, p. 47) 'now [it] is seen that the true ruler, the king of all creatures, prevails in strength' [type 2]

[4.20]　*Ne gedafenað þe, nu þe dryhten geaf welan ond wiste ond woruld-spede, ðæt ðu ondsware mid oferhygdum* (OX/3 XX XX AND, p. 11f.) 'it does not befit you, since the Lord has given you wealth and sustenance and wordly success, that you answer with arrogance' [type 3]

[4.21]　*hergað dryhten ða soecað hine* (OX/2 XX OLDT VESP, p. 19) '[those] who seek him praise the Lord' [type 4]

In the subject clauses of my corpus the subjunctive is the preferred realisation possibility of the verbal syntagm (cf. examples [4.17] and [4.20]). Noun clauses which function as objects are governed by verbs. Consequently, they are a subclass of the constructions which in studies of PDE go under the label mandative subjunctive/mandative constructions:

[4.22]　*se cyngc bit ðe þæt ðu cume to his gereorde* (O3 NI FICT APOLL, p. 22) 'the king asks you that you come to his feast'

Subject complements are in a copular relationship to the subject of the clause. Subject complement noun clauses are therefore restricted to complex sentences with a copular verb in the matrix clause. Whereas in PDE the subject precedes the verb and the subject complement follows the verb, this is not necessarily the case in OE. Examples [4.23]–[4.24] illustrate the arrangements 'subject + copular verb + subject complement' and 'copular verb + subject + subject complement'.[11]

[4.23]　*Gif þin willa sie, wuldres aldor, þæt me wærlogan wæpna ecgum, sweordum, aswebban* (OX/3 XX XX AND, p. 5) 'if [it] is your will, king of glory, that the traitors kill me with the edges of [their] weapons, with [their] swords'

[4.24]　*Drihten leof, lof sy þe selfum and wuldor ealra þære goda, þe þu me dest and gedon hæfst, and get is min hopa, þæt þu don wille aa in*

---

[11]　Since subjects as well as subject complements can be realised by nominal syntagms and by noun clauses, word order is the guiding principle in my analysis. I analyse the first nominal constituent as the subject, the second as the subject complement, cf. *mæst ðearf is, þæt æghwelc mon his að & his wed wærlice healde* (O2 STA LAW ALFLAW, p. 46) '[it] is the utmost necessity that everyone keeps his oath and his pledge' [*mæst ðearf* = subject, *that*-clause = subject complement].

ealra worulda woruld (O3/4 NN BIL MARGOE, p. 175f.) 'dear Lord, praise be to yourself and thanks for all the good that you do me and have done, and which is still my hope that you will do forever until the end of the world'

Noun clauses with the function <u>NP complement</u> are governed by nominal syntagms which themselves can realise several functions. My data attest the functions subject, subject complement, object and complement in a prepositional syntagm:

[4.25]   *Hyht is onfangen <u>þæt nu bletsung mot bæm gemæne, werum ond</u>* <u>*wifum, a to worulde forð in þam uplican engla dreame mid soðfæder*</u> <u>*symle wunian*</u> (OX/3 XX XX CHRI, p. 5f.) 'Hope is conceived that now a blessing may rest on both, men and women henceforth to eternity in the heavenly joy of the angels with the father of truth' (NP *hyht*: subject)

[4.26]   *þis synd þænne þa forewyrd <u>þæt Ægelric hæbbe þæt land æt Cert his</u>* <u>*dæg*</u> (O3 XX DOC ROB101, p. 188) 'these are then the arrangements, that Æthelric shall have the estate at Chart for his lifetime' (NP *þa forewyrd*: subject complement)

[4.27]   *Gif he mægnes hæbbe, <u>þæt he his gefan beride</u>* (O2 STA LAW ALFLAW, p. 74) 'if he has the power to besiege his enemy' (NP *mægnes*: genitive object)

[4.28]   *Ac we wyllað, þæt ælc man ofer XII wintre sylle þone að, <u>þæt he nelle</u>* <u>*þeof beon ne þeofes gewita*</u> (O3 STA LAW LAW11C, p. 324) 'but we wish that every person above the age of twelve years swears an oath that he does not want to be a thief or a thief's accessory' (NP *þone að*: accusative object)

[4.29]   *Hwy ge ymb ðæt unnet ealnig swincen, <u>þæt ge þone hlisan habban</u>* <u>*tiliað ofer ðioda ma þonne eow þearf sie?*</u> (O2/3 XX XX MBO, p. 165) 'why should you always struggle for that folly, that you try to have more fame among people than you need? (NP *ðæt unnet*: complement in a prepositional syntagm)

The function <u>adjectival complement</u> is only sparsely attested in my corpus. The adjectival syntagm which is expanded by a noun clause can only function as a subject complement:

[4.30]   *weorðe se carfull hu he swyþast mæge gecweman his Drihtne* (O3 IR HOM WULF10C, p. 207) 'he ought to be mindful how he may best please his Lord' (adjectival syntagm: *carfull*)

The distribution of these functions and their realisation possibilities are displayed in Table 4.5.

Table 4.5 The distribution of the realisation possibilities of the verbal syntagm in OE noun clauses with the functions subject, object, subject complement, NP complement and adjectival complement

Function	Subjunctive		Indicative		Modal		Total	
Subject	52	60.47%	28	32.56%	6	6.97%	86	100%
Object	277	57.23%	147	30.37%	60	12.40%	484	100%
Subject complement	74	88.10%	5	5.95%	5	5.95%	84	100%
NP complement	44	55.00%	23	28.75%	13	16.25%	80	100%
Adjectival complement	3	75.00%			1	25.00%	4	100%
Total	450	60.98%	203	27.51%	85	11.51%	738	100%

Object is by far the most frequent function of noun clauses; 65 per cent of all noun clauses are object clauses. Yet it is the function subject complement where we find the largest share of subjunctives. Table 4.5 also reveals that a simple distinction between subject clauses and object clauses does not tell us much about the functional preferences of the subjunctive. It remains to be seen if one of the constituents of the matrix clause has an influence on the form of the verbal syntagm of the dependent clause.

4.2.5 The parameter meaning

In this section the focus is on the influence of the meaning of constituents of the matrix clause on the distribution of subjunctives and its competitors in dependent noun clauses with different functions. The relevant constituents are the matrix verbs of object clauses, the subjects of sentences containing subject complement clauses and the NP of NP complement clauses.

4.2.5.1 The matrix verbs of object clauses[12]

The 484 object clauses of my corpus depend on ninety-nine different verbs; forty-eight of these matrix verbs occur only once, and the other fifty-one account for the remaining 436 examples. Some matrix verbs show a very characteristic distribution: forty-four of them govern only object clauses with subjunctive forms, another fifteen govern only object clauses with a verbal syntagm realised by a modal construction, and another four govern object clauses with verbal syntagms realised by either a subjunctive or a modal construction. These sixty-three verbs account for 194 of the 484 examples. The bulk of the examples follow matrix verbs that can govern object clauses with verbal syntagms of

---

[12] I will use this 'short' term instead of the correct but clumsy expression 'the verb in the matrix clause which governs an object clause'.

different realisation possibilities (cf. 'Appendix I: Matrix verbs of Old English object clauses').

The majority of the high-frequency matrix verbs of my corpus which govern only or preferably object clauses with subjunctive verbs share the semantic feature volition. Among them are *bebeodan* 'command, require', *beodan* 'command, decree', *biddan* 'ask, command, require', *ceosan* 'decide', *forbeodan* 'forbid', *gieman* 'take heed to', *halsian* 'entreat', *hedan* 'take heed to', *læran* 'teach, persuade', *willan* 'will, wish, desire'. They govern 138 of the 277 object clauses with subjunctive (~57 per cent). If we add the subjunctives in object clauses which are governed by matrix verbs with a volitional meaning that are attested only once, this is strong support for the hypothesis that verbs of volition preferably govern object clauses with a subjunctive verb form. These matrix verbs together with object clauses with subjunctive verb forms express root modality. This also holds when the verbal syntagm of the object clause is realised by a modal construction. Since the expression of root modality extends over the whole sentence, this is another instance of modal harmony (Huddleston and Pullum 2002: 179), which was also detected in OE relative clauses (cf. section 3.2.7).

[4.31]   *gif we hine biddað mid inneweardre heortan, þæt he us mildsige* (O3 IR HOM AELFR2/8, p. 533) 'if we ask him with sincere heart that he should show mercy on us'

The meaning which stretches across the whole construction is the speakers' plea for mercy. It is through the combination of the meaning of the verb *biddan* in the matrix clause and the subjunctive mood of the verb form *mildsige* in the object clause that the root modality is expressed.

Behre (1934: 73) argues in a similar way: 'the subjunctive of the *þæt*-clause is not determined by the governing verb but by the speaker's conception of the content of the *þæt*-clause as desired'. This explains why the same matrix verb can be followed by the subjunctive or by the indicative in the dependent clause. The most frequent verb in my corpus which shows this behaviour is *secgan*. It occurs sixty-seven times, fifteen times followed by the subjunctive in the dependent clause, forty-nine times by the indicative and three times by a modal construction.

[4.32]   *sege hire þæt heo me fylste* (O3 IR HOM AELFR2/29, p. 255) 'tell her that she should help me'

[4.33]   *we secgað eow þæt nan man hine ne sceal beladian* (O3 IR HOM AELFR2/29, p. 258) 'we tell you that nobody shall excuse him'

[4.34]   *Soð ic eow secge, þæt ge sylfe ne becumað into heofonan rice* (O3 IR HOM AELFR15, p. 531) 'I tell you truly that you yourself do not get into the kingdom of heaven'

The verb forms of the object clauses in [4.32] and [4.33] express root modality (subtype deonticity). It is stronger in [4.32], where it is supported by the imperative *sege* in the matrix clause. The indicative in the object clause of [4.34] expresses epistemic modality.

The form of the verbal syntagm in the object clause may even disambiguate the meaning of the corresponding matrix verb.

[4.35]   *gedo þu þet heo hider cuman* (O2/4 NN BIL CHAD, p. 172) 'make that they come hither'

[4.36]   *do þæt þe gehaten is* (O3/4 NN BIL MARGOE, p. 179) 'do what you are told'

The meaning of the matrix verb *don* in [4.35] can be paraphrased as 'cause'; that of the same matrix verb in [4.36] with 'perform'.

The regular correspondence between matrix verbs of volition and subjunctives or modal constructions in the dependent clause, which holds in my corpus, is not parallelled by a similar correspondence between matrix verbs of thinking and saying or matrix verbs of mental affection and subjunctives or modal constructions in the dependent clause, which was claimed in previous studies.[13] By contrast, the frequent verbs of saying and thinking (with the exception of *cweþan*) and verbs of mental affection, namely *seon*, *þencan*, *understandan* and *witan*, favour the indicative (cf. 'Appendix I: Matrix verbs of Old English object clauses'). This is also a case of modal harmony, since the meaning of these verbs expresses epistemic modality, and they usually govern object clauses with verbal syntagms that also express epistemic modality. Deviations from this default constellation are marked by the form of the verbal syntagm in the matrix and/or in the noun clause (cf. examples [4.32] and [4.33]).

4.2.5.2 The subjects of sentences containing subject complement clauses

In seventy-four out of the eighty-four examples (= 88 per cent) of subject complement clauses in my corpus the verbal syntagm is realised by a subjunctive. The vast majority of the subjects (fifty-one tokens) in the corresponding matrix clause is realised by a substantive with the meaning component volition: *gerædness* (15) 'decree', *þearf* (14) 'necessity', *willa* (8) 'will, wish', *niedþearf* (4) 'need', *neod* (3) 'desire', *riht* (3) 'right', *þegenlagu* (2) 'rights of a thane', *bebod* (2) 'command'.

[4.37]   *þonne is min willa þæt hit hæbbe min wiif* (O1 XX DOC HARM2, p. 3) 'then [it] is my will that my wife shall have it'

---

[13] Behre (1934: chapters VII, VIII), Traugott (1992: 239), Wilde (1939/1940: 303).

Four more substantives belong to the semantic classes of thinking/saying and mental affection: *cwyddung* (1) 'saying', *wundor* (2) 'wonder', *tweon* (1) 'doubt', *wen* (1) 'hope'. In seven subject complement clauses the subject is realised by substantives with different meanings: *gear* (2) 'year', *hlafordswice* (2) 'high treason', *hæðenscipe* (1) 'paganism', *þenung* (1) 'service', *fruma* (1) 'beginning'. Only in eleven examples is the subject realised by a neuter pronoun.

> [4.38]   *gyf hit geweorðe, þæt man mid tyhtlan & mid uncræftum sacerd belecge* (O3 STA LAW LAW11C, p. 284) 'if it happens that someone charges a priest with accusation and evil practices'

A similar distribution of subjects holds for the five examples in which the verbal syntagm of the noun clauses is expressed by a modal construction: *neod* 'desire' (1), *niedþearf* 'need' (1), *hopa* 'hope' (1), *þeaw* 'custom' (1), *soð* 'truth' (1). This correspondence is another instance of modal harmony. The subjects and subject complements express the same modality.

In the five sentences containing subject complement clauses whose verbal syntagm is an indicative the subject is a neuter pronoun; the other two subjects are realised by the substantives *gecynd* 'nature' and *untweo* 'certainty'. Here the meaning of the subject of the main clause and the form of the verbal syntagm in the subject complement syntagm are in modal harmony: both express epistemic modality.

The correspondence between the meaning of the subject of complex sentences containing a subject complement noun clause and the realisation of the verbal syntagm of this noun clause suggests the hypothesis that subjects with the meaning components volition, thinking/saying and mental affection strongly correlate with subjunctives or modal constructions in the corresponding subject complement clauses, whereas subjects with other meanings, in particular neuter pronoun subjects, favour indicatives in the subject complement clause. Both types of correspondence are instances of modal harmony. In the first case root modality extends over the whole sentence, in the second case epistemic modality extends over the whole sentence.

4.2.5.3 The NP of NP complement clauses
In forty-four instances of the eighty NP complement clauses of my corpus the verbal syntagm is realised by a subjunctive. The most frequent realisations of the nucleus of the governing NP of these noun clauses are *þearf* 'necessity' (7), *ræd* 'decree' (2) and *mægen* 'might' (2).[14] They

---

14 The nuclei of the remaining governing NPs are *geþeaht* 'thought' (1), *help* 'help' (1), *giefu* 'gift' (1), *ræden* 'condition' (1), *foreweard* 'condition' (1), *leafa* 'belief'

and some of the less frequently occurring NPs belong to the semantic classes of volition, thinking and saying, or mental affection (Behre 1934: chapters I, VII, VIII). But in twenty examples the NP is realised by one of the neuter pronouns *þæt*, *þis* or *hit*; this amounts to 45 per cent. The hypothesis of a correlation between the meaning of the governing NP and the subjunctive in the NP complement clause is therefore not supported. This is also true for the NP of NP complement clauses whose verbal syntagm is realised by a modal construction, where the share of NPs realised by a neuter pronoun amounts to 46 per cent. Yet indicatives in NP complement clauses correlate strongly with neuter pronouns in the NP position (sixteen out of twenty-three NPs = 69 per cent). This last result is reminiscent of the correspondence between neuter pronouns as subjects of complex sentences containing a subject complement noun clauses and the indicative of the verbal syntagm in the subject complement clause (cf. section 4.2.5.2).

4.2.6 *The parameter form of the matrix verb*

The focus in this section is on the potential influence of the form of the verbal syntagm in the matrix clause on the form of the verbal syntagm in the dependent clause. In my corpus the verbal syntagm of the relevant matrix clauses is realised by a subjunctive (149), an indicative (340), a modal construction (51), *Uton* + infinitive (10), a semi-modal construction (5) and by an imperative (54); the verbal syntagm of 129 matrix clauses is realised by none of these (= Others).[15] Table 4.6 shows the form of the verbal syntagm in the matrix clause vertically and that in the dependent clause horizontally.

Table 4.6 The relation between the form of the verbal syntagm in the matrix clause and in the noun clause in the OE corpus

Matrix \ Noun	Subjunctive	Indicative	Modal	Total
Subjunctive	108 72.48%	21 14.10%	20 13.42%	149 100%
Indicative	214 62.94%	81 23.82%	45 13.24%	340 100%
Modal	31 46.97%	26 39.39%	9 13.64%	66 100%
Imperative	18 33.33%	35 64.82%	1 1.85%	54 100%
Others	79 61.24%	40 31.00%	10 7.76%	129 100%
Total	450 60.98%	203 27.51%	85 11.51%	738 100%

(1), *milts* 'mercy' (1), *borg* 'pledge' (1), *ben* 'benefice' (1), *lufu* 'love' (1), *hopa* 'hope' (1), *þing* 'thing' (1), *oferþearf* 'great need' (1).

[15] The tokens of the patterns '*Uton* + infinitive' and 'semi-modal construction' are subsumed under 'Modal' in Table 4.6.

Matrix clauses with verbal syntagms realised by subjunctives tend to govern a subjunctive in the dependent noun clauses as well. The same tendency holds – although less strongly – for matrix clauses with verbal syntagms realised by a modal construction. Since subjunctives and modal constructions express root modality, this distribution can be interpreted as another instance of modal harmony.

Constructions with imperatives in the matrix clause, which favour indicatives in the dependent noun clause do not fit into this pattern. A closer look at the data reveals that the great majority of examples (twenty-three out of thirty-five examples) comes from one particular text (COSOLOMO) and that the relevant noun clauses are realised by interrogative clauses.

[4.39]   *Saga me hwilc wyrt ys betst and selust?* (Q OX/4 IR RELT SOLOM, p. 29) 'Tell me which plant is the best and the noblest'

So far I have not found an explanation for the large share of indicatives in noun clauses depending on matrix clauses with imperative verb forms. This corresponcence is all the more surprising since the other forms of the verbal syntagm in the matrix clause which express root modality, subjunctives and modal constructions, preferably trigger subjunctives in the noun clause.

4.2.7 The parameter clause type

The noun clauses of my corpus represent the following clause types: *that*-clause, *wh*-interrogative clause, nominal relative clause and *yes/no*-interrogative clause. The distribution of these clause types in the OE corpus is mapped in Table 4.7.

Table 4.7 The distribution of different types of noun clauses in the OE corpus

Clause type	Absolute number	Percentage
That-clause	580	78.59%
Wh-interrogative	101	13.69%
Relative clause	53	7.18%
Yes/no-interrogative	4	0.54%
Total	738	100%

Only *that*-clauses and *wh*-interrogative clauses occur in sufficient numbers in the OE corpus to merit an investigation into a potential influence of the clause type of the dependent clause on the form of its verbal syntagm.

Table 4.8 shows that such an influence is indeed given. The verbal syntagms of dependent *that*-clauses tend to be realised by a subjunctive, those of *wh*-interrogative clauses by an indicative.

Table 4.8 The distribution of the realisation possibilities of the verbal syntagm in different noun clause types of the OE corpus

Clause type	Subjunctive	Indicative	Modal	Total
That-clause	396 68.28%	121 20.86%	63 10.86%	580 100%
Wh-interrogative	29 28.71%	53 52.48%	19 8.81%	101 100%

4.2.8 Summary

In this section I have tried to discover the parameters which favour the occurrence of a subjunctive in OE noun clauses. Candidates were the date of the text and its text category as well as its format (prose vs. poetry), the function of the noun clause, the form of the verb in the matrix clause, the clause type of the noun clause and the meaning of several constituents of the matrix clause.

The analysis showed that in my corpus subjunctives are more frequent in earlier subperiods than in later subperiods, they are frequent in the text categories STA and IS, in early prose texts, in the function subject complement, in noun clauses depending on matrix clauses with a subjunctive verb form, and in the clause type *that*-clause. I also identified the meaning component volition in the matrix verbs of object clauses as well as the meaning components volition, thinking/saying and mental affection in the subjects of matrix clauses governing noun clauses with the function subject complement as triggers of subjunctives in the dependent noun clauses. Neuter pronouns realising the NP in NP complement clauses and neuter pronouns realising the subjects of sentences containing subject complement clauses were found to trigger the indicative in the dependent noun clauses. Both types of correspondence were interpreted as modal harmony. In the first case root modality extends over matrix and noun clause, in the second case epistemic modality is expressed in the matrix and noun clause.

Since a number of different parameters influences the probability of a subjunctive in the dependent noun clause, I wondered if their co-occurrence would increase this probability. It does indeed. I extracted the examples of subperiod O2, text category STA, clause type *that*-clause, and those with a subjunctive matrix verb. My corpus contains exactly fifteen examples which are characterised by a combination of these extralinguistic and linguistic features, and all of them occur in the same text (COLAW2). In fourteen of them (= 93.3 per cent) the verbal syntagm is realised by a subjunctive, in the only other example by a modal construction.[16]

---

[16] The earliest subperiod (O1) was not chosen because the text category STA is not

[4.39]   *locige <u>þæt hio hæbbe hrægl</u>* (O2 STA LAW ALFLAWIN, p. 30) 'he (should) take care that she has a dress'

I also discovered a similar effect in noun clauses of subperiod O4, of text category IR, of the clause types *wh*-interrogative, and in noun clauses with an imperative matrix verb. There are twenty-four examples with this combination of features, and all of them occur in the same text (COSOLOMO). In twenty-three of them (95.8 per cent) the verbal syntagm is realised by an indicative, in the only other example by a subjunctive.

[4.40]   *Saga me <u>hwæt ys God</u>?* (OX/4 IR RELT SOLOM, p. 25) 'Tell me who is God' (*ys* = indicative)

[4.41]   *Saga me for hwilcum ðingum heofon sy gehaten heofon?* (OX/4 IR RELT SOLOM, p. 25) 'Tell me why is the heaven called heaven' (*sy* = subjunctive)

The conclusion to be drawn from these results is that the choice between a subjunctive and an indicative as the realisation of the verbal syntagm in noun clauses depends most strongly on the combination of the values of the extralinguistic parameters 'date of composition' and 'text category' and of the linguistic parameters 'clause type of the noun clause' and 'form of the matrix verb'.

4.3 Middle English noun clauses: descriptive parameters

4.3.1 *Function*

The parameter function is dealt with in some detail by Fischer in her section on finite complement clauses. She lists the functions object of a verbal or adjectival predicate, apposition to another NP, and subject complement. Then she adds with some hesitation: 'There are constructions in Middle English that could be interpreted as subject clauses' (1992: 312). Her hesitation is motivated by the observation that these clauses rarely occupy initial position in ME. The constructions she has in mind contain a copular verb and an adjectival or a nominal subject complement. They are illustrated by examples [4.42] and [4.43].

[4.42]   *Wel is me <u>þat þu mayth hete</u>!* (M2 NI ROM HAVEL, p. 22) 'I am happy that you may eat'

represented in this subperiod. The parameter format was not included because all texts of the category STA are prose texts, but not vice versa. The parameter function was excluded, because seventy-seven out of the eighty-four subject complement clauses with their large share of subjunctives belong to the subperiods O3 and O4 and the subjunctive trigger is the meaning of the subject of their matrix clause.

[4.43] *Is hit a gret woundour <u>þat þu hast forsake styngyngge lust of body for</u>* <u>þe swete sauour of maydenhood</u>? (M2/3 IR RULE AELR3, p. 33) 'is it a great wonder that you have forsaken the fervent desire of the body for the sweet savour of maidenhood?'

With reference to Traugott's analysis of comparable OE constructions (Traugott 1992: 234) Fischer (1992: 313) prefers to interpret the *that*-clauses in [4.42] and [4.43] as 'complements to the adjective (. . .) and the noun (. . .) respectively'.

When potential subject clauses occur in constructions with impersonal verbs Fischer suggests analysing them as objects of the verb rather than as subjects. In the section where she deals with noun clauses which are realised as interrogative clauses, Fischer (1992: 279) is less hesitant to include subject as one of the possible functions.

Function as a descriptive parameter is not explicitly discussed in Moessner's (2007, 2010a) papers on ME mandative constructions. Rütten (2014), by contrast, requires that studies on mandative constructions should pay attention to functional equivalence. But already her examples (2)–(5) (2014: 377) show that she does not fulfil this requirement herself, mixing noun clauses with the functions subject and object in her study.

4.3.2 *Form*

Fischer (1992) deals with noun clauses under the headings 'Questions' and 'Complement clauses' (312–343). Questions are subdivided into *wh*-questions and *yes/no*-questions. Dependent interrogatives, and these are the question types which are at issue in this section, 'are found after nouns and predicates that are concerned with the truth value of the complementation, such as *ask*, (*not*) *know*, (*not*) *say*, *wonder*, *doubt*, etc.' (1992: 279). As a rule, the subjunctive is used in these clauses when an element of doubt or uncertainty is involved. Complement clauses are either finite or non-finite. When they are finite, their prototypical form is a *that*-clause, less frequently the conjunction *that* is deleted. The usual verb form in these clauses is the subjunctive, 'especially after (a) verbs expressing a wish, a command or exhortation, where the sub-clause denotes a prospective event . . . and (b) verbs expressing some mental activity' (1992: 314). Complement clauses can also be realised by nominal relative clauses. Non-finite complement clauses usually take the form of an infinitive construction.[17]

Kovács (2010) does not provide any new insights on the use of the

---

[17] Fischer (1992: 316) calls infinitive constructions 'the most frequent type' of non-finite complement clauses, and this is the only type she describes in more detail.

subjunctive in OE and ME, but for ME simply summarises Fischer's detailed analysis.

More specialised studies on ME noun clauses focus on the equivalent of Fischer's complement clauses. They are called mandative clauses/ constructions (Moessner 2007, 2010a, Rütten 2014, 2015). This is also the clause type which has received most attention in studies of the subjunctive in later periods (cf. section 4.5.1).

Moessner (2007: 212) explicitly excludes non-finite clauses, *wh*-clauses and imperative clauses, and she distinguishes the realisation possibilities subjunctive, modal construction, indicative and ambiguous in the verbal syntagm of object clauses. She comes to the conclusion that subjunctive frequency dropped between the beginning and the end of the ME period, and that this development was parallelled by an increase of modal constructions. She identified two sets of matrix verbs. One set with the verbs *bede*, *enact*, *loke* and *wille* contributed to the preservation of the subjunctive, the other set with the verbs *ordaine*, *pray* and *suppose* contributed to its replacement by modal constructions. In her data the instructive text categories show the largest numbers of subjunctives, and the narrative text categories the smallest.

Moessner (2010a) takes a wider perspective on the distribution of subjunctives in dependent mandative clauses, distinguishing the construction types *that*-clause, infinitive construction and direct speech with their different realisation possibilities of the verbal syntagm. She establishes *that*-clauses as the prevailing construction type in ME and the subjunctive as the prevailing realisation of the verbal syntagm in mandative *that*-clauses. Yet the subjunctive loses ground in favour of modal constructions between the beginning and the end of the ME period. In the construction type direct speech, the subjunctive as well as modal constructions play only a minor role; the preferred realisation of the verbal syntagm is the imperative. The introduction of construction types allows her not only to correlate text category and preferred realisation of the verbal syntagm, but also to correlate text category and preferred construction type. The second kind of correlation yields a particularly interesting result. The text categories statutory, instruction secular, instruction religious, documents and Bible prefer constructions with a strong mandative force. It is expressed by the combination of the suasive verb in the matrix clause and by a subjunctive or a modal construction in a *that*-clause or by an imperative in direct speech. These linguistic choices are in line with the communicative purpose of the corresponding authoritative and didactic texts. The text categories narration imaginative, narration non-imaginative, correspondence and mystery play prefer infinitive constructions. In this construction type the mandative force is much weaker, it relies only on the suasive verb in the matrix clause. This fits in well with the nature of the text categories involved. The authors of narrative texts have no didactic aims, and letters and mystery plays are at the oral end of the written-oral scale, where directive speech acts are usually expressed by indirect strategies (Trosborg 1995: 49).

Tanja Rütten (2014) is primarily interested in dependent mandative constructions in EModE, but she raises a question that is independent of the period in which mandative constructions are investigated. She points out that previous publications accepted only finite forms as competitors of the subjunctive and that studies that also considered infinitive constructions left them out in their statistics (Leech et al. 2009: 70) or judged them as of minor importance (Moessner 2010a: 157). Rütten argues that from a functional point of view, in addition to indicatives and modal constructions, not only infinitive constructions but also gerunds, deverbal nominalisations and primary substantives should be considered as competitors of the subjunctive (cf. Rütten 2014: 379, table 2).[18] This argument overlooks the fact that the replacement of the subjunctive by deverbal nominalisations or primary substantives transforms the dependent mandative construction expressing a direct directive speech act into an independent sentence expressing an indirect directive speech act (cf. Moessner 2010a: 161–162 for a discussion of the strength of the directive force in ME mandative constructions realised by subjunctives and infinitive constructions).[19] The inevitable change from a dependent to an independent mandative construction prohibits the inclusion of derived or primary substantives in a treatment of noun clauses.

4.3.3 *Governing elements*

The descriptions of governing elements, which abound in nearly all treatments of mandative constructions of all periods, share the semantic features wish, command, exhortation (Fischer 1992: 314), demand, recommendation, resolution, intention (Quirk et al. 1985: 156), volition (Övergaard 1995: 92, Visser 1963–1973: §869), requirement, suggestion (Jacobsson 1975: 162). The size of lists of these elements varies from seventeen (Johansson and Norheim 1988) to 240 (Kastronic and Poplack 2014). The problem with these lists is 'that there can be no question of giving a definitive list of mandative items' (Huddleston and Pullum 2002: 999). An important reason for this predicament is that mandative clauses can also be governed by expressions that have none of the semantic features mentioned above (Övergaard 1995: 82).[20]

---

[18] She envisages also the possibility of imperatives as competitors of subjunctives, but the example that nourishes this assumption is indeed ambiguous.

[19] For a discussion of descriptive models for the analysis of directive speech acts cf. Moessner (2010b: 221–225).

[20] For a discussion of these methodological issues cf. Moessner (2007: 210–212).

Most studies on mandative constructions focus on verbs as governing elements, yet some also include adjectives and nouns as triggers (Hoffmann 1997: 103–106, Hundt 1998b: 174, Kastronic and Poplack 2014: 76, Övergaard 1995: 113–121).[21] In their synchronic-diachronic investigation of noun clauses depending on the deontic-evaluative adjectives *important, essential, crucial, proper, fitting* and *appropriate*, Van Linden and Davidse (2009: 194) point out that mandative complements predominate after these adjectives and that propositional complements developed only after the EModE period. Many of the adjectives and nouns listed in these publications do not have a suasive meaning.

The descriptions of ME noun clauses which classify them primarily under the aspect of function list a wider variety of governing elements, including expressions of mental activities and verbs of saying (Fischer 1992, Visser 1963–1973).

4.4 Noun clauses in the ME corpus

My ME corpus contains 788 noun clauses (= 4.74/1,000 words). Their verbal syntagms are realised as subjunctives (302 = 1.82/1,000 words), as indicatives (283 = 1.70/1,000 words), as modal constructions (141 = 0.85/1,000 words), as semi-modal constructions (12 = 0.07/1,000 words) or as imperatives (50 = 0.30/1,000 words).[22] In the following sections the influence of several linguistic and non-linguistic parameters on the distribution of the realisation possibilities of their verbal syntagms will be presented and discussed.

4.4.1 *The parameter date of composition*

Table 4.9 contains the distribution of the realisation possibilities of the verbal syntagm in noun clauses across the four ME subperiods of the corpus.

The general trend is that the share of modal constructions increases whereas that of imperatives decreases; the shares of the other realisation possibilities fluctuate across the subperiods. The trends of decreasing subjunctive frequency and increasing indicative frequency noticed in the OE period are not continued. Concerning subjunctive frequency my results are not in line with the frequency decrease reported in Moessner

[21] Harsh (1968: 115) distinguishes three types of dependent noun clauses in which he found subjunctives in his corpora. His type 5 covers noun clauses depending on adjectival subject complements. It is attested only once in his ME corpus (cf. table 7, p. 160f.). By contrast, there are twenty-two examples of object clauses – his types 3 and 4 – depending on verbs in his ME corpus.
[22] Semi-modal constructions are subsumed under 'Modal' in the tables of this chapter.

Table 4.9 The distribution of the realisation possibilities of the verbal syntagm in noun clauses across subperiods M1–M4

Subperiod	Subjunctive	Indicative	Modal	Imperative	Total
M1	77 35.98%	76 35.51%	31 14.49%	30 14.02%	214 100%
M2	24 24.74%	45 46.39%	20 20.62%	8 8.25%	97 100%
M3	116 49.15%	78 33.05%	37 15.68%	5 2.12%	236 100%
M4	85 35.27%	84 34.85%	65 26.97%	7 2.91%	241 100%
Total	302 38.32%	283 35.91%	153 19.42%	50 6.35%	788 100%

(2010a: 158). This discrepancy is probably due to the fact that the clause types she investigated do not coincide with the ones here.[23]

4.4.2 *The parameter text category*

The text categories with the largest absolute numbers of noun clauses are IR (328 = 1.97/1,000 words) and XX (176 = 1.06/1,000 words). With the exception of category EX, which is least frequently attested, the other categories contain about the same number of examples. Table 4.10 shows the distribution of the realisation possibilities of the verbal syntagm in noun clauses across the text categories of the ME corpus.

The subjunctive is the preferred realisation in the prototypical text categories STA, IS and XX, modal constructions dominate in EX, and in all other text categories the indicative is the preferred realisation.

Since imperatives in noun clauses are only possible in direct speech passages, their distribution reflects the frequent occurrence of direct speech in narrative texts. The frequency of subjunctives in texts of the categories STA and IS is a consequence of their directive nature.

The category STA is represented by the proclamation of Henry III and by extracts from *The Statutes of the Realm* (subperiod M4). Compared to the OE period, subjunctive frequency has decreased by a little more than 10 per cent in ME. Since this decrease is compensated by just over an 8 per cent increase of modal constructions, it can be concluded that the degree of directiveness remained unchanged but that its expression partly shifted from subjunctives to modal constructions.[24] In terms of modality this means that the preferred expression of root modality shifted from subjunctives to modal constructions.

The category IS is represented by two handbooks with instructions about how to recognise a good horse and how to treat it when it is ill, about the appropriate moment for blood-letting, about the duties of watch officers, about how to prepare ink, and many other useful recipes. These instructions are usually expressed by subjunctives.

> [4.44]   Loke *þat he be hardi & coragious of herte* (M3 IS HANDM HORSES, p. 87) 'make sure that it is strong and courageous of character'
>
> [4.45]   *ȝe schul first pryncypaly take hede þat þe pees be kepte in ȝour towne* (M4 IS HANDO REYNES, p. 154) 'you must first of all make sure that the peace be kept in your town'

---

[23]   Moessner (2010a) does not include dependent interrogative and nominal relative clauses.

[24]   In current descriptive models of directive speech acts both realisations belong to the type direct directive (cf. Moessner 2010b: 221–225).

Table 4.10 The distribution of the realisation possibilities of the verbal syntagm in ME noun clauses across prototypical text categories

Category	Subjunctive	Indicative	Modal	Imperative	Total
STA	43 74.14%	4 6.90%	11 18.96%		58 100%
IS	46 66.67%	12 17.39%	10 14.49%	1 1.45%	69 100%
IR	84 25.61%	167 50.91%	61 18.60%	16 4.88%	328 100%
NI	17 21.52%	32 40.51%	19 24.05%	11 13.92%	79 100%
NN	19 28.36%	22 32.84%	5 7.46%	21 31.34%	67 100%
EX	2 18.18%	2 18.18%	7 63.64%		11 100%
XX	91 51.70%	44 25.00%	40 22.73%	1 0.57%	176 100%
Total	302 38.32%	283 35.91%	153 19.42%	50 6.35%	788 100%

The heterogeneous category XX contains five files with extracts from prologues and epilogues by William Caxton (file 7), mystery plays (file 10), petitions (file 12), depositions (file 13) and official letters (file 23). Official letters and, in particular, petitions contribute most to the large subjunctive frequency of the prototypical text category XX (cf. Table 4.11).

4.4.3 *The parameter prose vs. poetry*

In my ME corpus the share of subjunctives is still greater in prose texts than in verse texts, although it declines in both text formats between OE and ME (cf. Table 4.12).

In verse texts the clearly preferred realisation is the indicative. Modal constructions occupy third place on the frequency scale in both text formats. The proportion of subjunctives to modal constructions in prose texts, which started to decline in the OE period, witnesses a further decline in ME from 6.2:1 to 2.1:1. In verse texts the ratio subjunctives to modal constructions changes from 1.9:1 to 1.05:1, i.e. the absolute numbers of the two realisation possibilities are almost the same.

4.4.4 *The parameter noun clause function*

The noun clauses of my ME corpus are coded for the functions subject, object, subject complement, NP complement, adjectival complement and 'Others'. The distribution of the realisation possibilities of the verbal syntagm in the noun clauses with these functions is mapped in Table 4.13.

The function 'Other' was introduced for nine noun clauses which did not fit the expected categories subject, object, subject complement, NP complement and adjectival complement. These noun clauses are special in that the element on which they depend is not part of a well-formed clause. The seven noun clauses with a subjunctive verb depend on the element *dahet* 'misfortune, woe' – attested as a substantive in a ME text – which is not part of my corpus.[25] All instances of *dahet* in my corpus occur in the romance *Havelok*, where they are glossed as 'a curse on' (interj.). The following noun clause denotes the target of the curse.

[4.46]   *Daþeit wo ne smite sore!* (M2 NI ROM HAVEL, p. 52) 'A curse on [everybody] who does not attack furiously'

---

[25] *Dahet habbe þat ilke best þat fuleþ his owe nest* (Owl and Nightingale, l.99f.) 'the animal which dirties its own nest may have misfortune'.

Table 4.11 The distribution of the realisation possibilities of the verbal syntagm in ME noun clauses in the texts of the prototypical text category XX

File	Subjunctive	Indicative	Modal	Imperative	Total
7	4 16.67%	11 45.83%	9 37.50%		24 100%
10	5 50.00%	4 40.00%		1 10.00%	10 100%
12	55 62.50%	11 12.50%	22 25.00%		88 100%
13	12 46.16%	7 26.92%	7 26.92%		26 100%
23	15 53.57%	11 39.29%	2 7.14%		28 100%
Total	91 51.70%	44 25.00%	40 22.73%	1 0.57%	176 100%

Table 4.12 The distribution of the realisation possibilities of the verbal syntagm in ME noun clauses in prose and in verse texts

Format	Subjunctive	Indicative	Modal	Imperative	Total
Prose	279 41.39%	226 33.53%	131 19.44%	38 5.64%	674 100%
Poetry	23 20.18%	57 50.00%	22 19.30%	12 10.52%	114 100%
Total	302 38.32%	283 35.91%	153 19.42%	50 6.35%	788 100%

Table 4.13 The distribution of the realisation possibilities of the verbal syntagm in ME noun clauses with different functions

Function	Subjunctive	Indicative	Modal	Imperative	Total
Subject	75 46.01%	58 35.58%	30 18.41%		163 100%
Object	192 35.29%	195 35.85%	107 19.67%	50 9.19%	544 100%
Subject complement	17 36.96%	18 39.13%	11 23.91%		46 100%
NP complement	7 36.84%	10 52.63%	2 10.53%		19 100%
Adjectival complement	4 57.14%		3 42.86%		7 100%
Others	7 77.78%	2 22.22%			9 100%
Total	302 38.32%	283 35.91%	153 19.42%	50 6.35%	788 100%

The two noun clauses with an indicative verb occur in the religious treatise *Ancrene Wisse*, and they depend on the element *lo*, which the *OED*
classifies as an interjection equivalent with the imperative *look!*

[4.47]   *lo <u>hu grurefulliche godd seolf þreateð þe</u>* (M1 IR RELT ANCR, p. 164)
'look how terribly God threatens you'

The seven noun clauses which function as <u>adjectival complements</u>
depend on the adjectives *wurþi* 'worthy', *able* 'suitable', *war* 'wary',
uncuð 'unacquainted'.

[4.48]   *Ne deme ðe nog[[t[] wurdi, <u>ðat tu dure loken up to ðe heueneward</u>*
(M2 IR RELT BEST, p. 6f) 'do not consider yourself worthy to dare
to look up to heaven'

[4.49]   *Ne hope þu to oðres mannes deaðe, uncuð <u>hwa lengest libbe</u>* (MX/1
IS PHILO VESPD3, p. 4) 'do not hope for another person's death, not
knowing who lives longest'

The distribution of the realisation possibilities of the verbal syntagm in
the noun clauses with this function is the same in OE and in ME. Only
subjunctives and modal constructions are attested. The share of subjunctives decreases between OE and ME. It should be borne in mind,
however, that adjectival complements play only a minor role among the
noun clauses.

Noun clauses like those in examples [4.50] and [4.51] are analysed as
<u>NP complements</u>.

[4.50]   *For unto a povre ordre for to yive Is signe <u>that a man is wel yshryve</u>*
(M3 NI FICT CTPROL, p. 27) 'for giving alms to a poor order is a
sign that a person has been well shriven'

[4.51]   *And over that, that opyn proclamacion be made in every Shire of
this youre seid Realme <u>that no man bye ne selle after the seid feste of
Seynt Mighell by eny other Weight or mesure than is according to the
seid Standard</u>* (M4 STA LAW STAT2, p. 552) 'and additionally that
open proclamation be made in every shire of this your said realm that
nobody buy nor sell after the said feast of St. Michael by any other
weight or measure than is according to the said standard'

Fischer's description of this function as apposition to another NP evokes
the idea of referential identity. When Quirk et al. (1985: §17.26) call
PDE noun clauses with this function appositive clauses, this is justified
by their definition of apposition as a relation between items such that 'the
reference of one must be included in the reference of the other' (Quirk et
al. 1985: §17.65), and they point out that the head of the construction

is a general abstract noun, often a nominalisation. This description fits the examples in the ME corpus exactly. The heads of the noun clauses in [4.50] and [4.51] are the abstract noun *signe* and the nominalisation *proclamacion* respectively. The number of NP complements as well as the frequency of subjunctives in noun clauses with this function has decreased after the OE period. Whereas in OE the preferred realisation of the verbal syntagm in NP complement clauses was the subjunctive, in ME it is the indicative.

The same development can be observed in <u>subject complement clauses</u>. Whereas in OE the relative frequency of this noun clause type was 0.66/1,000 words, with 0.28/1,000 words it has more than halved in ME, and the percentage share of subjunctives has dropped from 88.10 per cent to 36.96 per cent. The prototypical ME complex sentence with a noun clause as subject complement has the form 'subject + copular verb + noun clause with an indicative verb'.

> [4.52]   *And the cause is <u>that ther is almost none / that entendeth to the comyn</u>*
>   *<u>wele but only euery man for his singuler prouffyte</u>* (M4 XX PREF
>   CAXTON, p. 77) 'and the reason is that there is almost nobody who
>   has the common weal in mind, but everybody [works for] his own
>   profit'

Traugott's argument (1992: 234) that in OE noun clauses cannot occur in initial position and therefore cannot function as <u>subject clauses</u> is no longer valid for ME, because nominal relative clauses are attested in initial position (cf. examples [4.53] and [4.54]).

> [4.53]   *<u>who so is absent at þilk masses wiþ-oute verry cause</u> schal paie to*
>   *þe brotherede a pound wex* (M3 XX DOC RET, p. 42) 'whoever is
>   absent from these masses without a plausible reason shall pay one
>   pound of wax to the brotherhood'
> [4.54]   *<u>Whoso wil be perfiȝt and lyue aftir þis chapitil</u>, do as Catoun seiþ*
>   (M3/4 IR RELT HILTON, p. 4) 'who wants to be perfect and live
>   according to the chapter shall do as Cato says'

Noun clauses functioning as subjects in non-initial position are often accompanied by an impersonal pronoun *hit* or *that* in initial position. This is what Mitchell calls a 'formal pronoun subject' in his OE examples (Mitchell 1985: §1963). For PDE, Quirk et al. (1985: §18.33) deal with this construction under the heading 'extraposition of a clausal element':

The subject is moved to the end of the sentence, and the normal subject position is filled by the anticipatory pronoun *it*. The resulting sentence thus contains two subjects, which we may identify as the 'postponed subject' (the one

which is notionally the subject of the sentence) and the 'anticipatory subject (*it*)'.

Whereas in PDE the extraposition of the notional subject makes the anticipatory subject *it* obligatory, it is an optional element in ME.

[4.55]   *it may be take þat he ne hath nouȝt of his owene to helpe hym self with* (M3 XX DOC RET, p. 50) 'it may be assumed that he has nothing of his own to help himself with'

[4.56]   *Also is ordeined þat no man ne woman be receyued in to þis fraternite bot onliche men & women of gode fame & of gode name* (M3 XX DOC RET, p. 43) '[it] is also ordained that no man nor woman shall be received into this fraternity except men and women of good reputation and of good name'

The possibility of a formal subject *hit* has a consequence on the analysis of noun clauses in matrix clauses with a copular verb. When the copular verb is accompanied by an adjectival or a prepositional syntagm and a noun clause, the latter functions as the subject irrespective of the presence or absence of the formal subject *hit*. This is the case in examples [4.57] and [4.58].

[4.57]   *Betere is þat þu þider go* (M2 NI ROM HAVEL, p. 27) '[it] is better that you go there'

[4.58]   *Hit byð dysig þat man speca ær, þone he þænce* (MX/1 IS PHILO VESPD3, p. 5) 'it is stupid that a man speaks before he thinks'

If the copular verb is accompanied by a substantival syntagm and a noun clause, the former functions as the subject and the noun clause functions as the subject complement, if there is no formal subject *hit*. If there is an additional formal subject *hit*, the noun clause functions as the subject and the substantival syntagm functions as the subject complement. These constellations are illustrated in examples [4.59] and [4.60].

[4.59]   *The firste tokene of loue is, þat þe louier submytte fully his wille to þe wille of him þat he loueþ* (M3/4 IR RELT HILTON, p. 1) 'the first token of love is that the lover submits his will fully to the will of the person that he loves'

[4.60]   *Also hit ys my wyl that hit be, be the wyll & be the devyce of Robert pygeon* (M3 XX DOC TEST, p. 215) 'also it is my will that it shall be according to the will and according to the plan of Robert Pygeon'

In example [4.59] the noun clause functions as subject complement, in [4.60] the noun clause is the extraposed/notional subject; it is accompanied by the formal subject *hit*.

The construction types with a noun clause as subject listed for OE (cf. section 4.2.4) have to be only slightly modified for ME to accomodate the formal subject *hit* and the possibility of a subject noun clause in initial position:

a.   (*hit*) + BE + adjectival/prepositional syntagm + noun clause
b.   (*hit*) + passive verbal syntagm + noun clause
c.   (*hit*) + (NPdat.) + impersonal verb + noun clause
d.   personal verb + (object) + noun clause
dd. noun clause + personal verb + (object)
e.   *hit* + BE + substantival syntagm + noun clause

Since noun clauses functioning as subjects stand out as favouring subjunctives more than noun clauses with other functions, it seemed worthwhile to check the distribution of the realisation possibilities of the verbal syntagm in subject clauses of the different construction types. The results are given in Table 4.14.

Table 4.14 The distribution of the realisation possibilities of the verbal syntagm in ME subject clauses of different construction types

Type	Subjunctive	Indicative	Modal	Total
a	16 59.26%	7 25.93%	4 14.81%	27 100%
b	28 58.33%	9 18.75%	11 22.92%	48 100%
c	17 50.00%	12 35.29%	5 14.71%	34 100%
d	1 16.67%	4 66.67%	1 16.66%	6 100%
dd	9 24.32%	24 64.87%	4 10.81%	37 100%
e	4 36.36%	2 18.18%	5 45.46%	11 100%
Total	75 46.01%	58 35.58%	30 18.41%	163 100%

Construction types (a) and (b) clearly contribute most to the significant share of subjunctives in subject clauses. This is particularly interesting because in most studies on subjunctives in noun clauses these constructions are neglected.

Noun clauses following substantival or adjectival syntagms are acknowledged in some publications on PDE mandative constructions (Crawford 2009, Hoffmann 1997, Hundt 1998b, Kastronic and Poplack 2014), but the function of these noun clauses is not discussed. Mindt (2008) deals with PDE *that*-clauses following adjectives (= construction type a), and she analyses them as adjectival complements. Yet she is primarily interested in the semantic relation between the adjectives and the form of the verbal syntagm in the dependent clauses, and her data contain both adjectival complements and subjects.[26] This is why her results are only of marginal interest in the present context. Övergaard (1995: 31–35) is the only one who argues that noun clauses following (emotive) adjectives have to be treated separately because 'the noun clause is invariably the subject of the whole structure'. She notes that the subjunctive is far more frequent in this construction in American English than in British English, but that there is a frequency rise in both regional varieties in the twentieth century. Yet the percentage figure for her 1990 British corpus (= 33 per cent) is below that of my ME corpus. Therefore, a long-term diachronic study of this construction type would be highly welcome.

When voice is analysed in complex sentences at all, the focus is on the voice in the dependent noun clause, not on that of the matrix clause. Subject clauses depending on passive matrix clauses (= construction type b) cluster in two files of the ME corpus, in CMDOCU3 and in CMLAW. The former contains mainly petitions, but also extracts from gild-books and some wills; the latter is a collection of acts and statutes. The set of verbs in the passive verbal syntagms which take a subject clause with subjunctive is quite small. It comprises the items *ordenen* (seventeen examples), *enact* (six examples), *finden* (three examples), *cnawen* (one example), *taken* (1 example). The small number of files and the small number of verbs involved suggest that the pattern is a style-marker of formal official prose in ME.

[4.61] *Also is ordeined <u>þat what brother þat ne comeþ nouȝt atte somons of</u> <u>þe maistres atte forseid four tymes of þe ȝer, þat he paie a pound wex</u> <u>bot if he haue verrey excusacion of his abscense</u>* (M3 XX DOC RET, p. 43) '[it] is also ordained that any brother who does not come at the summons of the masters at the agreed four times of the year shall pay a pound of wax unless he has a good excuse for his absence'

As in the OE period, <u>object</u> is the most frequent function of <u>noun clauses</u> in the ME corpus as well; object clauses have a share of 69 per cent of all noun clauses. Although indicative is the preferred option in object noun clauses, the shares of both indicatives and subjunctives do not deviate much from each other. In the following sections a potential influence of the meaning and form of the matrix verb on the form of the verb in dependent clauses – in particular on those with object function – will be investigated.

---

[26] She illustrates the first functional type by the example *Scarlet was glad that Brian wasn't present* and the second by *It may be possible that I shall meet them all again one day* (Mindt 2008: 142). Her analysis of the second functional type differs from that by Quirk et al. (1985: §16.70).

4.4.5 *The parameter matrix verb*

4.4.5.1 The meaning of the matrix verb of object clauses

The 544 object clauses of the ME corpus depend on 104 different verbs; forty-nine of them occur only once, and the other fifty-five account for the remaining 495 examples (cf. 'Appendix II: Matrix verbs of Middle English object clauses'). Table 4.15 contains the ten matrix verbs governing more than ten object clauses in the corpus.

Table 4.15 The distribution of the realisation possibilities of the verbal syntagm in the ME object clauses depending on the most frequent matrix verbs

Verb	Subjunctive	Indicative	Modal	Imperative	Total
cnawen	2	13	11		26
cweðen	4		3	29	36
lokien	30	5			35
ordenen	33		3		36
preien	7		5		12
seggen	1	28	26	18	73
þenchen	3	13	3		19
understanden	1	7	3		11
willen	34	1	1		36
witen	7	19	13		39
Total	122	86	68	47	323

Indicatives and subjunctives show a characteristic distribution in object clauses. Subjunctives are the preferred option after the verbs *lokien, ordenen, preien* and *willen*. Object clauses with indicative verb forms do not occur or are extremely rare after these verbs. They all share the semantic feature of volition. This is in line with the situation in the OE corpus, where verbs of volition preferably govern object clauses with subjunctive verb forms (cf. section 4.2.5.1). The root modality which is expressed by the meaning of the matrix verb is in harmony with that of the verbal syntagm in the dependent clause realised by the subjunctive.

> [4.62] *And also we wile þat none of her breþeren make no sengler conseill by hem self* (M3 XX DOC RET, p. 57) 'and we also wish that none of their brethren shall make an individual decision by himself'

The verbs *cnawen, seggen, þenchen, understanden* and *witen* favour the indicative. They belong to the category of verbs of thinking and saying, and their object clauses with indicative verbs are assertive speech acts; their verbal syntagms express epistemic modality.

[4.63] *ye knowe better þanne we doo / <u>how þe said Duc Iohan gouerneþ him</u>*
<u>*towardes vs / and oure Rewme of Englande / and oure suggettes*</u> (M3
XX CORO HENRY5C, p. 105) 'you know better than we do how the
said Duke John behaves towards us and our Realm of England and
our subjects'

Some of the verbs of thinking and saying have an additional peculiar-
ity; besides the indicative or the subjunctive they govern object clauses
with imperatives or modal constructions. Since modal and imperative
constructions express root modality, the behaviour of these verbs asks
for an explanation.

[4.64] *First ȝee schull wel knowe <u>þat the naturell bawme is full cleer</u>* (M3 NI
TRAV MAND, p. 33) 'first you shall know that the natural balm is
completely clear'
[4.65] *Bi þe which þou maist knowe <u>fro which þou schalt fle</u>* (M3/4 IR RELT
HILTON, p. 10) 'by it you may know from which you shall flee'
[4.66] *Thou seist to me <u>it is a greet meschief To wedde a povre womman</u>* (M3
NI FICT CTPROL, p. 108f.) 'you say to me it is a great misfortune to
marry a poor woman'
[4.67] *Þen he saythe þus: <u>Man, thynke þat þou art but eskys</u>* (M3/4 IR SERM
MIRK, p. 82) 'then he says this: Man, remember that you are but ash'

These examples document that – unlike volitional matrix verbs – matrix
verbs of thinking and saying can govern object clauses that are assertive
speech acts expressing epistemic modality and others that are directive
speech acts expressing root modality. In the first case the verbal syntagm
in the object clause is an indicative, in the second it is an imperative or
a modal construction, very rarely is it a subjunctive.[27] A similar correspondence between verbs of thinking and saying and the form of the verb
in the object clause could also be established in the OE corpus.

4.4.5.2 The form of the matrix verb
The verbal syntagms of the matrix clauses which govern the relevant
noun clauses in the ME corpus are realised by subjunctives (92 tokens),
indicatives (251 tokens), modal constructions (58 tokens) and imperatives (63 tokens); the verbal syntagm of 324 matrix clauses is realised by
none of these (= Others). The relation between the form of the matrix
verb and the form of the verb in the dependent noun clause is shown in
Table 4.16.

Subjunctives in the noun clauses of the ME corpus have the biggest

---

[27] Only the verb *cweðen* is not attested with an indicative in the object clause. This is
probably a matter of chance.

Table 4.16 The relation between the form of the matrix verbs and the form of the verbs in the noun clauses of the ME corpus

Noun \ Matrix	Subjunctive	Indicative	Modal	Imperative	Total
Subjunctive	60 65.22%	20 21.74%	11 11.96%	1 1.08%	92 100%
Indicative	71 28.29%	117 46.61%	61 24.30%	2 0.80%	251 100%
Modal	17 29.31%	27 46.55%	14 24.14%		58 100%
Imperative	38 60.32%	15 23.81%	6 9.52%	4 6.35%	63 100%
Others	116 35.80%	104 32.10%	61 18.83%	43 13.27%	324 100%
Total	302 38.32%	283 35.91%	153 19.42%	50 6.35%	788 100%

Table 4.17 The relation between the form of the matrix verbs and the form of the verbs in ME object clauses

Object \ Matrix	Subjunctive	Indicative	Modal	Imperative	Total
Subjunctive	20 54.06%	12 32.43%	4 10.81%	1 2.70%	37 100%
Indicative	24 22.02%	53 48.62%	30 27.52%	2 1.84%	109 100%
Modal	5 15.63%	17 53.13%	10 31.24%		32 100%
Imperative	38 61.29%	15 24.19%	5 8.07%	4 6.45%	62 100%
Others	105 34.54%	98 32.24%	58 19.08%	43 14.14%	304 100%
Total	192 35.29%	195 35.85%	107 19.67%	50 9.19%	544 100%

share after subjunctives and imperatives in the corresponding matrix clauses. The subjunctive triggering force of imperatives in the matrix clause has greatly increased after the OE period, whereas the probability of a matrix subjunctive being followed by a subjunctive in the dependent clause has decreased. The unexplained preference of OE indicative matrix verbs to favour subjunctives in the dependent clause was replaced by a preference of the indicative in the dependent clause (cf. Table 4.6 in section 4.2.6).

Since an influence of the meaning of the matrix verb on the form of the verb in ME object clauses could be established in section 4.4.5.1, the next step was to check if there was a similar influence of the form of the matrix verb on the verb in <u>object clauses</u>. Table 4.17 shows that indeed this is so, but the influence is a little less pronounced than when all noun clauses are considered.

In object clauses, the share of subjunctives after matrix clauses with a subjunctive or an imperative verb is 58.58 per cent (fifty-eight object clauses with a subjunctive after ninety-nine matrix clauses with a subjunctive or imperative), whereas in all noun clauses it amounts to 63.23 per cent (ninety-eight noun clauses with a subjunctive after 155 matrix clauses with a subjunctive or imperative). The conclusion to be drawn from these figures is that modal harmony between the form of the verb of the matrix clause and that of the object clause is less strong than that betweeen the form of the verb of the matrix clause and that of a noun clause of any function. Additionally, a comparison with the analysis of the relation between the meaning of the verb in the matrix clause and the form of the verb in the object clause reveals that modal harmony between these is stronger than between the forms of the verbs in the matrix and in the object clause (cf. section 4.4.5.1).

4.4.6 *The parameter clause type*

The noun clauses of the ME corpus are coded for the following clause types: *that*-clause, *wh*-interrogative, relative, imperative and *yes/no*-interrogative.

Examples [4.68]–[4.72] illustrate the different clause types, and Table 4.18 shows their distribution in the ME corpus.

[4.68] *Lauerd, we pray þe <u>þis resun be halden with vs</u>* (M3 IR RULE BENEDME, p. 14) 'Lord, we pray you [that] this command be kept by us'[28]

[4.69] *In boke is ðe turtres lif writen o rime, <u>wu lagelike ge holdeð luue al hire lif time</u>* (M2 IR RELT BEST, p. 22) 'in [the] book is the turtle-dove's

---

[28] The conjunction *that* can be deleted.

life described in rhyme, how loyally it keeps to its lover during all its life-time'

[4.70]   *what-so þat oon likiþ, þat oþir likiþ* (M3/4 IR RELT HILTON, p. 20) 'whatsoever pleases the one, pleases the other'

[4.71]   *Ful loude he soong „Com hider, love, to me!"* (M3 NI FICT CTPROL, p. 34.C1) 'he sang very loudly "Come hither, love, to me!"'

[4.72]   *he askeð ham 3ef ham biluueð to heren him ane hwile* (M1 IR HOM SWARD, p. 178) 'he asks them if [it] would please them to listen to him for a while'

Table 4.18 The distribution of the clause types of noun clauses in the ME corpus

Clause type	Absolute number	Percentage
That-clause	518	65.74
Wh-interrogative	103	13.07
Relative	99	12.56
Imperative	50	6.35
Yes/no-interrogative	18	2.28
Total	788	100

As in the OE corpus, the clause types *that*-clause and *wh*-interrogative are attested most frequently. Since the frequency of relative clauses lags only a little behind, they are also included in Table 4.19, which shows the distribution of the realisation possibilities of the verbal syntagm in these clause types.

Table 4.19 The distribution of the realisation possibilities of the verbal syntagm in noun clauses of different types in the ME corpus

Clause type	Subjunctive	Indicative	Modal	Total
That-clause	260 50.19%	147 28.38%	111 21.43%	518 100%
Wh-interrogative	18 17.48%	62 60.19%	23 22.33%	103 100%
Relative	18 18.18%	68 68.69%	13 13.13%	99 100%

That-clauses show a preference for subjunctives; *wh*-interrogatives and relative clauses show an even more pronounced preference for indicatives. The same distribution was already observed in *that*-clauses and *wh*-interrogatives in the OE corpus (cf. section 4.2.7).

4.4.7 *Summary*

In the ME corpus, 788 relevant noun clauses were identified, i.e. finite noun clauses with verbal syntagms in the second or third person singular. They are realised as subjunctives (302 tokens), indicatives (283 tokens), imperatives (50 tokens) and modal or semi-modal construction (153 tokens).

Across the four subperiods of ME the frequency of modal constructions increases, whereas that of imperatives decreases. The trends of a decreasing subjunctive frequency and a compensatory increasing indicative frequency noticed in the OE corpus were not continued. The frequency values of all realisation possibilities fluctuate in ME without showing a steady development.

The largest shares of subjunctives were found in the text categories STA, IS and XX, and of imperatives in NI and NN. The distribution of the latter reflects the frequent occurrence of direct speech in narrative texts. The frequency of subjunctives in statutory and instructive texts was interpreted as a consequence of their directive and authoritative character. Although the share of subjunctives is lower in the ME than in the OE corpus, the text categories that favour the subjunctive are the same in both periods.

The comparison of prose and verse texts revealed that the share of subjunctives is greater in prose texts than in verse texts. This distribution is the same as in the OE corpus. The proportion of subjunctives to modal constructions in prose texts, which started to decline in the OE period, witnesses a further decline in ME from 6.2:1 to 2.1:1.

The distribution of the realisation possibilities of the verbal syntagm was established for noun clauses with the functions subject, object, subject complement, NP complement, adjectival complement and 'Others'. This last function was introduced for a couple of noun clauses which did not fit into one of the well-established categories. They depend on an interjection, and together with the noun clauses with the function adjectival complement they play only a minor role.

Noun clauses with the function NP complement are saliently less frequent in the ME corpus than in the OE corpus, and the subjunctive which was the preferred form of their verbal syntagms in OE was replaced by the indicative.

A similar development was noticed for noun clauses with the function subject complement. Whereas in OE the relative frequency of this noun clause type was 0.65/1,000 words, its frequency has more than halved in ME with 0.28/1,000 words, and the percentage share of subjunctives has dropped from 88.10 per cent to 36.96 per cent.

Subject clauses were found in initial and in non-initial position. They favour the subjunctive more than noun clauses with other functions and more than negligible numbers of occurrences. This subjunctive preference was investigated in several construction types, and it turned out that instances of the construction types '(hit) + BE + adjectival/prepositional syntagm + noun clause' and '(hit) + passive verbal syntagm + noun clause' contributed most to the large share of subjunctives in subject clauses. The first construction type has not been investigated at all for OE and ME, and with the exception of Övergaard (1995) it was not analysed as a subject clause in studies of PDE mandative constructions. The second construction type has been neglected completely in previous studies on subjunctive constructions. In my ME corpus, instances of this construction type cluster in two files, which contain petitions, extracts from gild-books, wills, acts and statutes. Although the number of passive matrix verbs which take subject clauses with subjunctive verb forms is quite small, it was suggested that this construction type is a style-marker of formal official prose in ME. With 0.98/1,000 words the frequency of subject clauses is much greater in the ME corpus than in the OE corpus, where it amounts to only 0.67/1,000 words. Although the preferred realisation possibility of the verbal syntagm is still the subjunctive, its percentage share has decreased from 60.47 per cent in the OE corpus to 46.01 per cent in the ME corpus.

Object clauses are the most frequent function type in the ME corpus; they have a share of 69 per cent of all noun clauses. The indicative is the preferred realisation of their verbal syntagm, but the percentage shares of both subjunctive and indicative do not deviate much from each other.

An influence of the matrix verb on the choice of the form of the verbal syntagm in noun clauses was discovered with respect to meaning and form in object clauses. Among the 104 verbs which govern object clauses in the ME corpus, fifty-five are attested more than once. The ten matrix verbs governing more than ten object clauses show a characteristic distribution of the realisation possibilities of the verbal syntagm in the object clauses. Volitional matrix verbs, which express root modality by their meaning, govern the subjunctive nearly exclusively. The verbal syntagms in the corresponding object clauses express root modality by their form. Matrix verbs of thinking and saying favour the indicative. Some of them alternatively govern object clauses with modal or imperative constructions. In the first case the object clauses are assertive speech acts expressing epistemic modality, in the second case they are directive speech acts expressing root modality.

The form of the matrix verb also influences the realisation of the verbal syntagm in the dependent clause. Subjunctives in the noun clauses of the ME corpus have the biggest share after subjunctives and imperatives in the corresponding matrix clauses. The subjunctive triggering force of matrix imperatives has greatly increased from OE to ME, whereas that of matrix subjunctives has decreased. The unexplained preference of OE indicative matrix verbs to favour subjunctives in the dependent clause was replaced by a preference of the indicative in the dependent clause. When only object clauses are considered in ME, the influence of matrix imperatives on the form of the verbal syntagm is even greater than on that of all noun clauses; that of the subjunctive is much smaller.

Correlations between the meaning of the governing NP in NP complement clauses and the form of the verbal syntagm in the dependent clauses was not investigated, because with nineteen examples this function type is not attested frequently enough in the ME corpus. The same holds for possible relations between the meaning of subjects and the form of the verbal syntagm in subject complement clauses.

The last parameter to be examined was the clause type of the dependent clause. *That*-clauses proved to be the most frequent clause type and also the clause type with the largest share of subjunctives. *Wh*-interrogative clauses and relative clauses showed a preference for indicatives. Concerning *that*-clauses and *wh*-interrogative clauses, the same findings were reported about the OE corpus.

4.5 Early Modern English noun clauses: descriptive parameters

4.5.1 *Function*

The most straightforward functional classification of noun clauses is into subject clauses and object clauses (Visser 1963–1973: §§863–875). Visser's examples of EModE subject clauses occur in impersonal constructions as extraposed subjects, which are accompanied by a formal subject, usually *it*. The same constructions were attested in ME, too, but because of their non-initial position they were not readily accepted as subject clauses (cf. section 4.3.1).

Rissanen (1999: 282), who posits the functions subject, object and appositive complement for EModE noun clauses, quotes a passage from a scientific treatise of the HC which demonstrates that initial position of subject clauses became possible in the sixteenth century. The subject noun clauses in this passage are nominal relative clauses. Rissanen's function 'appositive complement' corresponds to Fischer's term 'apposition to another NP' in her description of the functions of ME noun clauses. He takes over her claim that the governing nouns are abstract and 'convey an experience or the content of a statement, fact, etc.' (Fischer 1992: 312).

Noun clauses with object function are the topic of studies on EModE mandative constructions (Fillbrandt 2006, Rütten 2014, 2015). Fillbrandt's data were extracted from the EModE part of the HC, and she analysed only the noun clauses governed by the verbs from Visser's list (Visser 1963–1973: §869). Rütten's data come from the EModE part of *The Corpus of Religious Prose*, and she analyses the distribution of verbal and non-verbal objects of the verbs from the same list. Although she uses the term mandative constructions for the topic of her studies, she uses it with a meaning, which was probably inspired by *The Cambridge Grammar*'s terminology. Huddleston and Pullum (2002: 995) 'apply the term mandative not only to the subordinate clause but also to the verb, noun, or adjective which licenses or governs them', and according to the form of the governed element they distinguish between subjunctive mandatives, *should*-mandatives and covert mandatives. Rütten's non-verbal objects which are governed by mandative verbs could be understood as one type of covert mandatives.

4.5.2 *Form*

In his detailed description of EModE noun clauses, Rissanen (1999) distinguishes finite and non-finite types of noun clauses. The former are introduced by *that* or *lest*, by interrogative pronouns, or by zero, the latter are realised as infinitive or gerund constructions. In finite noun clauses the subjunctive alternates with the indicative and with modal constructions. The subjunctive as a marker of modality occurs in noun clauses 'indicating wish, request, exhortation, doubt, etc.' and in reported speech 'in contexts in which uncertainty (. . .) is indicated' (1999: 285). For Rissanen, the typical modal auxiliaries are *shall*, *will* and *may*.

In handbooks of EModE, noun clauses are not treated in a separate chapter, but their authors agree that the subjunctive is used in *that*-clauses after expressions of commanding and entreating (Barber 1997: 173, Nevalainen 2006: 96).

EModE noun clauses after suasive verbs, so-called mandative constructions, are the topic of papers by Fillbrandt (2006) and Rütten (2014, 2015). Whereas Fillbrandt follows the traditional path and considers only the subjunctive, the indicative and modal constructions as realisation possibilities of the verbal syntagm in these noun clauses, Rütten argues that the traditional approach neglects the aspect of functional equivalence. In her opinion the subjunctive competes not only with the indicative and with modal constructions, but also with *to*-infinitive constructions, gerunds, nominalisations and noun phrases (2014: 377). There is, however, a flaw in her argument. The 'triggers', as she calls the suasive verbs, govern objects that can be realised by (*that*)-clauses, *to*-infinitive constructions, gerunds, nominalisations and ordinary noun phrases; they do not govern subjunctives, indicatives or modal constructions. Therefore, there is no functional equivalence between the former and the latter. The former compete on the part of speech, the latter on the phrase level.[29] Although this crucial difference is acknowledged in her 2015 e-article, Rütten insists that 'it seems reasonable to discuss them [= infinitival constructions, gerunds and noun phrases] alongside the subjunctive'.

---

[29] For a model of ME mandative constructions along these lines cf. Moessner (2010a: figure 1, p. 154).

4.5.3 Governing elements

This topic is particularly relevant in the context of noun clauses functioning as objects, i.e. in mandative constructions. The most detailed account of governing elements is to be found in Visser's historical syntax (1963–1973). His often-used lists contain volitional expressions (§869), expressions of emotion and other mental activities (§872), verbs of believing, trusting and understanding (§873), and verbs of saying, declaring, lying and denying (§874). Traugott (1972: 149–150) mentions similar elements without, however, providing explicit lists. Fillbrandt (2006) bases her study on EModE mandative constructions on the verbs in Visser's lists; Rütten (2014, 2015) considers only suasive verbs as governing elements. This is one of the reasons why the results of the development of the subjunctive in these papers are difficult to compare.

In his section about noun clauses, Rissanen (1999: 285) deals with governing elements only implicitly, when he states that the subjunctive is used 'in nominal clauses indicating wish, request, exhortation, doubt, etc.', and he adds that it is also common in reported speech 'particularly in contexts in which uncertainty (. . .) is indicated'.

4.6 Noun clauses in the EModE corpus

My EModE corpus contains 792 noun clauses (= 4.10/1,000 words). Only those noun clauses are included whose verbal syntagm is in the third person singular, and noun clauses with second person singular verbal syntagms only in those texts in which the personal pronoun of the second person singular is realised by a *th*-form. The verbal syntagms of the relevant noun clauses are realised as subjunctives (75 = 0.39/1,000 words), as indicatives (480 = 2.49/1,000 words), as modal constructions (211 = 1.09/1,000 words), as semi-modal constructions (11 = 0.06/1,000 words)[30] and as imperatives (15 = 0.08/1,000 words). In the following sections, the influence of several linguistic and non-linguistic parameters on the distribution of these realisation patterns will be analysed and discussed.

4.6.1 The parameter date of composition

The chronological classification of the texts of the EModE part in the HC into three seventy-year subperiods (E1: 1500–1570, E2: 1570–1640, E3: 1640–1710) was taken over, and the distribution of the realisations of the verbal syntagm in the relevant noun clauses is mapped in Table 4.20.

---

[30] They are realised as '*be* + *to* + infinitive' or as '*ought* + *to* + infinitive'. Because they occur rarely they are subsumed under 'Modal' in the tables.

Table 4.20 The distribution of the realisation possibilities of the verbal syntagm in noun clauses across subperiods E1–E3

Subperiod	Subjunctive	Indicative	Modal	Imperative	Total
E1	49 16.61%	183 62.03%	53 17.97%	10 3.39%	295 100%
E2	22 10.23%	119 55.35%	73 33.95%	1 0.47%	215 100%
E3	4 1.42%	178 63.12%	96 34.04%	4 1.42%	282 100%
Total	75 9.41%	480 60.23%	222 26.47%	15 1.88%	792 100%

Table 4.21 The distribution of the realisation possibilities of the verbal syntagm in EModE noun clauses across prototypical text categories

Category	Subjunctive	Indicative	Modal	Imperative	Total
STA	46 32.62%	6 4.26%	89 63.12%		141 100%
IS	8 7.21%	82 73.87%	21 18.92%		111 100%
IR	4 5.48%	51 69.86%	16 21.92%	2 2.74%	73 100%
NI	2 9.09%	8 36.37%	6 27.27%	6 27.27%	22 100%
NN	4 6.45%	42 67.74%	15 24.20%	1 1.61%	62 100%
EX	2 2.25%	67 75.28%	20 22.47%		89 100%
XX	9 3.06%	224 76.19%	55 18.71%	6 2.04%	294 100%
Total	75 9.41%	480 60.23%	222 26.47%	15 1.88%	792 100%

Indicatives are by far the most favoured realisation, and their shares are almost constant throughout the whole EModE period. Subjunctive frequency drops, and this trend is particularly drastic between E2 and E3. Modal constructions show a rising trend, which is most pronounced between E1 and E2. These findings correspond nicely to Fillbrandt's results (2006: 144), although she analysed a more restricted set of data. Looking at Table 4.20, one is inclined to expect the complete loss of the subjunctive right after the EModE period and not only in the twentieth century as predicted by Fowler (1926/1965: 595). Yet the massive frequency loss of the subjunctive had set in already between the end of the ME and the beginning of the EModE periods (cf. Table 4.9). A similar leap in the other direction can be observed in indicative frequency, which almost doubled between ME and EModE. The frequency rise of modal constructions, which was noticed in ME, continues at about the same speed in EModE.

4.6.2 *The parameter text category*

Noun clauses are unevenly spread across the text categories with a frequency peak in category XX, where they reach a relative frequency of 11.49/1,000 words.[31] The files of my corpus which represent this text category are translations of Boethius's dialogue *De consolatione philosophiae*. The distribution of all realisation possibilities of the verbal syntagm is shown in Table 4.21.

Leaving aside category XX, the largest number of noun clauses and at the same time the largest share of subjunctives is found in the category STA with files from the *Statutes of the Realm*. This is the genre which corresponds to the earlier law-codes. Among the other realisation types only modal constructions are worth mentioning. Like subjunctives they cluster in the texts of the category STA. The lesson to be learned from this distribution is that verbal syntagms expressing root modality are a style feature of statutory texts. From a closer look at the STA files two more interesting insights can be gained. First, noun clause density in STA decreases from subperiod to subperiod (E1: 5.09, E2: 3.99, E3: 2.58 per 1,000 words). Second, in all subperiods verbal syntagms expressing root modality by far outnumber those expressing epistemic modality, and the relation between subjunctives and modal constructions changes such that after E1 the share of modal constructions surpasses that of subjunctives. In subperiod E3 verbal syntagms expressing root modality are almost exclusively represented by modal constructions, cf. Table 4.22.

---

[31] The subcorpus of category XX contains 25,590 words.

Table 4.22 The distribution of the realisations of the verbal syntagm in noun clauses of category STA across subperiods E1–E3

Subperiod	Subjunctive	Indicative	Modal	Total
E1	41 68.33%	1 1.67%	18 30.00%	60 100%
E2	4 8.51%	2 4.26%	41 87.23%	47 100%
E3	1 2.94%	3 8.82%	30 88.24%	34 100%
Total	46 32.62%	6 4.26%	89 63.12%	141 100%

4.6.3 The parameter noun clause function

Following the classification of the noun clauses in the ME corpus, the functions subject, object, subject complement, NP complement and adjectival complement are distinguished. The distribution of the realisation possibilities of the verbal syntagm of EModE noun clauses with these functions is shown in Table 4.23.

Object and subject are the preferred functions of EModE noun clauses, all other functions play only a minor role. Yet it is extraordinary that the share of subjunctives is greatest in the adjectival complement clauses, which are attested by twelve tokens only, cf. example [4.73].

> [4.73] *in the churning thereof let your stroakes goe slow, and be sure that your churne be cold when you put in your creame* (E2 IS HANDO MARKHAM, p. 112) [governing adjective: *sure*)

Following the functional classification of the noun clauses in the earlier periods, I use the term NP complement for constructions that Rissanen calls 'appositive complement'. The governing element is an abstract noun or a neutral pronoun, and the preferred realisation of the verbal syntagm is the indicative or a modal construction, cf. examples [4.74] and [4.75].

> [4.74] *And when any thing is donne untowardly the common saying will passe upon them, That it is suitable to their breeding* (E3 IS EDUC LOCKE, p. 49) [governing element: *the common saying*)
>
> [4.75] *And the great principle and foundation of all vertue and worth is placed in this, That a man is able to deny himself his owne desires* (E3 IS EDUC LOCKE, p. 50) [governing element: *this*]

Noun clauses with subject complement function are also only infrequently attested in the EModE corpus, and their verbal syntagms are nearly always realised by an indicative verb form, cf. example [4.76].

> [4.76] *The seconde cause is, that the thing that is caried about from place to place, is of so precious a treasure that it had the more neede of good keeping* (E1 EX SCIM VICARY, p. 59)

Table 4.23 The distribution of the realisation possibilities of the verbal syntagm of EModE noun clauses with different functions

Function	Subjunctive	Indicative	Modal	Imperative	Total
Subject	40 16.53%	108 44.63%	94 38.84%		242 100%
Object	30 6.20%	326 67.36%	113 23.34%	15 3.10%	484 100%
Subject complement		15 88.24%	2 11.76%		17 100%
NP complement	3 8.11%	25 67.57%	9 24.32%		37 100%
Adjectival complement	2 16.67%	6 50.00%	4 33.33%		12 100%
Total	75 9.41%	480 60.23%	222 26.47%	15 1.88%	792 100%

The construction types set up for OE and ME subject clauses (cf. sections 4.2.4 and 4.4.4) were also used for the analysis of the subject clauses of my EModE corpus. Probably as a consequence of the regularisation of SVO word order construction type d (= personal verb + (object) + noun clause) is not attested in the EModE corpus.

Table 4.24 The distribution of the realisation possibilities of the verbal syntagm in EModE subject clauses of different construction types

Type	Subjunctive	Indicative	Modal	Total
a	2 10.53%	16 84.21%	1 5.26%	19 100%
b	38 25.17%	38 25.17%	75 49.66%	151 100%
c		26 70.27%	11 29.73%	37 100%
dd		27 81.82%	6 15.15%	33 100%
e		1 50.00%	1 50.00%	2 100%
Total	40 16.53%	108 44.63%	94 38.84%	242 100%

Table 4.24 tells a very straightforward story: with their large shares of subjunctives and modal constructions subject clauses of construction type b favour verbal syntagms expressing root modality. Subject clauses with these verbal syntagms also have a characteristic distribution across text categories. With two exceptions they occur in the texts from *The Statutes of the Realm,* and the range of triggering verbs comprises just four elements, namely *enact, ordain, enquire* and *declare* (cf. example [4.77]).

> [4.77]   *Be it enacted by the aucthoritie aforesaide, That it shall not be laufull to any person or persons to inclose or take in any parte of the Commons or Waste Groundes* (E2 STA LAW STAT4, p. IV, 853)

Subject clauses of construction type b with a verbal syntagm expressing root modality thus turn out as style-markers of EModE written legislative texts.

As in the earlier periods, object clauses occupy top position on the frequency scale of noun clauses; with 61 per cent, their share is only slightly smaller than in the ME corpus. Since they are the focus of earlier studies on EModE mandative constructions, the next sections will look at the potential influence of the meaning and the form of the verb in the matrix clause on the form of the verbal syntagm in the object clause.

4.6.4 *The parameter matrix verb*

4.6.4.1 The meaning of the matrix verb of object clauses

The 484 object clauses of the EModE corpus depend on ninety-five different verbs; forty-three of them occur only once, and the other fifty-two account for the remaining 441 examples (cf. 'Appendix III: Matrix verbs of Early Modern English object clauses'). The ten verbs *confess, hear, know, ordain, perceive, say, see, show, tell* and *think* govern more than ten object clauses each. The matrix verb *ordain* stands out in that all its object clauses contain verbal syntagms expressing root modality. It contains the meaning component 'volition'. In the object clauses depending on the other nine matrix verbs the indicative is the preferred realisation of their verbal syntagms. They belong to Visser's two categories expressions of mental activities and verbs of saying. This is more or less the same distribution as in the ME corpus. Yet the preferred expression of root modality shifted from the subjunctive to modal constructions after the ME period.

4.6.4.2 The form of the matrix verb

The verbal syntagms of the matrix clauses of the relevant noun clauses of the EModE corpus are realised by subjunctives (104 tokens), indicatives (242 tokens), modal constructions (72 tokens), semi-modal constructions (11 tokens) and imperatives (37 tokens); the verbal syntagms of 326 matrix clauses are realised by none of these (= Others).[32] The relation between the form of the matrix verb and the form of the verbal syntagm in the dependent clause can be derived from Table 4.25.

As in the ME corpus, subjunctives in EModE noun clauses have the largest share after subjunctives and imperatives in the corresponding matrix clauses. Their subjunctive triggering force, however, is weaker in the EModE corpus than in the ME corpus. Modal constructions dominate in noun clauses depending on matrix clauses with verbal syntagms realised by subjunctives, and there is a clear correspondence between large shares of indicatives in the matrix and the dependent clauses. These results suggest a high degree of modal harmony. The only flaw is the preference of matrix clauses with verbal syntagms realised by modal constructions for indicatives in the corresponding noun clauses. Further studies of the modal auxiliaries are needed to explain this deviation from the general trend.

In a next step I checked if the triggering force of the form of the verbal syntagm in the matrix clause on that of the verbal syntagm in the dependent clause was equally strong if not all noun clauses were considered but only object clauses (cf. Table 4.26).

The dominance of the indicative in object clauses is even more salient than in all noun clauses. It is also the preferred realisation of the verbal syntagm in object clauses depending on matrix clauses with verbal syntagms realised by modal constructions. This corrrespondence was already noticed when all noun clauses were considered. In object clauses, too,

---

[32] These are ambiguous or non-finite forms.

Table 4.25 The relation between the form of the verbal syntagm in the matrix clause and that of the verbal syntagm in the noun clause in the EModE corpus

Matrix \ Noun	Subjunctive	Indicative	Modal	Imperative	Total
Subjunctive	36 34.62%	2 1.92%	66 63.46%		104 100%
Indicative	15 6.20%	179 73.97%	46 19.01%	2 0.82%	242 100%
Modal		55 66.27%	28 33.73%		83 100%
Imperative	6 16.22%	22 59.46%	9 24.32%		37 100%
Others	18 5.52%	222 68.10%	73 22.39%	13 3.99%	326 100%
Total	75 9.41%	480 60.23%	222 26.47%	15 1.88%	792 100%

Table 4.26 The relation between the form of the matrix verbs and the form of the verbs in EModE object clauses

Matrix \ Object	Subjunctive	Indicative	Modal	Imperative	Total
Subjunctive		2 100%			2 100%
Indicative	11 8.80%	83 66.40%	29 23.20%	2 1.60%	125 100%
Modal		19 70.37%	8 29.63%		27 100%
Imperative	4 11.43%	22 62.86%	9 25.71%		35 100%
Others	15 5.08%	200 67.80%	67 20.68%	13 4.41%	295 100%
Total	30 6.20%	326 67.36%	113 23.34%	15 3.10%	484 100%

further studies on the modal auxiliaries involved are needed to explain this strange combination of verbal syntagms expressing different types of modality. A comparison with the results of the corresponding analysis of the ME corpus reveals that this combination gained in importance after the ME period.

4.6.5 *The parameter clause type*

The noun clauses of the EModE corpus are coded for the same clause types as those of the ME corpus: *that*-clause, *wh*-interrogative, relative, imperative and *yes/no*-interrogative. They are illustrated by examples [4.78]–[4.82].

[4.78] *we have reason to conclude <u>that great care is to be had of the formeing childrens mindes</u>* (E3 IS EDUC LOCKE, p. 19)

[4.79] *thou knowest now, <u>what be the true good</u>* (E2 XX PHILO BOETHEL, p. 59)

[4.80] *<u>what shall be adjudged by the said Justices or recovered upon such Action</u> shall be paid out of His Majesties Revenue of Excise* (E3 STA LAW STAT7, p. PVIII, 457)

[4.81] *But I charge the <u>keepe thys secret vntyll all bee fynesed</u>* (E1 NI FICT HARMAN, p. 70)

[4.82] *we are charged to examine, and to trie our hearts <u>whether God bee in vs of a truth or no</u>* (E2 IR SERM HOOKER, p. 39)

With eleven and twenty-seven attestations respectively, imperative and *yes/no*-clauses play only a minor role. Attestations of the clause types *that*-clause, *wh*-interrogative and relative amount to over 95 per cent of all noun clauses of the EModE corpus. The distribution of the realisation possibilities of the verbal syntagms in these clause types is shown in Table 4.27.

The indicative is the preferred realisation in all three clause types. Its share is smallest in *that*-clauses. Compared to the ME corpus, the replacement of the subjunctive by the indicative in *that*-clauses is the most noteworthy change.

4.6.6 *Summary*

Information of a rather general nature about EModE noun clauses, which comes from language histories and handbooks, concerns their function (subject, object, appositive complement), their form (*that*-clauses, nominal relative clauses or indirect questions), the realisation possibilities of their verbal syntagm, and the semantic components of the verbs in the matrix clauses on which they depend. Only two authors

Table 4.27 The distribution of the realisation possibilities of the verbal syntagm in EModE noun clauses of different clause types

Clause type	Subjunctive	Indicative	Modal	Imperative	Total
That-clause	60 10.08%	343 57.65%	188 31.60%	4 0.67%	595 100%
Wh-interrogative	3 2.73%	90 81.82%	17 15.45%		110 100%
Relative	2 4.08%	40 81.64%	7 14.28%		49 100%

(Fillbrandt 2006, Rütten 2014, 2015) used corpus-linguistic methods in their analyses of EModE noun clauses, and both deal only with mandative constructions.

My EModE corpus contains 792 relevant noun clauses (= 4.10/1,000 words). Their verbal syntagms are realised as subjunctives (75 = 0.39/1,000 words), as indicatives (480 = 2.49/1,000 words), as modal constructions (211 = 1.09/1,000 words), as semi-modal constructions (11 = 0.06/1,000 words) and as imperatives (15 = 0.08/1,000 words).

During the EModE period, the relative frequency of subjunctives decreases, whereas that of modal constructions rises. The same trends were observed in the ME corpus. The relative frequency of indicatives does not change much across the subperiods of EModE, but it increases considerably between ME and EModE.

Leaving aside text category XX, the statutory texts of category STA, which are the successors of the earlier law-codes, contain the highest number of noun clauses and at the same time the largest share of subjunctives and of modal constructions. These root modality expressing verbal syntagms far outnumbers the epistemic modality expressing verbal syntagms in this text category, but after subperiod E1 modal constructions change place with subjunctives as the most frequent realisation. In subperiod E3 root modality expressing verbal syntagms are nearly exclusively represented by modal constructions. This is a change which had already started in ME.

Object and subject are the preferred functions of EModE noun clauses, all other functions play only a minor role. There is a complementary frequency distribution of subjunctives and modal constructions on the one hand and indicatives on the other hand in noun clauses with these two functions. Subject clauses prefer verbal syntagms expressing root modality, object clauses prefer verbal syyntagms expressing epistemic modality. The preferred verbal syntagms of subject clauses occur most frequently in constructions of the type '(hit) + passive verbal syntagm + noun clause'. This distribution is the same as in the ME corpus.

When all noun clauses of the EModE corpus are considered, it is very obvious that indicative verbal syntagms of matrix clauses preferably combine with indicative verbal syntagms in the dependent clauses, whereas subjunctive verbal syntagms in matrix clauses preferably govern noun clauses with verbal syntagms realised by modal constructions. If under these circumstances we can speak of modal harmony at all, it holds only for epistemic modality.

This result is even more obvious when only the object clauses of the EModE corpus are considered. Among the ten matrix verbs which govern more than ten object clauses each there is only one verb, namely *ordain*, which expresses root modality by its meaning, and which governs only object clauses with verbal syntagms expressing the same modality. By contrast, the other matrix verbs governing more than ten object clauses belong to the categories of saying and mental activitiy; they govern object clauses with indicative verbs. There are also only thirty-five matrix verbs of object clauses which by their form (= imperative) express root modality, and even they govern object clauses with verbal syntagms preferably realised by indicatives.

The last parameter which was tested for its influence on the form of the verbal syntagm in the noun clauses of the EModE corpus was clause type. Only *that*-clauses, *wh*-interrogatives and relative clauses occur in sufficiently large numbers, and all three clause types prefer the indicative. This preference is least pronounced in *that*-clauses.

5

The subjunctive in adverbial clauses

In this chapter I will adopt the classical classification method of adverbial clauses; namely, according to their semantic roles (cf. OE: Mitchell 1985: §§2416–3721, ME: Fischer 1992: 343–361, EModE: Rissanen 1999: 304–319, PDE: Quirk et al. 1985: §§15.24–15.56).

5.1 Old English adverbial clauses: descriptive parameters

The analysis of OE adverbial clauses meets with several difficulties: some introductory elements can be used as adverbs and as conjunctions (e.g. *þeah*, *æfter*); some elements can introduce not only adverbial clauses but also clauses with other functions (e.g. *þær* introduces nominal relative clauses and clauses of place); some conjunctions can introduce adverbial clauses with different semantic roles (e.g. *þonne* introduces clauses of time and clauses of comparison); some adverbial clauses combine different semantic roles (e.g. purpose and result). These difficulties made it impossible to use an automatic search for the identification of the relevant adverbial clauses, although the set of introductory elements is finite and spelling differences could have been overcome by an appropriate routine. With the method of close reading adopted for the analysis of the subjunctive and its competitors in the construction types described in Chapters 2–4, I identified OE adverbial clauses of the following types: clauses of time, of place, of reason, of concession, of condition, of purpose and result, and of comparison. Statements about the realisations of their verbal syntagms are unfortunately rather vague.

5.1.1 Clauses of time

Their introductory conjunction is the variable with the strongest influence on the mood distribution in clauses of time. Behre (1934: chapter 5), Mitchell (1985: §§2530–2801), Traugott (1992: 259–261) and Wilde (1939/1940: 363–367) treat clauses of time introduced by *ær* apart from those introduced by other temporal conjunctions. They agree that *ær*-clauses favour the use of the subjunctive. Mitchell and Behre restrict the subjunctive in *ær*-clauses to complex sentences with affirmative matrix clauses. The other temporal conjunctions govern the indicative, unless the matrix clause contains an expression of volition mainly realised by an imperative or a subjunctive verb form. Visser's treatment of mood in temporal clauses (1963–1973: §879) is very detailed; he lists the temporal conjunctions with their mood preferences alphabetically. Examples of OE temporal clauses with subjunctive are listed for the conjunctions *æfter, ær, mid þy/þæm þæt,*[1] *oðþæt, siððan, þenden, þonne,*[2] *þy dæge þe, þe hwile (þæt).*

The only systematic treatment of the subjunctive in OE clauses of time is Callaway's book *The Temporal Subjunctive in Old English* (1931). He distinguishes three types of temporal subjunctives according to the relationship between the dependent clause and the superordinate clause. These types are the subjunctive of antecedent action, the subjunctive of subsequent action, and the subjunctive of contemporaneous action. The last category is subdivided into the subjunctive of time-limitation, the subjunctive of duration of time, and the subjunctive introduced by particles denoting contemporaneousness without suggesting limitation or duration of time.

Clauses with subjunctives of antecedent action are introduced by conjunctions with the meaning 'after', most often by *siððan* and *sona swa*. Clauses with subjunctives of subsequent action are introduced by conjunctions with the meaning 'before'. All of them include the element *ær*. Clauses with subjunctives of contemporaneous action are introduced by conjunctions meaning 'until', if they belong to the time-limit subclass, by conjunctions meaning 'while', if they belong to the duration subclass, and by conjunctions meaning 'when', if they belong to the subclass denoting contemporaneousness without suggesting limitation or duration of time. The most frequent conjunction of the first subclass is *oð ðæt*, that of the second subclass is *ðenden* and that of the third subclass is *ðonne*.

Subjunctives expressing antecedent action are not very frequent in Callaway's data; among his 1,230 subjunctives only fifty-one belong to this type. The other two types occur with about the same frequency.

The factors whose potential influence on the frequency of the different types of temporal subjunctives is discussed are the subjunctive in the Latin source text and the form of the verbal syntagm in the superordinate clause (Callaway 1931: 114–128). On the basis of his data, Callaway argues that only the subtype time-limit of the subjunctive of contemporaneous action is clearly favoured in texts with a Latin original. The

---

[1] He notes: 'These conjunctive phrases have a strong connotation of cause and manner.'

[2] He notes: 'There is a strong connotation of conditionality.'

temporal subjunctive in these texts often corresponds to a subjunctive in the Latin original. By contrast, all other types of temporal subjunctive are established as native OE constructions. The hypothesis that the subjunctive in clauses of time is triggered by an imperative or a subjunctive in the superordinate clause is clearly rejected by Callaway for subjunctives expressing antecedent and subsequent action and for the subtype duration of the subjunctive of contemporaneous action. Only for the subtype time-limit and for the subtype of contemporaneous action which does not suggest limitation or duration does he not completely exclude it.

Although he did not test his data for the feature negation in the superordinate clause, he mentions that in other Germanic languages the presence of a negative element favours the indicative in temporal clauses of subsequent action and the subjunctive in other types of clauses of time.

5.1.2 Clauses of place

Information on mood in clauses of place is to be found in the reference works by Mitchell (1985: §§2450–2529) and Visser (1963–1973: §895). According to the former '[t]he prevailing mood in both definite and indefinite clauses of place in OE prose and poetry is the indicative' (§2508), and the latter considers the context as the factor which determines the use of indicative and subjunctive: 'Clauses of place have the verb in the modally marked form when there is some doubt as to the finding or the existence of the locality referred to in the clause . . . When the clause expresses mere fact the modally zero form is normal . . .' (§895).

5.1.3 Clauses of reason

There is general agreement that the verb in clauses of reason is usually in the indicative form. If the subjunctive occurs, the clause expresses a denied cause (Traugott 1992: 255) or the speaker's meditative rejecting attitude towards the content of the clause (Behre 1934: 307).

5.1.4 Clauses of concession

OE clauses of concession are introduced by *þeah*, and their verb is in the subjunctive mood. This is the unanimous statement in all treatments of this clause type. None of them, however, completely excludes the possibility of indicative verb forms. Wilde (1939/1940: 360) even provides percentage figures: his 56 per cent of subjunctives contrast with 4 per cent for indicatives, 31 per cent for ambiguous forms, 5.5 per cent for modal constructions and 2.5 per cent for modal constructions with subjunctive.

5.1.5 *Clauses of condition*

The most frequent introductory conjunction is *gif* 'if'. This is probably
the reason why Behre (1934: chapter 4), Mitchell (1985: §§3541–3721),
Traugott (1992: 256–258) and Wilde (1939/1940: 338–352) treat these
conditional clauses in more detail. The subjunctive in *gif*-clauses is used
when the matrix clause contains an expression of volition realised by an
imperative or a subjunctive verb form. Wilde additionally notes that this
constellation is very frequent in law texts and charters. Visser (1963–
1973: §880) discusses the argument put forward by Behre and others
that the mood of the verb in *gif*-clauses expresses the speaker's attitude
towards the assumed event in the subordinate clause, and he comes to
the conclusion that 'in the existing Old English documents there was a
tendency to consider the modality of the conditional clause already sufficiently expressed by the conjunction'.

Conditional clauses introduced by *buton, nymþe, nefne, nemne* usually
occur with subjunctive verb forms (Behre, Mitchell, Wilde).

5.1.6 *Clauses of purpose and result*

Behre (1934: chapters 2 and 11), Visser (1963–1973: §877–878, §§891–
893) and Wilde (1939/1940: 352–355, 369–371) treat clauses of purpose
and clauses of result in separate chapters. They agree that in the former
the subjunctive is the appropriate verb form, whereas in the latter the
indicative is used. Both also see the problem that clauses of purpose and
clauses of result are introduced by the same conjunction, namely *þæt*,
and that the analysis of one clause as a clause of purpose and the other as
a clause of result depends on the context. They do not realise that their
argument is circular, because it implies that clauses of purpose have a
subjunctive verb form and adverbial *þæt*-clauses with subjunctive verb
forms are clauses of purpose. The circularity of this argument is one
of Mitchell's explicit reasons for treating clauses of purpose and result
together (Mitchell 1985: §§2802–3006).[3] Traugott (1992: 250–252) uses
the same approach without motivating it. Despite explicitly subscribing
to the argument that clauses of purpose and clauses of result are difficult,
if not impossible, to distinguish from each other, Callaway (1933) sets
out to produce a separate description of clauses of result. He claims that
the subjunctive is used in these clauses when the result is looked upon as

---

[3] '... OE scholars make the basic distinction between them [= clauses of purpose
and result] by the mechanical and circular test of mood, on the assumption that the
subjunctive implies that the aim has not been attained and therefore the clause is
one of purpose whereas the indicative implies that the aim has been attained and
therefore the clause is one of result' (Mitchell 1985: §2803).

contingent. Other, but less important, factors which favour the use of the subjunctive in clauses of result are the mood of the verb in the superordinate clause and the corresponding form of the verb in the Latin originals of translated texts.

5.1.7 Clauses of comparison

Descriptions of OE clauses of comparison differ with respect to the types to be distinguished: comparisons of equality vs. comparisons of inequality (Traugott 1992: 262–265, Wilde (1939/1940: 371–373), clauses of comparison vs. clauses of hypothetical similarity (Visser 1963–1973: §§888–890), *þonne*-clauses vs. *swa/swilce*-clauses (Behre 1934: chapter 10), *þonne*-clauses vs. *swa*-clauses vs. *swilce*-clauses (Mitchell 1985: §§3202–3385). All of them agree, however, on the introductory conjunctions of clauses of comparison, namely *þonne*, *swa* and *swilce*.[4] They also agree on the distribution of the subjunctive and the indicative after these conjunctions: *swa* is usually followed by the indicative, unless the superordinate clause contains an expression of volition; *þonne* is followed by the subjunctive, when the superordinate clause is affirmative, and by the indicative, when the superordinate clause is negative; *swilce* is followed by the indicative, unless it expresses a hypothesis ('as if').

5.1.8 Summary

There are few general truths about the mood of the verb in adverbial clauses. Concessive clauses have a strong preference for the subjunctive, clauses of place and clauses of reason clearly favour the indicative. Linguistic factors influencing the occurrence of one or the other mood include the conjunctions, the existence of a negative element in the matrix clause, and the form of the verb in the matrix clause.

5.2 Adverbial clauses in the OE corpus

My OE corpus contains 1,642 adverbial clauses with a verbal syntagm with a second or third person singular or a plural present tense form (= 12.81/1,000 words). This restriction is necessary because only in these forms is the subjunctive overtly marked. The verbal syntagms of these clauses are realised as subjunctives (865 = 6.75/1,000 words), as indicatives (599 = 4.67/1,000 words) or as modal constructions (178 = 1.39/1,000 words). An example of each realisation possibility is given under [5.1]–[5.3].

---

[4] Wilde considers only the first two.

[5.1]   *læt us on eorðan gerestan. oððæt god us eft arære* (O3 IR HOM
AELFR2/27, p. 248) 'let us remain on earth until God raises us up
again' [subjunctive]

[5.2]   *þonne hie restað, þonne restað hie buton bedde & bolstre* (O2/3
NI TRAV ALEX, p. 47) 'when they rest, they rest without bed and
cushion' [indicative]

[5.3]   *acwel ðu hine mid isene oððe mid attre, þæt þu mage freodom onfon*
(O3 NI FICT APOLL, p. 8) 'kill him with sword or with poison that
you may receive [your] freedom' [modal construction]

In the following sections I will explore which linguistic and non-linguistic
features favour these realisation possibilities.

5.2.1 *The parameter date of composition*

Table 5.1 maps the distribution of the realisation possibilities of the verbal
syntagm in adverbial clauses across the subperiods O1–O4 of the corpus.

Table 5.1 The distribution of the realisation possibilities of the verbal syntagm
in adverbial clauses across subperiods O1–O4

Subperiod	Subjunctive	Indicative	Modal	Total
O1	30 78.95%	7 18.42%	1 2.63%	38 100%
O2	335 65.56%	127 24.85%	49 9.59%	511 100%
O3	469 48.35%	397 40.93%	104 10.72%	970 100%
O4	31 25.20%	68 55.29%	24 19.51%	123 100%
Total	865 52.68%	599 36.48%	178 10.84%	1,642 100%

The relative frequencies show a very clear trend. The shares of indicatives and modal constructions increase, whereas the share of subjunctives
decreases.

5.2.2 *The parameter text category*

The distribution of the realisation possibilities of the verbal syntagm
in the adverbial clauses of the different text categories can only be ade-
quately assessed when they are related to the frequency of adverbial
clauses in the corpus. This is shown in Table 5.2.

The relative frequency of adverbial clauses is greatest in the texts of
the categories STA, EX and IS. Consequently, the distribution of the
realisation possibilities of the verbal syntagm in the adverbial clauses
of these text categories will tell us most about subjunctive preferences
in individual text categories. This is what we need to take into account
when interpreting Table 5.3.

Table 5.2 The distribution of adverbial clauses across different text categories of the OE corpus

Text category	Adverbial clauses/ absolute numbers	Adverbial clauses/ 1,000 words
STA	670	39.09
IS	122	17.45
IR	196	11.93
NI	59	4.27
NN	59	2.87
EX	118	22.01
XX	418	8.73
Total	1,642	12.81

Table 5.3 The distribution of the realisation possibilities of the verbal syntagm in OE adverbial clauses across prototypical text categories

Category	Subjunctive		Indicative		Modal		Total	
STA	486	72.54%	121	18.06%	63	9.40%	670	100%
IS	80	65.57%	31	25.41%	11	9.02%	122	100%
IR	63	32.14%	105	53.57%	28	14.29%	196	100%
NI	21	35.59%	28	47.46%	10	16.95%	59	100%
NN	14	23.73%	33	55.93%	12	20.34%	59	100%
EX	26	22.03%	87	73.73%	5	4.24%	118	100%
XX	175	41.87%	194	46.41%	49	11.72%	418	100%
Total	865	52.68%	599	36.48%	178	10.84%	1,642	100%

Two of the three text categories with a large relative frequency of adverbial clauses also stand out as those with a large share of subjunctives. The text category with the largest relative frequency of adverbial clauses, namely STA, is at the same time the text category with the largest share of subjunctives. This text category will prove to be particularly relevant for the study of OE subjunctive constructions in other respects as well (cf. section 5.2.5). Characteristic examples of subjunctives in adverbial clauses of OE law texts are quoted under [5.4]–[5.6].

[5.4] *Ara ðinum fæder & þinre medder, ða þe Dryhten sealde, þæt ðu sie þy leng libbende on eorþan* (O2 STA LAW ALFLAWIN, p. 28) 'honour your father and your mother, whom the Lord gave you, so that you may live the longer on earth'

[5.5] *Sunnandæges freols healde man georne, swa þærto gebyrige* (O3 STA LAW LAW11C, p. 240) 'the feast-day of Sunday one should dutifully respect as is appropriate'

[5.6] *gyf he maran gærses beðyrfe, ðonne earnige ðæs* (O3/4 STA LAW LAWLAT, p. 447) 'if he need more grass, he may labour for it'

The only other text category in which the subjunctive is the preferred realisation of the verbal syntagm is IS, with 65.57 per cent of subjunctives.

5.2.3 The parameter dialect

Since the texts of the HC are coded for the parameter dialect, a potential influence of this parameter on the realisation possibilities of the verbal syntagm in adverbial clauses was also checked. To this end, the texts of my corpus were subsumed under the dialect categories West Saxon, Anglian and Kentish.[5]

Table 5.4 The distribution of the realisation possibilities of the verbal syntagm in adverbial clauses across the dialects Anglian, Kentish and West Saxon

Dialect	Subjunctive	Indicative	Modal	Total
Anglian	96 59.63%	56 34.78%	9 5.59%	161 100%
Kentish	18 60.00%	6 20.00%	6 20.00%	30 100%
West Saxon	751 51.76%	537 37.01%	163 11.23%	1,451 100%
Total	865 52.68%	599 36.48%	178 10.84%	1,642 100%

The result of the dialect analysis as shown in Table 5.4 is quite telling. Kentish texts stand out for their large shares of subjunctives and modal constructions.

5.2.4 The parameter prose vs. poetry

Callaway argues that in some clauses of time subjunctives are due to the influence of the Latin original of the corresponding texts (cf. section 5.1.1). This claim can only be checked in prose texts because only among these are translations or adaptations from Latin originals. The distribution of the realisation possibilities of the verbal syntagm in adverbial clauses in prose texts and in poetry is mapped in Table 5.5.

Table 5.5 The distribution of the realisation possibilities of the verbal syntagm in OE adverbial clauses of prose and verse texts

Format	Subjunctive	Indicative	Modal	Total
Prose	803 56.55%	472 33.24%	145 10.21%	1,420 100%
Verse	62 27.93%	127 57.21%	33 14.86%	222 100%
Total	865 52.68%	599 36.48%	178 10.84%	1,642 100%

---

[5] The HC parameter codings A/X, AM, AM/X and AN are subsumed under Anglian, the parameter codings K and K/X under Kentish, and WS, WS/K, WS/A, WS/AM and WS/X under West Saxon.

In the prose texts of my corpus the preferred realisation of the verbal syntagm is the subjunctive, whereas in verse texts it is the indicative. The shares of modal constructions do not vary much between prose and verse texts. Yet from the figures in Table 5.5 an influence of the structure of the Latin originals of prose texts cannot be derived, since they represent the distribution of the realisations of the verbal syntagm in all adverbial clauses of my corpus. A detailed analysis of native OE prose texts and texts based on Latin originals would be necessary to assess the claim of a Latin influence on subjunctive frequency in OE adverbial clauses.

5.2.5 *The parameter clause type*

The adverbial clauses of the corpus are coded for the following types: clauses of time, of place, of reason, of concession, of condition, of purpose and result, and of comparison. Table 5.6 shows the distribution of the realisation possibilities of the verbal syntagm in these clause types.

Table 5.6 The distribution of the realisation possibilities of the verbal syntagm in OE adverbial clauses across clause types

Clause type	Subjunctive	Indicative	Modal	Total
Time	121 41.44%	154 52.74%	17 5.82%	292 100%
Place	9 29.03%	18 58.07%	4 12.90%	31 100%
Reason		72 91.14%	7 8.86%	79 100%
Concession	56 91.67%	2 3.33%	3 5.00%	61 100%
Condition	478 62.73%	199 26.12%	85 11.15%	762 100%
Purpose/Result	112 65.12%	19 11.04%	41 23.84%	172 100%
Comparison	89 36.33%	135 55.10%	21 8.57%	245 100%
Total	865 52.68%	599 36.48%	178 10.84%	1,642 100%

Clauses of reason and clauses of concession form the extreme points on the subjunctive frequency scale. The non-occurrence of subjunctives in the former and the very frequent occurrence of subjunctives in the latter are in line with the findings in earlier studies (cf. sections 5.1.3 and 5.1.4). The almost exclusive occurrence of the indicative in clauses of reason tallies with common experience that reasons for an action or a state of affairs are usually given as facts. In the seven examples with a modal construction in clauses of reason, the modal is either *may* or *shall* (cf. examples [5.7] and [5.8]).

[5.7]   *þis he deð þonne, forðam þe he ne mæg locian on þæt sar and on þone micelan wop* (O3/4 IR HOM SUND6, p. 169) 'he does so, because he may not look on that pain and that loud weeping'

[5.8]   *þe ic me betæce ungewæmmode, þæt þu me gehealde togeanes þæs*
deofles costnung strange and staþolfæste on þinre þære sweteste lufa,
<u>*forþan þe to þe nu is and æfre wæs and þurh þin help æfre beon sceal*</u>
<u>*min hiht and min hope and min soþe lufu*</u> (O3/4 NN BIL MARGOE,
p. 171) 'I entrust me to you unblemished that you hold me against the
devil's temptation strong and firm in your dearest love, because on
you is and ever was and by your help always will be my joy and my
hope and my true love'

As example [5.8] shows, *shall* need not always express deontic modality, it can also occur as a marker of futurity and thus express epistemic
modality; and in example [5.7] *ne mæg locian* is more idiomatically
translated as 'does not like to', also expressing epistemic modality.[6]

In the <u>concessive clauses</u> of the corpus relative subjunctive frequency
notably exceeds the value mentioned by Wilde (cf. section 5.1.4), whereas
the percentage figures for indicatives and modal constructions do not
deviate greatly from his. On the basis of my corpus I can even claim that
in clauses of concession the subjunctive is the default option in OE texts.
Example [5.9] proves, however, that the indicative is not completely
excluded.

[5.9]   <u>*þeah to þe seo gefylde gleawnis & snyttro næniges fultumes abædeð*</u>
<u>*sio lar þæs rihtes*</u> *hwæþere ic wolde þæt þu mine dæde ongeate* (O2/3
NI TRAV ALEX, p. 1f.) 'although in you consummate wisdom and
erudition and teaching of what is right require no assistance, yet I
wished that you should learn of my deeds'

In two more clause types the subjunctive is the preferred realisation of
the verbal syntagm, namely in clauses of condition and clauses of purpose
and result. In their treatment of <u>conditional clauses</u> earlier studies distinguish between conditional clauses introduced by *gif* and conditional
clauses introduced by other conjunctions (cf. section 5.1.5). In my corpus
the following conditional conjunctions are attested: *gif, buton, nymðe,*
nemne, swa, wiþ þon þe. All conjunctions apart from *gif* and *buton* are
only attested once or twice, and they govern a subjunctive. The distribution of the realisation possibilities of the verbal syntagm after *gif* and
buton are shown in Table 5.7.

Table 5.7 shows that the large share of subjunctives in conditional
clauses is due to the subjunctive preference of the conjunctions other than
gif. It is also noteworthy that in all fourteen modal constructions after
buton the modal is a subjunctive form of *willan* (11), *mot* (2) or *dearr*

---

[6] On the development of *sculan* as a marker of obligation to a marker of futurity, cf.
Wischer (2008: 125–143).

Table 5.7 The distribution of the realisation possibilities of the verbal syntagm in OE conditional clauses after different conjunctions

Conjunction	Subjunctive	Indicative	Modal	Total
Gif	418 60.84%	198 28.82%	71 10.34%	687 100%
Buton	55 78.57%	1 1.43%	14 20.00%	70 100%
Others	5 100%			5 100%
Total	478 62.68%	199 26.15%	85 11.17%	762 100%

(1). Strictly speaking, they could be added to the ordinary subjunctives so that after conjunctions other than <u>gif</u> only one example of a realisation remains that does not express root modality. It is quoted as example [5.9].

> [5.9] *þonne plihton hy heora are & eallon heora æhtan, <u>butan hit friðbenan</u>*
> <u>syndan</u> (O3 STA LAW LAW11C, p. 256) 'then they shall imperil their
> honour and all their possessions unless they are refugees'

Another reason for the large share of subjunctives in conditional clauses is their frequent occurrence in the prototypical text category STA: 66 per cent of all conditional clauses occur in the law texts of my corpus, and in these subjunctives have a share of 75 per cent, indicatives have a share of 16 per cent and modal constructions have a share of 9 per cent.

The <u>clauses of purpose and result</u> of my corpus are introduced by the conjunctions *þæt* (145), *þy læs þe* (18), *to þon þæt* (4), *wiþ þan þe* (2), *for þy þe* (1) and *wiþ þæt* (2). As the numbers in parentheses indicate, the last four occur significantly less often than the first two, and they are always followed by the subjunctive. In my corpus they introduce only clauses of purpose (cf. examples [5.10]–[5.13]).

> [5.10] *Theophile, <u>to þon þæt þu ðe gebeorge</u>, sege hluddre stæfne hwa ðe*
> *hete me ofslean* (O3 NI FICT APOLL, p. 40) 'Teophilus, in order to
> save yourself, say in a loud voice who asked you to kill me'
>
> [5.11] *mon selle to Folcanstane in mid minum lice X oxan & X cy & C eawa*
> *& C swina & higum ansundran D pending <u>wið ðan ðe min wiif þær</u>*
> <u>benuge innganges</u> (O1 XX DOC HARM2, p. 3) 'at my funeral, ten
> oxen, ten cows, one hundred ewes, and one hundred swine are to be
> given to Folkestone, and to the community severally, five hundred
> pence, in order that my wife may have the privilege of entering there'
> (transl. Harmer 1914: 41)
>
> [5.12] *hio forgifeð fiftene pund <u>for ðy ðe mon ðas feorme ðy soel gelæste</u>* (O1
> XX DOC HARM2, p. 5) 'she remits fifteen pounds in order that this
> food-rent may be the better provided' (transl. Harmer 1914: 42)
>
> [5.13] <u>*Wið þæt cildum butan sare teð wexen*</u>, *haran brægen gesoden, gnid*

> *gelome mid þa toðreoman* (O2/3 IS HANDM QUADR, p. 27) 'in
> order that children's teeth grow without pain, rub the gums often with
> a boiled hare's brain'

The conjunction *þy læs þe* introduces clauses of negative purpose.
Therefore, it does not come as a surprise that in these clauses the share of
subjunctives is very large. They strengthen the root modality expressed
by the conjunction. As a matter of fact, out of the eighteen occurrences
of *þy læs þe*, seventeen are followed by a subjunctive; the only other
example is followed by a modal construction.

A competition between all three realisation possibilities of the verbal
syntagm is only attested after the conjunction *þæt*. In the 145 passages of
my corpus *þæt* is followed by the subjunctive in eighty-six cases, by the
indicative in nineteen cases and by a modal construction in forty cases.
A closer look at the passages with indicative reveals that all of them are
clauses of result. In most cases this reading is supported by the occurrence of the element *swa* in the immediate context (cf. examples [5.14]
and [5.15]).

[5.14] *Seo eorðe stent on ælemiddan ðurh Godes mihte swa gefæstnod, þæt*
        heo næfre ne bihð, ufor ne neoðor (O3 EX SCIA TEMP, p. 42) 'the
        earth stands so firm through God's might that it never bends, neither
        upward nor downward'

[5.15] *þurh þæt man gebringeð ealles to manege on yfelan geþance & on*
        undæde, swa þæt hy ne scamað na þeah hy syngian swyðe (O3 IR
        HOM WULF8C, p. 273) 'through this, man puts bad ideas and inten-
        tions into all too many [persons' minds] so that they are not ashamed
        although they sin greatly'

So far my data support the hypothesis mentioned in section 5.1.6 that
in clauses of purpose the subjunctive is the rule, whereas in clauses of
result the indicative prevails. This complementary distribution is a consequence of clauses of purpose expressing root modality and clauses of
result expressing epistemic modality.

Clauses of time occupy the second rank on the frequency scale of
adverbial clauses, yet the dominant realisation of their verbal syntagms
is the indicative. Prompted by earlier studies I sorted them according to
their introductory conjunction. Table 5.8 shows the result of this more
detailed analysis.

When we remove the conjunctions with very few attestations to the
end and arrange the others according to Callaway's model (cf. section
5.1.1), Table 5.9 is the result.

Since Callaway counted only subjunctives and no alternative forms,
and since he presents only absolute numbers, a comparison of his figures

Table 5.8 The distribution of the realisation possibilities of the verbal syntagm after individual conjunctions in OE clauses of time

Conjunction	Subjunctive	Indicative	Modal	Total
Ær	30 85.71%	5 14.29%		35 100%
Nu		1 100%		1 100%
Oþþæt	26 68.42%	11 28.95%	1 2.63%	38 100%
Siþþan	3 21.43%	11 78.57%		14 100%
Þenden	2 28.57%	4 57.14%	1 14.29%	7 100%
Þonne	41 25.31%	110 67.90%	11 6.79%	162 100%
Þe hwile	16 59.26%	8 29.63%	3 11.11%	27 100%
Swa			1 100%	1 100%
Hwonne	3 100%			3 100%
Þa		1 100%		1 100%
Þæt		3 100%		3 100%
Total	121 41.44%	154 52.74%	17 5.82%	292 100%

Table 5.9 The distribution of the realisation possibilities of the verbal syntagm in OE clauses of time after temporal conjunctions of antecedent, subsequent and contemporaneous action

Conjunction	Subjunctive	Indicative	Modal	Total
Siþþan Antecedent	3 21.43%	11 78.57%		14 100%
Ær Subsequent	30 85.71%	5 14.29%		35 100%
Oþþæt Contemporaneous a)	26 68.42%	11 28.95%	1 2.63%	38 100%
Þenden Contemporaneous b)	2 28.57%	4 57.14%	1 14.29%	7 100%
Þe hwile Contemporaneous b)	16 59.26%	8 29.63%	3 11.11%	27 100%
Þonne Contemporaneous c)	41 25.31%	110 67.90%	11 6.79%	162 100%
Others	3 33.33%	5 55.56%	1 11.11%	9 100%
Total	121 41.44%	154 52.74%	17 5.82%	292 100%

with those in Table 5.9 is difficult. It is to be noted, however, that the share of subjunctives in clauses of time denoting antecedent action is very low in my corpus and inversely the share of indicatives is very high. This distribution was to be expected, because antecedent action is usually expressed as a fact, and the indicative is the default realisation of fact. It also corresponds to Callaway's observation that subjunctives of antecedent action are less frequent in his corpus than in the other types of temporal clauses. The following is one of the few corpus examples of a subjunctive of antecedent action.[7]

> [5.16]   *Sing ðis wið toðece, <u>syððan sunne beo on setle</u>, swiðe oft* (O2/3 IS
>   HANDM LACN, p. 104) 'sing this very often against toothache as
>   soon as the sun goes down'

Table 5.9 also supports the hypothesis reported in section 5.1.1 that clauses of time introduced by *ær* usually govern a subjunctive verb form. In my corpus the share of subjunctives is greatest in these clauses (cf. example [5.17]).

> [5.17]   *ne mægen hi swa leohtne leoman ansendan, <u>ær se þicca mist þynra</u>
>   <u>weorðe</u>* (O2/3 XX XX MBO, p. 158) 'they cannot send forth such a
>   bright ray of light, before the thick mist may become thinner'

The dominance of the subjunctive in temporal clauses of subsequent action was also to be expected, because actions or states of affairs that have not yet materialised at the time of speaking are usually not presented as facts but as possibilities, wishes or commands.

Clauses of comparison are similar to clauses of time in that they are among the clause types with a relatively high frequency, but a small share of subjunctives. As Table 5.10 shows, subjunctive frequency depends on the introductory conjunction in clauses of comparison.

Table 5.10 The distribution of the realisation possibilities of the verbal syntagm in OE clauses of comparison

Conjunction	Subjunctive	Indicative	Modal	Total
Swa	70 32.26%	129 59.45%	18 8.29%	217 100%
Þonne	8 61.54%	3 23.08%	2 15.38%	13 100%
Swilce	11 73.33%	3 20.00%	1 6.67%	15 100%
Total	89 36.33%	135 55.10%	21 8.57%	245 100%

Clauses of comparison introduced by *swa* favour the indicative, those introduced by *þonne* or *swilce* the subjunctive. Examples [5.18]–[5.20] illustrate these patterns.

> [5.18]   *Hu mæg ic, dryhten min, ofer deop gelad fore gefremman on feorne
>   weg swa hrædlice, heofona scyppend, wuldres waldend, <u>swa ðu worde</u>
>   <u>becwist</u>?* (OX/3 XX XX AND, p. 8) 'how can I, my Lord, undertake

---

[7]   The subjunctive in example [5.16] may be conditioned by the imperative of the
   verbal syntagm in the matrix clause (cf. section 5.2.6.1).

the journey on a distant course over the deep waterway as quickly, creator of the heavens, ruler of glory, as you tell me by your word?

[5.19] *mid nanum leohtran ðinge gebete þonne him mon aceorfe þa tungon of* (O2 STA LAW ALFLAWIN, p. 66) '[he] shall not make amends with an easier thing than one shall cut his tongue off'

[5.20] *ic biddo higon ðaet ge me gemynen aet ðere tide mid suilce godcunde gode suilce iow cynlic ðynce* (O1 XX DOC HARM1, p. 2) 'I pray the community that ye remember me on this anniversary with such divine service as may seem to you becoming' (transl. Harmer 1914: 40)

The particle *swilce* is dealt with in great detail by Mitchell (1985: §§3323–3333). After discussing passages where *swilce* can be analysed as an indefinite pronoun or as a conjunction, he suggests two analyses of the conjunction *swilce*, either as a conjunction of comparison or as a conjunction of manner. In the first case it is to be translated as 'just as' and is followed by the indicative, in the second case it is to be translated as 'as if' and is followed by the subjunctive. When Mitchell's meaning-based classification of *swilce* is adopted, my corpus contains ten clauses of comparison introduced by *swilce*. Yet in only three of them is *swilce* followed by the indicative (cf. example [5.21]).

[5.21] *ic cweþe on wordum be Æscmere on minum geongum magum swelce me betst gehieraþ* (O2 XX DOC ROB26, p. 52) 'I shall verbally bequeath Æscmere to such of my young kinsmen as obey me best' (transl. Robertson 1956: 53)

The remaining five *swilce*-clauses are clauses of manner in Mitchell's terminology, and accordingly their conjunction is followed by a subjunctive (cf. example [5.22]).

[5.22] *On ðam ylcan earde norðeweardan beoð leohte nihta on sumera, swilce hit ealle niht dagige* (O3 EX SCIA TEMP, p. 50) 'in this same country towards the north the nights are bright in summer as if it was day all night'

This distribution supports Mitchell's claim that in clauses of manner, i.e. in *as if*-clauses introduced by *swilce*, the subjunctive is the rule. On the other hand, my data do not support his claim that in clauses of comparison the conjunction *swilce* is followed by the indicative. Therefore, I do not adopt Mitchell's distinction between clauses of manner and clauses of comparison but stick to the latter term. Then my data support the hypothesis that clauses of comparison introduced by *swilce* preferably govern the subjunctive.

The clauses of place in my corpus are introduced by *þær*, and as was to be expected their preferred mood is the indicative (cf. example [5.23]).

[5.23] *gif þu þinum clænsungdagum, þær þu færest geond eorðan ymb-*
hwyrft, hys flæsc gesoden etest & þigest, hyt byþ god þe & þinum
weorudum (O2/3 IS HANDM QUADR, p. 7) 'if on your days of
purging, wherever you travel across the expanse of the earth, you eat
and taste its flesh boiled, it is good for you and your armies'

5.2.6 *The parameter matrix clause*

The matrix clauses of the adverbial clauses in my corpus are coded for
the features negation and volition; the latter is expressed by subjunctive
or imperative mood. The most serious problem during the coding procedure was the identification of the matrix clause of a given adverbial
clause (cf. examples [5.24 and [5.25]).

[5.24] *Se ðe slea his agenne þeowne esne oððe his mennen, & he ne sie*
idæges dead, ðeah he libbe twa niht oððe ðreo, ne bið he ealles swa
scyldig, forþon þe hit wæs his agen fioh (O2 STA LAW ALFLAWIN,
p. 32) 'the person who kills his own female servant or his male servant
and he is not dead on the same day, although he lives two or three
nights more, he is yet not guilty, because it was his own property'

Is the adverbial clause *ðeah he libbe twa niht oððe ðreo* directly dependent on the main clause *ne bið he ealles swa scyldig* or on the relative
clause *ðe slea his agenne þeowne esne oððe his mennen, & he ne sie*
idæges dead? In the first case the verb of the matrix clause is indicative,
in the second it is subjunctive.

[5.25] *þis sind þa landmearca to Byligesdyne, of ða burnan æt Humelcyrre,*
fram ∣[Humelcyrre∣] Heregeresheafode, fram Heregeresheafode
æfter ðam ealdan hege to ðare grene æc, þonne forð þæt hit cymð
to þare stanstræte, of þare stanstræte andlang scrybbe þæt hit cymð
to Acantune, fram Acyntune þæt hit cymð to Rigendune, fram
Rigindune æft to þara burnan (O3 XX DOC WHIT15, p. 40) 'These
are the boundaries of Balsdon: from the stream at *Humelcyrre*; from
Humelcyrre to *Heregeresheafod* from *Heregeresheafod* along the old
hedge to the green oak; then on until one comes to the paved road;
from the paved road along the shrubbery until one comes to Acton;
from Acton until one comes to Roydon; from Roydon back to the
stream' (transl. Whitelock 1930)

Which is the matrix clause of the three adverbial clauses *þæt hit cymð*
to þare stanstræte, *þæt hit cymð to Acantune* and *þæt hit cymð to*
Rigendune? Strictly speaking, they do not have a matrix clause at all.

5.2.6.1 Volition

The expression of volition in the matrix clause as a subjunctive favouring feature is mentioned in previous studies in the context of clauses of time, of condition, of purpose and result, and of comparison. Among the 1,642 adverbial clauses of my corpus 997 (= 60.72 per cent) depend on a matrix clause with a verbal syntagm marked for the feature volition.[8] Table 5.11 provides an overview of the distribution of the realisation possibilities of the verbal syntagm in all types of adverbial clauses depending on matrix clauses with and without an expression of volition.

Table 5.11 The distribution of the realisation possibilities of the verbal syntagm in OE adverbial clauses depending on matrix clauses with and without expressions of volition

Adv. cl. \ Matrix	Subjunctive	Indicative	Modal	Total
Subjunctive	541 77.18%	89 12.69%	71 10.13%	701 100%
Imperative	100 67.57%	31 20.94%	17 11.49%	148 100%
Modal	42 28.38%	77 52.03%	29 19.59%	148 100%
Non-volition	182 28.22%	402 62.32%	61 9.46%	645 100%
Total	865 52.68%	599 36.48%	178 10.84%	1,642 100%

Quite obviously the subjunctive in adverbial clauses correlates with expressions of volition in the corresponding matrix clauses. This correlation is strongest when the expression of volition is realised by a subjunctive verb form, and it is weakest when it is expressed by a modal construction.

Since large shares of subjunctives in some contexts were explained previously by other factors (e.g. clause type, introductory conjunction), the influence of the structure of the verbal syntagm in the matrix clause was tested in the remaining contexts, namely in clauses of purpose and result (cf. section 5.1.6), in clauses of time introduced by a conjunction other than *ær* (cf. section 5.1.1), in clauses of condition introduced by *gif* (cf. section 5.1.5), and in clauses of comparison introduced by *swa* (cf. section 5.1.7). The results of this more detailed analysis are displayed in Table 5.12.

Table 5.12 shows that an expression of volition in the matrix clause correlates more strongly with a subjunctive in the dependent clause in the selected types of adverbial clause than with all adverbial clauses in the corpus. There is a saliently strong correlation in conditional clauses introduced by *gif*. An expression of volition in the matrix clause raises

---

[8] As in the analysis of relative and noun clauses the verbal syntagm of the matrix clause is analysed as expressing volition when it is realised by a subjunctive, an imperative or a modal construction.

Table 5.12 The distribution of the realisation possibilities of the verbal syntagm in selected OE adverbial clauses depending on matrix clauses with expressions of volition

Clause type	Subjunctive	Indicative	Modal	Total
Time ≠ ær	74 60.16%	40 32.52%	9 7.32%	123 100%
Condition gif	377 74.07%	75 14.73%	57 11.20%	509 100%
Purpose/Result	71 76.34%	1 1.08%	21 22.58%	93 100%
Comparison swa	62 52.99%	43 36.75%	12 10.26%	117 100%
Total	584 69.36%	159 18.88%	99 11.76%	842 100%

the share of subjunctives from 60.84 per cent to 74.07 per cent (cf. Table 5.7). Examples [5.26]–[5.29] illustrate subjunctive occurrence in the selected adverbial clauses.

[5.26]   *syððan heora begra dæg agan si, Ægelrices & þæs arcebisceopes Eadsiges, þænne ga þis foresprecene land into Cristes cyricean mid mete & mid mannan* (O3 XX DOC ROB101, p. 188) 'as soon as the life of both of them is over, of Æthelric and of Archbishop Eadsige, this land mentioned before shall pass to Christchurch with its produce and its men'

[5.27]   *Gif þu sunu age oððe swæsne mæg, oððe on þissum folcum freond ænigne eac þissum idesum þe we her on wlitað, alæde of þysse leodbyrig, þa ðe leofe sien, ofestum miclum* (OX/3 XX XX GEN, p. 73) 'if you have a son or a male kinsman dear among this people or a friend of these maidens whom we here behold, lead those who are dear to you in great haste from this town'

[5.28]   *Ond eac swelce ecelice min gemynd stonde & hleonige oðrum eorðcyningum to bysne, ðæt hie witen þy gearwor þæt min þrym & min weorðmynd maran wæron, þonne ealra opra kyninga þe in middangearde æfre wæron* (O2/3 NI TRAV ALEX, p. 49f.) 'And also my memory shall thus stand forever and tower as an example for other earthly kings so that they know the more readily that my power and my glory were greater than those of all other kings that ever were in the world'

[5.29]   *ic ðe bebiode ðæt ðu do swæ ic geliefe ðæt ðu wille, ðæt ðu ðe ðissa worulddinga to ðæm geæmetige swæ ðu oftost mæge, ðæt ðu ðone wisdom ðe ðe God sealde ðær ðær ðu hiene befæstan mæge, georne befæste* (O2 XX PREF PRCP, p. 5) 'I command that you do as I believe that you wish [namely] that you disengage yourself from the

affairs of this world as often as you can, so that you may eagerly apply
the wisdom that God gave you wherever you can apply it'

Example [5.26] shows that an expression of volition in the matrix clause
is accompanied by a subjunctive even in a clause of time of the subclass
antecedent action, where the indicative is the prevailing mood (cf. also
example [5.16]). The subjunctive *age* in the *gif*-clause of example [5.27]
corresponds to the subjunctive *alæde* of the main clause. The translation
of *þæt* as 'so that' in example [5.28] indicates that the adverbial clause is
interpreted as a clause of result, and yet the mood of the verb is subjunctive. This is in line with Callaway's claim that one of the conditioning
factors of the subjunctive in clauses of result is the mood of the verb
in the superordinate clause. In the complex example [5.29], the clause
of comparison with the subjunctive *mæge* depends on the object clause
ðæt ðu ðe ðissa woruldðinga to ðæm geæmetige with the subjunctive
geæmetige. It illustrates the claim which is derived from the figures in
Table 5.12 that the share of subjunctives in comparative clauses introduced by *swa* is nearly twice as great when the matrix clause contains an
expression of volition as when this is not the case (cf. Table 5.10).

5.2.6.2 Negation
Negation is mentioned in the studies by Behre (1934), Callaway (1931),
Mitchell (1985), Traugott (1992) and Wilde (1939/1940) as a factor
favouring special mood constellations in clauses of time and in clauses of
comparison. According to Mitchell and Behre (cf. section 5.1.1) clauses
of time introduced by *ær* disfavour the subjunctive after negated matrix
clauses. My corpus contains 35 *ær*-clauses with a subjunctive frequency
of 85.71 per cent (cf. Table 5.8). In the thirteen occcurrences of *ær*-
clauses depending on a negated clause the share of subjunctives is only
76.92 per cent (= 10 tokens). This distribution supports Mitchell's and
Behre's claims. It should, however, be borne in mind that the absolute
numbers from which this support is derived are very small. The hypothesis that a negated matrix clause raises the relative frequency of indicatives in clauses of comparison introduced by *þonne* cannot be supported
from my data, since out of the thirteen relevant clauses only one depends
on a negated matrix clause.

5.2.7 Summary

In the first part of this chapter I reviewed earlier studies on OE adverbial
clauses on the basis of the semantic roles of adverbial clauses. In the
analysis of the adverbial clauses of my corpus I tested the influence of the
parameters date of composition, text category, dialect, prose vs. poetry,
clause type, and matrix clause. The following results were achieved:

The relative frequency of subjunctives steadily decreases from subperiods O1 to O4. The prototypical text category STA contains the highest number of adverbial clauses and at the same time the largest share of subjunctives. The Kentish dialect, which is represented by only one file in the corpus, has the largest share of subjunctives and modal constructions and the smallest share of indicatives. Prose texts contain more subjunctives than verse texts, and this result gives at least some support to the hypothesis that the Latin original of translated texts influenced the subjunctive frequency. Concessive clauses have the largest share of subjunctives, followed by clauses of purpose and result and by clauses of condition. A more detailed analysis of the clauses of purpose and result revealed a tendency for the subjunctive to dominate in clauses of purpose and for the indicative to prevail in clauses of result. The high overall frequency of subjunctives in conditional clauses could be attributed to the subjunctive preference of the conjunctions other than *gif*. Individual conjunctions were also identified as favouring the subjunctive in other types of adverbial clause, namely *ær*, *oþþæt* and *þe hwile* in clauses of time. The share of subjunctives is smallest in clauses of comparison, of place and of reason. Among the features volition and negation in matrix clauses, which were investigated as potentially influential on the mood in adverbial clauses, the former proved stronger than the latter. An expression of volition – i.e. a subjunctive, an imperative or a modal construction in the matrix clause – raises the relative subjunctive frequency in clauses of time introduced by conjunctions other than *ær*, in conditional clauses introduced by *gif*, in comparative clauses introduced by *swa*, and in clauses of purpose and result irrespective of the introductory conjunction. A negation in the matrix clause has a weakly disfavouring influence on subjunctive frequency in temporal clauses introduced by *ær*.

5.3 Middle English adverbial clauses: descriptive parameters

ME handbooks and diachronic reference works distinguish clauses of time, of place, of reason, of concession, of condition, of purpose, of result and of comparison. The difficulties listed for OE hold for the analysis of ME adverbial clauses as well: some elements can be used as adverbs and as conjunctions (e.g. *after*), some elements can introduce different types of clause (e.g. *that* introduces noun clauses and clauses of purpose), some conjunctions introduce different types of adverbial clause (e.g. *siþ* introduces clauses of reason and clauses of time), some adverbial clauses combine different semantic roles (e.g. purpose and result).

In the first part of this section the relevant features of adverbial clauses will be reviewed, and in the second part the influence of several linguistic and extralinguistic parameters on the realisation of the verbal syntagm in the adverbial clauses of my ME corpus will be analysed.

5.3.1 *Clauses of time*

Fischer (1992: 352–356) presents a very detailed description of temporal clauses. Her main division is between temporal clauses expressing overlap in time (introductory elements: *while, as long as*) and those indicating temporal sequence.[9] The latter order events in two ways: (1) the event in the subclause is anterior to that in the matrix clause, (2) the event in the subclause is posterior to that in the matrix clause. Clauses of type (1) are further subdivided according to whether the conjunction expresses simple sequence (introductory elements: *after (that), as soon as*), or whether it limits the duration of the action in the matrix clause (introduced by *sithen (that), from (that), when*). Clauses of type (2) can also either express simple sequence (introduced by *er/or/before (that)*) or delimit the duration of the action in the matrix clause (introduced by *till (that), until*). The subjunctive is frequent after the conjunctions *or/er/ before (that)* and *till (that)*. Factors which favour the use of the subjunctive are a negative element, an imperative or another expression of volition in the matrix clause.

Till and *er* are also singled out by Mustanoja (1960: 463) and by Burrow and Turville-Petre (1992: 49) as subjunctive favouring conjunctions. Visser (1963–1973: §879) additionally mentions a frequent use of the subjunctive after *when* during the ME period.

5.3.2 *Clauses of place*

Authors who deal with clauses of place at all (Burrow and Turville-Petre 1992: 49, Mustanoja 1960: 462, Visser 1963–1973: §895) note that the use of the subjunctive is a function of the degree of certainty on the part of the text producer.

5.3.3 *Clauses of reason*

Fischer (1992: 347) agrees with Visser (1963–1973: §894) that the indicative is the regular mood in clauses of reason.

5.3.4 *Clauses of concession*

The general tenor in treatments of concessive clauses is that they prefer the subjunctive (Burrow and Turville-Petre 1992: 49, Visser 1963–1973: §883). Yet the subjunctive seems to have lost ground in favour of the

---

[9] Although Fischer's descriptive model of clauses of time is reminiscent of Callaway's for OE (cf. section 5.1.1), the two models differ in the analysis of individual conjunctions, e.g. *þonne/when*, *oððæt/till*.

indicative during the ME period (Fischer 1992: 351, Mustanoja 1960: 467–469).

5.3.5 Clauses of condition

Opinions about the use of the subjunctive in ME clauses of condition vary among the authors of reference works. Whereas Visser (1963–1973: §880) does not detect a preference for either mood, Burrow and Turville-Petre (1992: 49) find a preference for the subjunctive, and Fischer (1992: 349–350) and Mustanoja (1960: 469–470) note a development from a preference for the indicative in OE and EME to the subjunctive in Late ME, and here especially in the north. In his chapter, which is based on Bible translations, Harsh (1968: 152–153) also found a rising subjunctive frequency in conditional clauses, which even continued into the EModE period.

The hypothesis of a rising subjunctive frequency in ME conditional clauses is supported in the specialised studies by Kihlbom (1939) and Moessner (2005). Kihlbom analysed private letters of the fifteenth century and found the subjunctive to be the prevailing form. Moessner's data come from the HC, the *Helsinki Corpus of Older Scots* (HCOS) and the *Corpus of Early English Correspondence Sampler* (CEECS). In addition to the factor date of composition her paper explores the influence of the regional dialect, the text category, the format and the dichotomy lexical verb vs. *be* on the distribution of the realisation possibilities of the verbal syntagm in conditional clauses. These are the results of her analysis: the relative frequency of subjunctives rises continually; the replacement of the indicative by the subjunctive started in the Southern and Midland dialect areas and moved northwards; although the share of subjunctives of lexical verbs drops, it is larger than the share of subjunctives of *be* even in the last subperiod; the text categories with the highest incidence of subjunctives are letters and instructive texts.

5.3.6 Clauses of purpose and result

The authors who describe these two types of clauses separately (Mustanoja 1960: 465–467, Visser 1963–1973: §§877, 891) use a circular argument (cf. section 5.1.6 for OE). They state that in clauses of purpose the subjunctive is used and in clauses of result the indicative is used, and the subjunctive indicates that a given clause is a clause of purpose, whereas the indicative indicates that a given clause is a clause of result. Harsh does not motivate his distinction of clauses of purpose and clauses of result, but from his figures of subjunctive frequency (1968: 160–161) it can be concluded that it is based on the prevailing use of the different mood forms.

The formal and semantic similarities are the motivation for Fischer (1992: 343) to treat both clause types together. She notes that 'the subjunctive mood is usual in purpose clauses, and the indicative in result clauses, but borderline cases show that the indicative and subjunctive may also occur in purpose and result clauses repectively'. The all-purpose conjunction is *that*, but there are also subordinators which formally distinguish purpose from result clauses. This holds in particular for the negative purpose conjunction *lest*, which is followed by the subjunctive.

Kikusawa (2012) studied the distribution of subjunctives and modal constructions in *lest*-clauses of Late ME prose texts, focusing on the influence of clause type, text category and medium. She found that in her data adverbial *lest*-clauses preferred the subjunctive, and noun clauses introduced by *lest* preferred modal constructions. Among the text categories with sufficient examples, religious texts favoured the subjunctive and romances favoured modal constructions. The category religious texts allowed a division into oral and written texts, and the latter showed a larger share of subjunctives than the former.[10]

5.3.7 Clauses of comparison

Under this heading usually two clause types are subsumed, namely clauses expressing equality and clauses expressing inequality (Fischer 1992: 356–361, Mustanoja 1960: 464–465, Visser 1963–1973: §§887–890).[11] There is only general agreement on the preference of the subjunctive in what Fischer calls conditional comparative clauses and Visser terms clauses of hypothetical similarity; they are introduced by *as if, as though, lyk as, swylce*.

5.3.8 Summary

Apart from clauses of reason with pervasive indicative and clauses of concession with equally pervasive subjunctive, all other adverbial clauses were found to occur with either mood. In some adverbial clauses the introductory conjunction proved to influence the choice of the subjunctive (e.g. *er, till* in clauses of time, *lest* in clauses of negative purpose). Extralinguistic factors which were identified as having an influence on subjunctive frequency were date of composition, dialect, text category and medium.

---

[10] The quality of the study is impaired by wrong examples, which suggest that the data collection was not conducted carefully enough, which casts also some doubt on the reliability of the results.

[11] Concerning clauses of comparison, of purpose, of condition and of concession, Kovács (2010: 64–66) echoes Fischer's description.

5.4 Adverbial clauses in the ME corpus

My ME corpus contains 1,475 relevant adverbial clauses, i.e. adverbial clauses with a verbal syntagm in the second or third person singular present tense. With 8.86/1,000 words, their normalised frequency is lower than in the OE corpus. This difference is easily explained because in the OE period verbs were also marked for mood in the forms of plural present. The verbal syntagms in the ME corpus are realised as subjunctives (531 = 3.08/1,000 words), as indicatives (711 = 4.27/1,000 words) or as modal constructions (233 = 1.40/1,000 words).[12] Examples [5.30]–[5.33] illustrate the realisation possibilities.

[5.30] *Al-though chastite be the flour of alle vertues, yit with-oute mekenesse she waxith drye and fadith his colour* (M4 IR RULE AELR4, p. 13) 'although chastity is the flower of all virtues, without meekness it becomes dry and loses its colour'

[5.31] *gef ðer is noman ðanne he falleð, he remeð and helpe calleð* (M2 IR RELT BEST, p. 21) 'if there is nobody when he falls, he shouts and calls for help'

[5.32] *ȝef þu wult mi nome witen; ich am katerine icleopet* (M1 NN BIL KATH, p. 26) 'if you wish to know my name, I am called Katherine'

[5.33] *þer arn iii dayes þat no man owyth to be lete blood* (M4 IS HANDO REYNES, p. 157) 'there are three days when nobody should be let blood'

In the following sections the influence of several linguistic and extralinguistic parameters on the distribution of the realisation possibilities of the verbal syntagm in adverbial clauses will be tested.

5.4.1 *The parameter date of composition*

The files of the ME corpus are coded for the subperiods M1 to M4. The distribution of the realisation patterns of the verbal syntagms across these subperiods is entered in Table 5.13.

The continuous developments observed in OE do not continue in the ME period. On the whole, subjunctive frequency as well as indicative frequency decreases, and this decrease is compensated for by an increase of modal constructions. Yet between the individual subperiods there is a wave-like development in all three realisation possibilities. This heterogeneous picture is in line with the more specific, yet conflicting, earlier

---

12 Under the heading modal constructions, the patterns 'modal auxiliary + infinitive' and 'semi-modal + *to* + infinitive' are subsumed. The semi-modals attested in my corpus are *ought* and *need*.

Table 5.13 The distribution of the realisation possibilities of the verbal syntagm in adverbial clauses across subperiods M1–M4

Subperiod	Subjunctive	Indicative	Modal	Total
M1	115 36.16%	165 51.89%	38 11.95%	318 100%
M2	37 27.82%	74 55.64%	22 16.54%	133 100%
M3	202 40.73%	222 44.76%	72 14.51%	496 100%
M4	177 33.52%	250 47.35%	101 19.13%	528 100%
Total	531 36.00%	711 48.20%	233 15.80%	1,475 100%

claims about subjunctive frequency increase in conditional clauses and subjunctive frequency decline in concessive clauses (cf. section 5.3.4 and 5.3.5).

5.4.2 *The parameter text category*

Following the argument put forward when dealing with subjunctive constructions in OE adverbial clauses, the first step was to establish the distribution of the adverbial clauses in the ME corpus across the prototypical text categories. The absolute numbers and the relative frequencies per 1,000 words are given in Table 5.14.

Table 5.14 The distribution of ME adverbial clauses across prototypical text categories

Category	Adverbial clauses/ absolute numbers	Adverbial clauses/ 1,000 words
STA	100	8.62
IS	202	13.60
IR	612	12.08
NI	134	5.95
NN	68	3.90
EX	71	11.04
XX	288	6.71
Total	1,475	8.86

It is not only the case that the ME corpus contains fewer adverbial clauses than the OE corpus – in absolute and in relative terms – but they are also differently distributed across the prototypical text categories. Corresponding to the lower relative frequency of adverbial clauses generally, one might expect that this decrease is reflected in all text categories. Yet this expectation is only fulfilled with respect to the categories STA, IS, EX and XX; in the remaining categories the relative frequency of adverbial clauses is even higher in the ME corpus than in the OE corpus.

The distribution of the realisation possibilities of the verbal syntagms of the texts in the different categories is shown in Table 5.15.

Table 5.15 The distribution of the realisation possibilities of the verbal syntagm in ME adverbial clauses across prototypical text categories

Category	Subjunctive	Indicative	Modal	Total
STA	44 44.00%	41 41.00%	15 15.00%	100 100%
IS	111 54.95%	71 35.15%	20 9.90%	202 100%
IR	181 29.58%	348 56.86%	83 13.56%	612 100%
NI	51 38.06%	59 44.03%	24 17.91%	134 100%
NN	17 25.00%	34 50.00%	17 25.00%	68 100%
EX	29 40.85%	25 35.21%	17 23.94%	71 100%
XX	98 34.03%	133 46.18%	57 19.79%	288 100%
Total	531 36.00%	711 48.20%	233 15.80%	1,475 100%

The text category which most clearly favours the subjunctive is IS, where more than every second verbal syntagm is realised by this mood. This result is all the more telling since IS is also the category with the highest density of adverbial clauses in the ME corpus. The category contains two representatives of the text type handbook; one of them describes how to choose a good horse and how to treat it when it falls ill, the other deals with the appropriate organisation of various aspects of public life (cf. examples [5.34] and [5.35]).

> [5.34] *3if þe schabbe be in þe dok of þe taile þen schalt þou take blak comyn & grynde it seþe a litel in swete mylke it when it is hote a-noynte þe schabbe ofte þer-with* (M3 IS HANDM HORSES, p. 109) 'if the scab is at the end of the tail, you must take black cumin and grind it and seethe it in a little sweet milk, and when it is hot anoint the scab often with it'
> [5.35] *if ony man dystruble or breke þe pees, 3e schall arest hym and brynge hym to þe Kyngis preson as wel be day as nyght* (M4 IS HANDO REYNES, p. 154) 'if anyone disturb or break the peace, you shall arrest him and take him to the King's prison by day as well as by night'

The text category which occupies the second rank on the frequency scale of subjunctives is STA. Its two representatives belong to the text types documents and laws, and it is in particular the law file that contributes to the large number of subjunctives. It contains a set of acts from *The Statutes of the Realm*; they point out public misconduct and aim at correcting it (cf. example [5.36]).

> [5.36] *this noble Reame within short processe of tyme without refourmacion be had therin shall not be of habilite ne power to defend it self* (M4

STA LAW STAT2, PII, p. 534) 'this noble realm shall not be able nor have power to defend itself within short time, if no reform is brought about'

These observations support the generalisation of Moessner's (2005) finding based only on conditional clauses that the subjunctive is the preferred realisation possibility in instructive text categories (cf. section 5.3.5). This result is of diachronic relevance as well, since the same text categories, namely STA and IS, also proved to prefer the subjunctive in the OE corpus.

5.4.3 The parameter dialect

The texts of the ME corpus are coded for the dialect areas East Midland, West Midland, Northern, Southern and Kentish.[13] The distribution of the realisation possibilities of the verbal syntagm in these dialect areas is shown in Table 5.16.

Table 5.16 The distribution of the realisation possibilities of the verbal syntagm in adverbial clauses across ME dialect areas

Dialect	Subjunctive		Indicative		Modal		Total	
East Midland	298	34.65%	413	48.02%	149	17.33%	860	100%
West Midland	67	27.46%	142	58.20%	35	14.34%	244	100%
Northern	3	13.04%	17	73.91%	3	13.04%	23	99.99%
Southern	107	45.92%	99	42.49%	27	11.59%	233	100%
Kentish	56	48.70%	40	34.78%	19	16.52%	115	100%
Total	531	36.00%	711	48.20%	233	15.80%	1,475	100%

The parameter dialect has a very strong influence on subjunctive and indicative frequency. The share of subjunctives rises from north to south and reaches its peak in the Kentish dialect; indicative frequency is inversely distributed. The share of modal constructions does not vary greatly between dialects. The stronghold of the subjunctive in Southern, especially in Kentish, texts is in line with Moessner's observation based on conditional clauses alone that Northern, especially Scottish, texts disfavour the subjunctive (Moessner 2005: 221–223).

---

[13] The HC codes EML and EMO are subsumed under East Midland, WML and WMO under West Midland, NL and NO under Northern, SL and SO under Southern, KL and KO under Kentish (Kytö 1996: 50).

5.4.4 *The parameter prose vs. poetry*

Although the influence of this parameter on subjunctive frequency was not investigated in earlier studies, the distribution of the realisation possibilities in the prose and verse texts of my corpus was analysed in order to compare it to the figures established for the OE corpus. In the ME corpus, too, all translations are prose texts. If Callaway's claim held for ME as well, the share of subjunctives should be larger in those (cf. section 5.1.1).

Table 5.17 shows that the parameter prose vs. poetry has no influence at all on subjunctive frequency in the texts of the ME corpus. From its figures it can be concluded that neither translations from Latin nor from French originals have a higher proportion of subjunctives than native English texts.

Table 5.17 The distribution of the realisation possibilities of the verbal syntagm in ME adverbial clauses in prose and verse texts

Format	Subjunctive	Indicative	Modal	Total
Prose	459 35.97%	613 48.04%	204 15.99%	1,276 100%
Verse	72 36.18%	98 49.25%	29 14.57%	199 100%
Total	531 36.00%	711 48.20%	233 15.80%	1,475 100%

5.4.5 *The parameter clause type*

The adverbial clauses of the corpus were coded for the following clause types: clauses of time, of place, of reason, of concession, of condition, of purpose/result, and of comparison. For the reasons given previously, clauses of purpose and clauses of result are treated as one clause type.[14] Table 5.18 contains the distribution of the realisation possibilities of the verbal syntagm in these clause types.

This table shows a clear preference for the subjunctive in clauses of concession and condition, for the indicative in clauses of time, place, reason and comparison, and for modal constructions in clauses of purpose and result. Typical examples are quoted under [5.37]–[5.42].

> [5.37] *Though the moder be angry, the child shalbe slayn*! (M4 XX MYST DIGBY, p. 102) 'though the mother be angry, the child shall be killed!' [concession]
>
> [5.38] *And if it plese the, sette on that oo syde an ymage of oure Lady and a-nother on that other syde of Seint Iohn* (M4 IR RULE AELR4, p. 15) 'and if it please you, put on the one side a picture of our Lady and another one on the other side of St. John' [condition]

---

[14] Cf. section 5.1.6

Table 5.18 The distribution of the realisation possibilities of the verbal syntagm in ME adverbial clauses across clause types

Clause type	Subjunctive		Indicative		Modal		Total	
Time	101	35.07%	164	56.94%	23	7.99%	288	100%
Place	8	12.70%	46	73.02%	9	14.28%	63	100%
Reason	1	1.64%	52	85.25%	8	13.11%	61	100%
Concession	41	93.18%	3	6.82%			44	100%
Condition	295	68.93%	78	18.22%	55	12.85%	428	100%
Purpose/Result	66	31.58%	47	22.49%	96	45.93%	209	100%
Comparison	19	4.97%	321	84.03%	42	11.00%	382	100%
Total	531	36.00%	711	48.20%	233	15.80%	1,475	100%

[5.39]   *She is honoured over al ther she gooth* (M3 NI FICT CTPROL, p. 108. C1) 'she is greatly respected wherever she goes' [place]

[5.40]   *Corn is an euel & it is cleped þe corn for-as-myche as þe hyde of þe hors with þe flesche. or ellus þe flesche bi him-self. is so harde as þouȝ it were an horne* (M3 IS HANDM HORSES, p. 117) 'corn is an evil, and it is called corn because the skin of the horse together with the flesh or the flesh alone is so hard as if it were a horn' [reason]

[5.41]   *Beoð ofdred of euch mon alswa as þe þeof is* (M1 IR RELT ANCR, p. 90f.) 'be afraid of everybody as the thief is' [comparison]

[5.42]   *Leorne æfre æthweige æt þan wisen, þæt þu muge læren þa unwise*; (MX/1 IR HOM VESPD32, p. 6) 'learn always somewhat from the wise, so that you may teach the unwise;' [purpose/result]

The relative frequency of subjunctives in <u>clauses of concession</u> is even higher in ME than in OE, and although the three examples of indicatives date from subperiod M3 their low number does not confirm the alleged rise of indicative frequency during the ME period (Fischer 1992: 351, Mustanoja 1960: 467–469).

In <u>conditional clauses</u>, too, the share of subjunctives is greater in ME than in OE. In view of the results presented in Moessner's paper (2005: 220–221), which is based on an even larger corpus, this was to be expected. The conjunctions which introduce the conditional clauses of my ME corpus are *if, but (if), how, on this condition, so, without (that)* and *provided (that)*. Only the equivalents of OE *gif* and *buton* occur frequently enough to allow generalisations on the realisation of the following verbal syntagm (cf. Table 5.19).

Obviously the conjunction *if* contributes least to the large shares of subjunctives in ME conditional clauses. The picture obtained from the analysis of the conditional clauses of the ME corpus is more or less the same as that found in the OE corpus.

Table 5.19 The distribution of the realisation possibilities of the verbal syntagm after different conditional conjunctions in the ME corpus

Conjunction	Subjunctive	Indicative	Modal	Total
If	230 66.09%	70 20.12%	48 13.79%	348 100%
But (if)	46 80.70%	5 8.77%	6 10.53%	57 100%
Others	19 82.61%	3 13.04%	1 4.35%	23 100%
Total	295 68.93%	78 18.22%	55 12.85%	428 100%

The small share of subjunctives in <u>clauses of place</u> and <u>clauses of reason</u> confirms the findings of earlier studies (cf. sections 5.3.2 and 5.3.3).

Among the <u>clauses of comparison</u> in the ME corpus, the clauses of equality are introduced by *as*, *alswa as* and *so*, the clauses of inequality by *than*, and the clauses of hypothetical similarity by *swylce* and *as if*. As Table 5.20 shows, the expected subjunctive preference in clauses of hypothetical similarity is attested in the corpus.

Table 5.20 The distribution of the realisation possibilities of the verbal syntagm after different types of ME clauses of comparison

Clause type	Subjunctive	Indicative	Modal	Total
Equality	9 2.65%	295 86.76%	36 10.59%	340 100%
Inequality	6 15.79%	26 68.42%	6 15.79%	38 100%
Hypothetical similarity	4 100%			4 100%
Total	19 4.97%	321 84.03%	42 10.99%	382 99.99%

The only difference between OE and ME clauses of comparison concerns the clauses of inequality. In OE they preferred the subjunctive, in ME the preferred mood is the indicative (cf. example [5.43]).

> [5.43] *he hath a crest of fedres vpon his hed more gret <u>þan the poocok hath</u>* (M3 NI TRAV MAND, p. 31) 'it [= this bird] has a crest of feathers on his head bigger than the peacock has'

The <u>clauses of purpose and result</u> of my corpus are introduced by *that* and *lest*. The latter occurs only in clauses of purpose, whereas *that* can introduce either clause type. A separate analysis of clauses of purpose and result after these conjunctions yields the following distribution of the realisation possibilities of the verbal syntagm (cf. Table 5.21).

This distribution confirms Kikusawa's claim that adverbial *lest*-clauses prefer the subjunctive (2012: 133). This preference amounts to 64.2 per cent in Kikusawa's data, whereas in my corpus all adverbial *lest*-clauses are followed by the subjunctive (cf. example [5.44]).

Table 5.21 The distribution of the realisation possibilities of the verbal syntagm after *that* and *lest* in ME clauses of purpose and result

Conjunction	Subjunctive	Indicative	Modal	Total
That	56 28.14%	47 23.62%	96 48.24%	199 100%
Lest	10 100%			10 100%
Total	66 31.58%	47 22.49%	96 45.93%	209 100%

[5.44] *witeð þer ower ehenen <u>leaste þe heorte edfleo & wende ut</u>* (M1 IR RELT ANCR, p. 30) 'mind your eyes there, that the heart does not flee and go out'

Both the meaning of clauses of purpose introduced by *lest* and the form of their verbal syntagm express root modality. These clauses illustrate modal harmony.

Clauses of purpose and result introduced by *that* stand out for their large number of modal constructions. The modal auxiliaries attested in the corpus are *may* (57 tokens), *shall* (22 tokens), *can* (7 tokens), *will* (4 tokens), *must* (3 tokens), *dare* (2 tokens) and the combination *shall may* (1 token). Not all of them need to express root modality in combination with the following verb. Wischer (2008: 130) argues that in Late OE *willan* and *sculan* were usually used in periphrastic constructions and expressed the modalities volition and obligation, but 'occasionally the constructions with *willan* and *sculan* came close to mark mere future tense'. In ME the expression of future tense was foregrounded, and this development took place earlier in *sculan* than in *willan*. The rare combination *shall may* and most of examples of *shall* and *will* in my corpus suggest an interpretation of mere prediction (cf. examples [5.45] and [5.46]).

[5.45] *it schal ordeyne, rule and mesure þe feruours of Cristis loue and þe visitaciouns of his gracious presence so wiseli and so priuely and so sobirly, <u>þat it schal mowe laste esily and contynuely in þe feelingis and in þe goostli cunfortis of Cristis loue</u>* (M3/4 IR RELT HILTON, p. 25f.) 'it [= the soul] shall ordain, rule and measure the fervours of Christ's love and the visitations of his gracious presence so wisely and so intimately and so soberly that it will easily and continuously be able to remain in the feelings and in the spiritual comfort of Christ's love'

[5.46] *it peliþ awei þe heere up bi þe rotes so <u>þat þe hors wille rubbe him-self þat þe necke & þe dok of his taile schal be al bare</u>* (M3 IS HANDM HORSES, p. 103) 'it [= the scab] uproots the hair so that the horse is going to rub itself so that the neck and the end of its tail will be completely bare'

The interpretation of these examples as clauses of result, the occurrence of *so* in the matrix clause and the denotation of future of the modal auxiliary *shall* are features expressing epistemic modality.

The overall result to be derived from the more detailed analysis of clauses of purpose and result is that the clauses introduced by *lest* are unambiguous clauses of purpose and express root modality, which is underlined by their subjunctive verbal syntagms. The majority of the clauses of purpose and result introduced by *that* are unambiguous clauses of result and express epistemic modality, which is underlined by modal constructions with *shall* and *will* as markers of futurity.

If one only considers the figures for clauses of time in Table 5.18, this clause type clearly belongs to those favouring the indicative. Earlier studies suggest, however, that the form of the verbal syntagm in clauses of time depends on the introductory conjunction. The clauses of time in my corpus are introduced by the following conjunctions: *when, what tyme that, ayen, ere, as soon as, oþþæt, unto the time, that, on that dai that, while, as, as long as, so, during the time, till, unto, þonne, siððen, nu* and *after*. When we assign these conjunctions according to the time relation between adverbial clause and matrix clause to the subclasses anteriority, posteriority and temporal overlap, the distribution of the realisation possibilities of the verbal syntagm yields the picture presented in Table 5.22.

Table 5.22 The distribution of the realisation possibilities of the verbal syntagm in the subclasses anteriority, posteriority and temporal overlap of the ME corpus

Time relation	Subjunctive	Indicative	Modal	Total
Anteriority	18 12.16%	122 82.43%	8 5.41%	148 100%
Posteriority	79 79.00%	13 13.00%	8 8.00%	100 100%
Overlap	4 10.00%	29 72.50%	7 17.50%	40 100%
Total	101 35.07%	164 56.94%	23 7.99%	288 100%

Only clauses of time which denote an event that is posterior to that in the corresponding matrix clause show a clear preference for the subjunctive. The conjunctions of the corpus which were assigned to this subclass are *ayen, ere, oþþæt, unto the time, unto, till*. The prominent representatives are *ere* (17 tokens) and *till* (74 tokens).

When these figures are compared with those from from OE corpus, it turns out that the conjunctions *ere* and *oþþæt* are preferably followed by the subjunctive in both periods, whereas *þe hwile/while* changed its mood preference from subjunctive in OE to indicative in ME.[15]

---

[15] In the diachronic assessment it is neglected that Callaway assigned *oþþæt* to the subclass contemporaneous actions.

5.4.6 The parameter matrix clause

Statements about the influence of features of the matrix clause on the form of the verbal syntagm in adverbial clauses are rare in earlier studies. Fischer (1992: 356–357) mentions a positive influence of a negative main clause on the use of the subjunctive in temporal clauses introduced by *ere*, and of an imperative or a volitional verb in the matrix clause on the use of the subjunctive in temporal clauses introduced by *till*, and she reminds her readers that in OE clauses of inequality favoured the subjunctive when they were followed by an affirmative main clause. Since an influence of the features negation and volition in the matrix clause on the form of the verbal syntagm in the adverbial clauses was tested in the OE corpus, the ME corpus was coded for the same features. The identification of the matrix clauses was again one of the difficulties in the coding process (cf. example [5.47]).

[5.47] *þou schalt neuere praie þe lasse, <u>whanne grace of deuocioun is</u>*
        <u>wiþdrawe, and temptaciouns and tribulaciouns comen upon þe</u>, þan
        <u>whanne þou hast grace of deuocioun withoute temptacioun</u> (M3/4 IR
        RELT HILTON, p. 3) 'you shall never pray the less when the grace
        of devotion is withdrawn and temptations and tribulations come over
        you than when you have the grace of devotion without temptation'

The matrix clause of the first temporal clause is *þou schalt neuere praie þe lasse*, that of the second is deleted.

5.4.6.1 Volition
Verbal syntagms in the matrix clause expressed by subjunctives, imperatives or modal constructions were coded as expressions of volition. In a first step I tested the feature volition in all types of adverbial clauses.

Only little more than one third (35.93 per cent) of the adverbial clauses depend on matrix clauses that are marked for volition. Strong markers of volition, namely imperatives, are exactly twice as frequent as subjunctives, but both volition markers have the same influence on the form of the verbal syntagm in adverbial clauses. This is different from OE, where the influence of a subjunctive in the matrix clause was greater than that of an imperative. Although ME modal constructions in the matrix clause trigger a smaller share of subjunctives in the dependent clause than the other markers of volition, their influence on subjunctive frequency in the dependent clause is greater than in OE. The figures in Table 5.23 support the general claim that an expression of volition in the matrix clause favours the occurrence of a subjunctive in the corresponding adverbial clause. The share of subjunctives in all adverbial clauses (36 per cent) is raised to 51.32 per cent when only those 530 adverbial

Table 5.23 The distribution of the realisation possibilities of the verbal syntagm depending on ME matrix clauses with expressions of volition

Volition	Subjunctive	Indicative	Modal	Total
Subjunctive	60 58.82%	29 28.43%	13 12.75%	102 100%
Imperative	117 57.35%	61 29.90%	26 12.75%	204 100%
Modal	95 42.41%	80 35.71%	49 21.88%	224 100%
Non-volition	259 27.41%	541 57.25%	145 15.34%	945 100%
Total	531 36.00%	711 48.20%	233 15.80%	1,475 100%

clauses are considered that depend on a matrix clause with an expression of volition.

In a second step I tested the influence of an expression of volition in the matrix clause on selected types of adverbial clauses. To this end, the adverbial clauses depending on matrix clauses with the feature volition which had already proved to prefer the subjunctive were separated from the rest. Among the first group are all concessive clauses, conditional clauses introduced by conjunctions other than *if*, clauses of inequality and of hypothetical similarity, clauses of negative purpose introduced by *lest*, and temporal clauses of the subclass posteriority. The second group contains clauses of place, clauses of reason, clauses of condition introduced by *if*, clauses of purpose and result introduced by *that*, clauses of equality, and clauses of anteriority and of overlap. The distribution of the realisation possibilities of the verbal syntagm in these two groups of adverbial clauses is shown in Tables 5.24a and 5.24b.

From a comparison of the figures in Table 5.24a with those in Tables 5.18–5.22 we can derive a clear influence of the feature volition in the matrix clause on subjunctive frequency in the adverbial clauses of the first group. The feature volition increases the share of subjunctives in clauses of inequality and hypothetical similarity by nearly 20 per cent, and in clauses of concession and in clauses of posteriority by about seven per cent. It has no effect on clauses of purpose and result introduced by *lest*; all *lest*-clauses of the corpus have a subjunctive verb irrespective of the presence of the feature volition in the matrix clause. By contrast, in clauses of condition introduced by conjunctions other than *if* an expression of volition in the matrix clause has a negative effect on the share of subjunctives.

Table 5.24b also shows a positive effect of the feature volition in the matrix clause on the share of subjunctives in the dependent clause. The effect is greatest in clauses of place (nearly 14 per cent) and in the sub-clauses of anteriority and temporal overlap (ca. 10 per cent). Only in clauses of reason does the feature volition in the matrix clause have a negative effect on the share of subjunctives in the dependent clause.

By way of conclusion we note that the feature volition in the matrix clause leads to an increase of subjunctive frequency in nearly all types of

Table 5.24a The distribution of the realisation possibilities of the verbal syntagm in the first group of ME adverbial clauses depending on matrix clauses with expressions of volition

Clause type	Subjunctive	Indicative	Modal	Total
Concession	18 100%			18 100%
Condition ≠ *if*	20 71.43%	3 10.71%	5 17.86%	28 100%
Inequal/Hyp. similarity	6 42.86%	8 57.14%		14 100%
Purpose/Result *lest*	6 100%			6 100%
Posteriority	57 86.36%	3 4.55%	6 9.09%	66 100%
Total	107 81.06%	14 10.61%	11 8.33%	132 100%

Table 5.24b The distribution of the realisation possibilities of the verbal syntagm in the second group of ME adverbial clauses depending on matrix clauses with expressions of volition

Clause type	Subjunctive	Indicative	Modal	Total
Place	4 26.67%	11 73.33%		15 100%
Reason		13 86.67%	2 13.33%	15 100%
Condition *if*	124 68.89%	26 14.44%	30 16.67%	180 100%
Purpose/Result *that*	17 32.69%	2 3.85%	33 63.46%	52 100%
Equality	3 5.17%	49 84.48%	6 10.35%	58 100%
Time ≠ Posteriority	17 21.80%	55 70.51%	6 7.69%	78 100%
Total	165 41.46%	156 39.20%	77 19.34%	398 100%

adverbial clause. The influence of the feature volition is equally strong when it is expressed by the subjunctive or by the imperative.

5.4.6.2 Negation

An influence of the presence or absence of negation in the matrix clause on subjunctive frequency in the adverbial clause is observed by Fischer (1992: 356–357). Clauses of posteriority, in particular *ere*-clauses, are expected to favour the subjunctive after negative matrix clauses, and clauses of inequality are expected to favour the indicative after negative matrix clauses. The results of a test of the influence of an expression of negation in the matrix clause on the form of the verbal syntagm in the adverbial clause are presented in Table 5.25.

Only about 10 per cent of the adverbial clauses of my corpus depend on a matrix clause that contains a negative element. Therefore, generalisations

Table 5.25 The distribution of the realisation possibilities of the verbal syntagm in ME adverbial clauses depending on negated matrix clauses

Clause type	Subjunctive	Indicative	Modal	Total
Time	8 33.33%	14 58.34%	2 8.33%	24 100%
Place		5 83.33%	1 16.67%	6 100%
Reason		13 100%		13 100%
Concession	13 86.67%	2 13.33%		15 100%
Condition	34 75.56%	8 17.78%	3 6.66%	45 100%
Purpose/Result	6 85.71%		1 14.29%	7 100%
Comparison		32 84.21%	6 15.79%	38 100%
Total	61 41.22%	74 50.00%	13 8.78%	148 100%

about the form of the verbal syntagm in these clauses can have only a tentative nature. The share of subjunctives in conditional clauses and in clauses of purpose and result is larger after negated matrix clauses than after matrix clauses generally, in all other clause types it is smaller.

In clauses of inequality a large share of indicatives was expected. My corpus contains thirty-eight clauses of comparison after negated matrix clauses. Of these, ten belong to the subclass clauses of inequality, and in eight of them the verbal syntagm is an indicative (= 80 per cent), and in the remaining two it is a modal construction. This result strongly supports Fischer's claim, and a comparison with Table 5.20 shows that it is indeed the presence of a negative element in the matrix clause that increases indicative frequency in clauses of inequality.

As Fischer's observation about the form of the verbal syntagm in clauses of time was restricted to the subclass posteriority, I extracted clauses of posteriority from the overall number of time clauses after a negated matrix clause. This procedure left me with seven examples with these features, and in five of them the verbal syntagm is a subjunctive (= 71.43 per cent). This share is lower than that in clauses of posteriority after matrix clauses generally and thus does not support Fischer's claim. A negative influence of negation in the matrix clause on subjunctive frequency in clauses of posteriority was also observed in the OE corpus (cf. section 5.2.6.2).

5.4.7 *Summary*

In the first part of the ME section of this chapter earlier studies on subjunctive frequency in adverbial clauses were reviewed. They deal with the linguistic features clause type, choice of conjunction, presence or absence of expressions of volition in the matrix clause, negative elements in the matrix clause as well as the extralinguistic factors date of composition, regional dialect, text category, and the dichotomy prose vs. poetry.

The second part contains the analysis of the 1,475 relevant adverbial clauses in the corpus (= 8.86 adverbial clauses per 1,000 words). The relative frequency, which is lower than in the OE corpus, is a consequence of the fewer forms that are overtly marked for subjunctive: second and third person singular and plural present in OE, second and third person singular only in ME. The parameters which were identified previously as relevant for the distribution of the realisation possibilities of the verbal syntagm in adverbial clauses were tested one after the other, and the results were compared with those obtained for the OE corpus and with the expectations raised by the findings in previous studies.

Subjunctive frequency as well as indicative frequency decreases during the ME period, and this decrease is compensated for by an increase of modal constructions. Yet between the subperiods there is a wave-like development in all three realisation possibilities. The unilateral development observed in OE is not continued in ME. An explanation for this heterogeneous picture has to be sought in the different developments in individual clause types.

Adverbial clauses with a larger than average frequency occur in ME in the prototypical text categories IS, IR and EX. IS is the only text category which clearly favours the subjunctive. Next on the subjunctive frequency rank are the text categories STA and EX. The large share of subjunctives in the former was interpreted as a generalisation of Moessner's finding based on the analysis of conditional clauses only that the subjunctive is the preferred realisation of the verbal syntagm in instructive texts. Since the text categories IS and STA were identified as high-frequency text categories and at the same time also as subjunctive favouring text categories in OE adverbial clauses, the parameter text category was established as a diachronically robust parameter.

The parameter dialect has a notable influence on the form of the verbal syntagm in ME adverbial clauses as well. The relative subjunctive frequency rises from north to south and reaches its peak in the Kentish dialect; indicative frequency is inversely distributed. The share of modal constructions does not vary greatly between dialects. The subjunctive favouring tendency of the Kentish dialect could also be observed in OE. The stronghold of the subjunctive in southern, especially in Kentish texts, is in line with Moessner's finding (2005: 221–223) that northern texts disfavour the subjunctive.

An influence of the parameter prose vs. poetry on subjunctive frequency cannot be derived from the figures of the ME corpus.

The parameter clause type has a significant influence on subjunctive frequency in both periods. ME clauses of concession and condition show a clear preference for the subjunctive, and clauses of time, place, reason and comparison prefer the indicative. Clauses of purpose and result prefer the subjunctive in OE, whereas in ME they are characterised

by a large share of modal constructions. The rise of indicative frequency in ME clauses of concession claimed by Fischer (1992: 351) and
Mustanoja (1960: 467–469) is not confirmed by the three examples
in the ME corpus. The share of subjunctives in conditional clauses is
greater in ME than in OE, and this is in line with the results presented
in Moessner's paper (2005: 220–221), which is based on an even bigger
corpus.

In clauses of time, of condition, of comparison, and in clauses of
purpose and result, individual conjunctions were tested for their influence on the form of the verbal syntagm. The conjunction *gif/if* contributes
less to subjunctive frequency than the other conditional conjunctions.
Variants of the conjunction *swa*, which introduce the subclass clauses of
equality, are responsible for the large share of indicatives in clauses of
comparison. In clauses of purpose and result the conjunction *lest*, which
introduces clauses of negative purpose, governs only the subjunctive. The
subclass posteriority mostly introduced by *ere* and *till* raises the share of
subjunctive in clauses of time.

An expression of volition in the matrix clause leads to an increase
of subjunctive frequency in nearly all clause types. The influence of the
feature volition is equally strong when it is expressed by a subjunctive
or by an imperative, and is weaker when it is expressed by a modal
construction.

The number of adverbial clauses depending on a negated matrix clause
is low in the corpora of both periods, in particular in clauses of place and
in clauses of reason. More general claims about the influence of negation
in the matrix clause were difficult to test because of the small number of
examples in the ME corpus.

5.5 Early Modern English adverbial clauses: descriptive parameters

Kortmann (1997: 294) identified EModE as the period with the highest
number of adverbial subordinators. The inventory of conjunctions
changed from ME to EModE through the addition of new elements
(e.g. *albeit, because, considering, except, howbeit, provided, seeing, to
the end, to the intent*), but also through the acquisition of new meanings by already existing elements (e.g. the conjunction *while* acquired a
causal meaning in addition to its earlier temporal meaning, the conjunction *where* acquired a contrastive-concessive meaning in addition to its
original locative meaning). Although the amount of polyfunctionality of
EModE adverbial conjunctions is smaller than in the previous periods, it
is still large enough to require a careful scrutiny of the context before an
example can be confidently analysed as a representative of this or that
semantic clause type.

Information about EModE adverbial clauses can be gleaned from handbooks and from more specialised studies. I will deal with these sources first and then present the analysis of my corpus.

5.5.1 Clauses of time

EModE handbooks (Barber 1997, Franz 1939, Görlach 1991, Rissanen 1999) single out the conjunctions *before, ere* and *till* as those that prefer the subjunctive. More generally, the subjunctive is characterised as the mood which expresses hypothetical or unreal meaning (Nevalainen 2006). The authors do not agree on the competitors of the subjunctive: some suggest the indicative, others modal constructions. Among the former is Trnka (1930) in his diachronic study of the English verb from Caxton to Dryden. Indicatives are identified as the strongest competitor of subjunctives by Moessner (2006: 254).

5.5.2 Clauses of place

EModE clauses of place are not considered to be worth separate studies, and handbook authors seem to take it for granted that the mood of their verbal syntagms is the indicative.

5.5.3 Clauses of reason

Rissanen (1999: 305) notes that '[t]he mood of the causal clauses is mostly indicative'.

5.5.4 Clauses of concession

There is general agreement among the authors of EModE handbooks (Barber 1997, Franz 1939, Görlach 1991, Nevalainen 2006) that the subjunctive is often used in clauses of concession and that it signals doubt, hypothesis or incredulity; indicatives and modal constructions are mentioned as alternatives. Moessner's corpus study (2006) revealed a share of 80 per cent of subjunctives in concessive clauses in the first subperiod of the EModE part of the HC, which, however, shrinks to 45 per cent in the last subperiod.

5.5.5 Clauses of condition

EModE clauses of condition are the clause type which has received most attention, not only in general reference works but also in individual studies. The subjunctive is identified as the most frequent realisation when a hypothetical or unreal meaning is involved (Barber 1997, Franz

1939, Görlach 1991, Kovács 2009, Nevalainen 2006). Most of the specialised publications concentrate on conditional clauses with a particular
conjunction and/or are based on a particular text category (Schlüter
2009: the conjunction *on condition*; Claridge 2007: the conjunction *if* in
the politics and science files of the *Lampeter Corpus*; Facchinetti 2001:
the conjunction *if* in the law files of the HC and ARCHER; González-
Álvarez 2003: conditional clauses in two letter corpora). In Moessner
(2006) the distribution of the realisation possibilities of the verbal
syntagm in conditional clauses introduced by a variety of conjunctions is
investigated in the three EModE subperiods of the multi-genre HC. Her
figures show that conditional clauses are not only the most frequent type
of adverbial clauses in her corpus, but also that the share of subjunctives
in conditional clauses is well above average in all three subperiods.

5.5.6. *Clauses of purpose and result*

Subjunctives, modal constructions but also indicatives as realisations of
the verbal syntagm in clauses of purpose and result are mentioned in reference works (Barber1997: 173; Rissanen 1999: 304) and in the overview
article by Kovács (2009: 84). Trnka (1930: 70) reports an exclusive use
of the subjunctive in clauses of purpose. Only two research articles use
a corpus-linguistic approach and provide quantitative results. Moessner
(2006: 254) notes a decrease of subjunctives in clauses of purpose and
result from the beginning to the end of the EModE period. Auer (2008:
153), who studied *lest*-constructions, found that in these the subjunctive
survived only until the middle of the seventeenth century.

5.5.7 *Clauses of comparison*

In most EModE reference works the realisation of the verbal syntagm
in clauses of comparison is not mentioned at all. Only Rissanen (1999:
315–319) distinguishes clauses of equality, clauses of inequality and
clauses in which the basis of comparison is hypothetical. In this last type
the finite verb of the clause is in the subjunctive. Kovács's (2009: 85)
description of EModE clauses of comparison paraphrases Rissanen's.

5.5.8 *Summary*

A fair amount of subjunctives can be expected in EModE clauses of
time, condition, concession, and purpose and result. The analysis of
my corpus, which will be presented next, additionally includes clauses
of place, of reason and of comparison, allowing us to trace a complete
picture of the development of the subjunctive in all adverbial clauses
across the three periods investigated.

5.6 Adverbial clauses in the EModE corpus

My EModE corpus contains 1,126 relevant adverbial clauses. Relevant are adverbial clauses with a third person singular present tense verb form or with a second person singular present tense verb form after the subject *thou*. The relative frequency of adverbial clauses of 5.78 per 1,000 words is lower than in the ME corpus. The explanation of the steadily decreasing frequency of adverbial clauses from OE to ME and to EModE lies in the decreasing inventory of forms with an overtly marked subjunctive. The verbal syntagms in the EModE corpus are realised as subjunctives (312 = 1.62/1,000 words), as indicatives (557 = 2.88/1,000 words) or as modal constructions (257 = 1.33 words/1,000 words[16]). Examples [5.48]–[5.51] illustrate the realisation possibilities.

> [5.48] *And the Zenith in Sphericall bodies is the Centre of them all, <u>though it bee not so in Astrolabes</u>* (E2 EX SCIO BLUNDEV, p. 155V)
>
> [5.49] *Therefore power, is desired, <u>for it is thoughte also to be good</u>* (E1 XX PHILO BOETHCO, p. 76)
>
> [5.50] <u>*As a Cow must be gentle to her milker*</u>*, so she must bee kindly in her owne nature* (E2 IS HANDO MARKHAM, p. 107)
>
> [5.51] <u>*because it [= marriage] is to effect much of that which it signifies*</u>*, it concerns all that enter into those golden fetters* (E3 IR SERM JETAYLOR, p. 9)

In the following sections the influence of several linguistic and extralinguistic parameters on the distribution of the realisation possibilities of the verbal syntagm in adverbial clauses will be tested.

5.6.1 The parameter date of composition

The files of the EModE corpus are coded for the seventy-year subperiods E1–E3. The distribution of the realisation possibilities of the verbal syntagm across these subperiods is mapped in Table 5.26.

There is a continuous decrease of relative subjunctive frequency, which, however, is not accompanied by a similarly continuous frequency increase of one of its competitors. The share of indicatives decreases between the first two subperiods, but then rises to a value above the one in E1. Overall, there is also a frequency rise of modal constructions, although their frequency development is not linear.

It is quite interesting to compare these results with those reported in the earlier studies by Auer (2005, 2006) and Moessner (2006), which are

---

[16] This figure contains seven instances of the patterns 'be + to + infinitive' and 'be + wont + to + infinitive'.

Table 5.26 The distribution of the realisation possibilities of the verbal syntagm in adverbial clauses across subperiods E1–E3

Subperiod	Subjunctive	Indicative	Modal	Total
E1	129 34.13%	195 51.59%	54 14.28%	378 100%
E2	104 28.65%	158 43.53%	101 27.82%	363 100%
E3	79 20.52%	204 52.99%	102 26.49%	385 100%
Total	312 27.71%	557 49.47%	257 22.82%	1,126 100%

also based on the HC and cover several semantic classes of EModE adverbial clauses. All of them note a continuous decrease of relative subjunctive frequency in EModE, but when it comes to the question of which was the strongest competitor of the subjunctive, Auer's figures tell a different story from Moessner's (2006) and those in the present book. The answer to be derived from Auer's tables (2005: Table 3, 2006: Table 4) clearly is that modal constructions far outnumbered indicatives at the end of the EModE period. Moessner (2006: Table 4) comes to a different conclusion, namely that the subjunctive was replaced by the indicative. One explanation for the conflicting results may be the identification of the relevant verbal syntagms: Auer included only third person singular forms, whereas in the present book and in Moessner (2006) verbal forms of the second person singular are also included when they are combined with the subject *thou*. It should also be borne in mind that the bottom-up procedure adopted in the present book produced a larger inventory of introductory conjunctions than those in the earlier studies, which used semi-automatic search routines. This feature and the different corpus sizes of Moessner (2006) and in the present book explain the different absolute figures and relative frequencies.

5.6.2 *The parameter text category*

Adverbial clauses are unequally distributed across the different text categories of the EModE corpus. Table 5.27 shows their absolute numbers and their relative frequencies per 1,000 words.

The relative frequency of adverbial clauses is lower in the EModE corpus than in the corpora of the earlier periods. As in the ME corpus, the relative frequency of adverbial clauses is highest in the category IS; the categories XX and STA come next on the frequency rank scale. The distribution of the realisation possibilities of the verbal syntagm in these text categories is therefore most telling (cf. Table 5.28).

In six out of the seven text categories the indicative is the most frequent realisation of the verbal syntagm; more than every second adverbial clause contains an indicative verb form. IS is the only text category with a notably larger share of subjunctives than the other text categories. It is represented by extracts from educational treatises by Roger Ascham and

Table 5.27 The distribution of EModE adverbial clauses across prototypical text categories

Category	Adverbial clauses/ absolute numbers	Adverbial clauses/ 1,000 words
STA	290	7.89
IS	243	9.20
IR	113	7.32
NI	35	2.22
NN	67	1.35
EX	146	6.25
XX	232	9.07
Total	1,126	5.82

Table 5.28 The distribution of the realisation possibilities of the verbal syntagm in EModE adverbial clauses across prototypical text categories

Category	Subjunctive	Indicative	Modal	Total
STA	81 27.93%	83 28.62%	126 43.45%	290 100%
IS	85 34.98%	127 52.26%	31 12.76%	243 100%
IR	29 25.66%	75 66.37%	9 7.97%	113 100%
NI	9 25.72%	20 57.14%	6 17.14%	35 100%
NN	19 28.36%	40 59.70%	8 11.94%	67 100%
EX	35 23.97%	78 53.43%	33 22.60%	146 100%
XX	54 23.28%	134 57.76%	44 18.96%	232 100%
Total	312 27.71%	557 49.47%	257 22.82%	1,126 100%

John Locke and by extracts from handbooks that deal with the effects of several sorts of wine, with the proper handling of horses, with running a dairy and with successful angling of different sorts of fish. All these texts give advice on how to do things well in a particular situation. Examples [5.52]–[5.54] illustrate the use of the subjunctive in texts of category IS in the three subperiods:

[5.52] *But if the childe misse, either in forgetting a worde, or in chaunging a good with a worse, or misordering the sentence, I would not haue the master, either froune, or chide with him* (E1 IS/EX EDUC ASCH, p. 183)

[5.53] *then you shall adde to a woollen cloath, or more if neede require till his haire* [= the horse's] *fall smooth againe* (E2 IS HANDO MARKHAM, p. 75)

[5.54] *though a (^Chub^) be by you and many others reckoned the worst of (^fish^), yet you shall see I'll make it a good Fish, by dressing it* (E3 IS HANDO WALTON, p. 215)

One of the categories which had a large share of subjunctives in ME has an exceptionally large share of modal constructions in the EModE corpus. This is the category STA, which contributes the biggest number of adverbial clauses to the corpus and therefore requires particular attention. A replacement of the subjunctive by modal constructions with *shall* was detected by Facchinetti (2001: 140–141) in conditional clauses in texts of the category STA. The auxiliary *shall* plays an exceptional role in adverbial clauses – in particular in clauses of condition – in my corpus, too. In 112 out of the 126 modal constructions the auxiliary is *shall*, and the corresponding adverbial clauses denote qualifications of provisions as in example [5.55].

> [5.57] And *if any such Sheriff Goaler or Keeper of Prison shall forswear and perjure himselfe and shall bee thereof lawfully convicted* such Sheriff Goaler or Keeper of Prison shall incurr and suffer such Penalties as are now in Force and may by Law bee inflicted upon Persons convicted of Perjury (E3 STA LAW STAT7, p. VII, 75)

The verbal syntagms of these qualifications were usually expressed by adverbial clauses with a subjunctive verb form in the earlier periods (cf. sections 5.2.2 and 5.4.2).

5.6.3 *The parameter clause type*

The adverbial clauses of the EModE corpus were coded for the following clause types: clauses of time, of place, of reason, of concession, of condition, of purpose/result, and for comparison.[17] Table 5.29 contains the distribution of the realisation possibilities of the verbal syntagm in these clause types.

Table 5.29 The distribution of the realisation possibilities of the verbal syntagm in EModE adverbial clauses across clause types

Clause type	Subjunctive	Indicative	Modal	Total
Time	32 14.35%	166 74.44%	25 11.21%	223 100%
Place		20 55.56%	16 44.44%	36 100%
Reason		80 84.21%	15 15.79%	95 100%
Concession	19 52.78%	13 36.11%	4 11.11%	36 100%
Condition	228 64.23%	41 11.55%	86 24.22%	355 100%
Purpose/Result	31 29.81%	29 27.88%	44 42.31%	104 100%
Comparison	2 0.72%	208 75.09%	67 24.19%	277 100%
Total	312 27.71%	557 49.47%	257 22.82%	1,126 100%

---

[17] For the arguments in favour of treating the clauses of purpose and clauses of result under one heading, cf. section 5.1.6.

There is a complementary distribution of subjunctives and indicatives in clauses of concession and clauses of condition on the one hand, and in clauses of time, of place, of reason and of comparison on the other. The former favour subjunctives, the latter indicatives. Clauses of purpose and result do not really prefer one of the realisation possibilities. Although the subjunctive shares in clauses of concession and of condition are smaller in the EModE corpus than in the ME corpus, these clause types still contribute most to the overall number of subjunctives in adverbial clauses.

In view of the comments in EModE handbooks on subjunctive use, and in comparison with subjunctive frequency in the ME corpus, the small share of subjunctives in the clauses of time of the EModE corpus was not to be expected. Yet it is not so surprising when we focus on the conjunctions *before* and *till*, which introduce temporal clauses of posteriority. They introduce forty-four clauses of time in the EModE corpus, and in thirty of them (= 68.18 per cent) the verbal syntagm is realised by a subjunctive. This share is not much smaller than the 79 per cent of the ME corpus (cf. Table 5.22).

The tendency of clauses of place and clauses of reason to favour the indicative, which was already noted in the ME corpus, is even stronger in the EModE corpus, where the subjunctive is not used at all in these clause types.

The most noteworthy change in conditional clauses is not their slight decrease of subjunctive frequency between ME and EModE, but the frequency of subjunctives after *if*. As in the ME corpus, *if* is the most frequent conjunction in the EModE corpus, too, but it is followed by the subjunctive more often than the other conditional conjunctions; subjunctive share after *if*: 67.27 per cent, vs. subjunctive share after other conditional conjunctions: 53.57 per cent.

The share of subjunctives in clauses of purpose and result can be attributed to the conjunctions *to the entent*, *lest* and *so as*. Although *to the entent* and *lest* are low-frequency conjunctions with one and six occurrences respectively, the subjunctive is to be expected after them since both introduce clauses of purpose.[18] The conjunction *so as*, which is neither in Kortmann's list of conjunctions (1997: 292–294) nor in Quirk et al.'s (1985: 1107–1108), is attested in my corpus with twenty-one occurrences and with a share of 76.19 per cent of subjunctives.[19]

---

[18] The figures in Auer (2008: Table 1) differ from mine. It may be that Auer's fifteen tokens of *lest* with a subjunctive in subperiods E2 and E3 include some instances of the complementiser *lest*.

[19] The *OED* lists *so as* with a first attestation from 1523 and paraphrases it as 'in such away that, so that' (*OED*, s.v. *so*).

[5.56]   *then lay in your butter, and presse it downe hard within the same, and when your pot is filled, then couer the top thereof with salt <u>so as no butter be seene</u>* (E2 IS HANDO MARKHAM, p. 113)

[5.57]   *Againe the Azimuth of the Sunne is a great Circle, passing through the Zenith and the Centre of the Sunne in what part of the heauen so euer he be, <u>so as he be aboue the Horizon</u>, which Circle deuideth the Horizon into two equall parts by crossing the same in two points opposite* (E2 EX SCIO BLUNDEV, p. 155R)

The adverbial clause in example [5.56] can be interpreted as a clause of purpose or as a clause of result, thus supporting my decision to treat these clause types together. The adverbial clause in example [5.57] is undoubtedly a clause of result. The subjunctives in both examples show that a claim of a prevailing indicative in clauses of result cannot be supported from my data.

5.6.4 *The parameter matrix clause*

The form of the matrix clause seems to have lost its influence on the form of the verbal syntagm in adverbial clauses, since it is neither mentioned in the EModE reference works nor in the specialised studies on individual adverbial clause types. Since volition and negation in the matrix clause proved to influence subjunctive frequency in OE and in ME, my EModE corpus was also coded for these features.

5.6.4.1 Volition

Verbal syntagms in the matrix clauses realised by subjunctives, imperatives or modal constructions were coded as containing a feature of volition. Table 5.30 contains the distribution of the realisation possibilities of the verbal syntagm in adverbial clauses depending on matrix clauses with and without the feature of volition.

Table 5.30 The distribution of the realisation possibilities of the verbal syntagm in EModE adverbial clauses depending on matrix clauses with and without expressions of volition

Adv. cl. Matrix	Subjunctive	Indicative	Modal	Total
Subjunctive	29 51.79%	20 35.71%	7 12.50%	56 100%
Imperative	6 33.33%	9 50.00%	3 16.67%	18 100%
Modal	83 31.92%	94 36.16%	83 31.92%	260 100%
Non-volition	194 24.49%	434 54.80%	164 20.71%	792 100%
Total	312 27.71%	557 49.47%	257 22.82%	1,126 100%

As in the ME corpus, about one third of adverbial clauses depends on matrix clauses containing a feature of volition in the EModE corpus.

Unlike in the ME corpus, in the EModE matrix clauses only subjunctives as markers of volition govern adverbial clauses with subjunctives as the preferred realisation of the verbal syntagm. All markers of volition in the matrix clause have a weaker influence on the form of the verbal syntagm in the adverbial clause. This is why I did not test the influence of the feature volition in matrix clauses on the verbal syntagms of individual EModE adverbial clause types.

5.6.4.2 Negation

Table 5.31 contains the distribution of the realisation possibilities of the verbal syntagm in adverbial clauses depending on negated and on non-negated matrix clauses.

Table 5.31 The distribution of the realisation possibilities of the verbal syntagm in EModE adverbial clauses depending on negated and non-negated matrix clauses

	Subjunctive	Indicative	Modal	Total
+ Negation	61 34.46%	87 49.15%	29 16.39%	177 100%
– Negation	251 26.45%	470 49.53%	228 24.02%	949 100%
Total	312 27.71%	557 49.47%	257 22.82%	1,126 100%

With 15.72 per cent, the share of adverbial clauses depending on negated matrix clauses is larger than in the ME corpus (cf. section 5.4.6.2). Negation in the matrix clause contributes to a larger share of subjunctives and to a smaller share of modal constructions in adverbial clauses; it has no effect on the share of indicatives in adverbial clauses.

A test of the influence of negation in the matrix clause on the share of subjunctives in the different types of adverbial clauses led to the same result as in the ME corpus. Only in clauses of condition and in clauses of purpose and result is the share of subjunctives larger after negated matrix clauses than after adverbial clauses generally (cf. Table 5.29). Table 5.32

Table 5.32 The distribution of the realisation possibilities of the verbal syntagm in different types of EModE adverbial clauses after negated matrix clauses

Clause type	Subjunctive	Indicative	Modal	Total
Time	4 9.76%	29 70.73%	8 19.51%	41 100%
Place		4 80.00%	1 20.00%	5 100%
Reason		7 87.50%	1 12.50%	8 100%
Concession	1 33.33%	2 66.67%		3 100%
Condition	48 73.85%	9 13.85%	8 12.30%	65 100%
Purpose/Result	8 66.67%		4 33.33%	12 100%
Comparison		36 83.72%	7 16.28%	43 100%
Total	61 34.46%	87 49.15%	29 16.39%	177 100%

shows the distribution of the realisation possibilities of the verbal syntagm in different types of adverbial clauses after negated matrix clauses.

5.6.5 Summary

The review of EModE reference works and specialised studies on subjunctive use in adverbial clauses revealed that the subjunctive was to be expected only in a subset of clauses of time and of comparison, more frequently in clauses of condition, of concession, and of purpose and result.

The analysis of the 1,126 verbal syntagms of my EModE corpus showed that with 5.78 per 1,000 words the relative frequency of adverbial clauses is again lower than in the preceding period. The indicative is the most frequent realisation (557 occurrences = 2.88/1,000 words), followed by the subjunctive (312 occurrences = 1.62/1,000 words) and modal constructions (257 occurrences = 1.33/1,000 words).

There is a continually decreasing subjunctive frequency in EModE, whereas the frequency development of the other two realisations is not unidirectional. At the end of the EModE period the indicative is the preferred realisation. The discrepancy between this result and Auer's (2005, 2006) was explained as a consequence of different ways of identifying relevant data (inclusion vs. non-inclusion of second person singular verb forms) and different research methods (close reading vs. semi-automatic research routine).

The text category IS stands out as the one with the highest density of adverbial clauses, and at the same time it is the only one with a notably larger share of subjunctives than in the other clause types. This is a repetition of the situation in the ME corpus. The large share of modal constructions in the texts of category STA was interpreted as a consequence of a change of genre conventions, which according to Facchinetti (2001) is especially salient in conditional clauses in the provisions part of statutory texts.

The parameter clause type divides the EModE adverbial clauses into two groups. Clauses of concession and clauses of condition prefer the subjunctive; clauses of time, of place, of reason and clauses of comparison prefer the indicative. Although the subjunctive shares in clauses of concession and condition are smaller than in the ME corpus, these clause types still contribute most to the overall number of subjunctives in EModE adverbial clauses. In clauses of purpose and result, where the three realisations are more or less equally distributed, the conjunctions *to the entent*, *lest* and *so as* contribute most to the share of subjunctives.

Although an influence of the form of the verbal syntagm in the matrix clause on that of the verbal syntagm in EModE adverbial clauses has not been mentioned in earlier publications, the coding of the feature volition proved especially rewarding. As in the preceding periods it raises subjunctive probability in adverbial clauses, and in EModE this influence is strongest when volition is expressed by a subjunctive. Negation in the matrix clause also contributes to a larger share of subjunctives in adverbial clauses, in particular in clauses of condition and in clauses of purpose and result.

6

A bird's eye view of the English subjunctive

The fine-grained analysis in Chapters 2–5 of subjunctive use in the periods OE, ME and EModE in the different construction types where it is attested makes it now possible to take a bird's eye view and paint a series of four large-scale pictures. The first three are synchronic cuts through the individual periods, and the last meets the promise in the title of this book – it is a condensed history of the English subjunctive from the earliest documents to the beginning of the eighteenth century.[1]

6.1 The subjunctive in Old English

My OE corpus, which comprises 128,200 words, contains 5,969 relevant verbal syntagms. Of relevance are those with a verb form of the second or third person singular present tense or plural present tense. With 2,753 occurrences, main clauses contribute most to the overall figure; they are followed by adverbial clauses (1,642 verbal syntagms), relative clauses (836 verbal syntagms) and noun clauses (738 verbal syntagms).

6.1.1 The subjunctive and its competitors

A comprehensive description of subjunctive use in a given period needs to consider that the subjunctive competes with different forms in the individual construction types. It competes with imperatives and modal constructions in main clauses, with indicatives and modal constructions in all dependent clause types, i.e. in relative clauses, in noun clauses and in adverbial clauses. Table 6.1 shows the distribution of the subjunctive and its competitors in all construction types with absolute numbers in the first line and percentage shares in the second line of each cell.

Read horizontally the last line of Table 6.1 shows that the subjunctive is the preferred realisation of the relevant verbal syntagms of the whole OE corpus. Relative clauses differ from all other construction types, and

---

[1] The figures in the tables of this chapter are based on those of the relevant tables in Chapters 2–5.

Table 6.1 The distribution of the subjunctive and its competitors in the OE corpus

Construction type	Subjunctive	Modal	Imperative	Indicative	Total
Main clause	1,255 45.59%	341 12.39%	1,157 42.02%		2,753 100%
Relative clause	210 25.12%	86 10.29%		540 64.59%	836 100%
Noun clause	450 60.98%	85 11.52%		203 27.50%	738 100%
Adverbial clause	865 52.68%	178 10.84%		599 36.48%	1,642 100%
Total	2,780 46.58%	690 11.56%	1,157 19.38%	1,342 22.48%	5,969 100%

the indicative is the preferred realisation of their verbal syntagms.[2] In main clauses a large share of subjunctives was to be expected, because only main clauses with verbal syntagms expressing root modality (sub-types bouletic and deontic modality) were included in the corpus; main clauses with indicative verbal syntagms were excluded by definition.

Read vertically the table reveals that larger shares of subjunctives than in the whole corpus are found in noun clauses and adverbial clauses; in main clauses their share is only slightly below that of the whole corpus.[3] Modal constructions do not play a big role as markers of root modality in any of the four construction types in the OE corpus.

The lesson to be learnt from these figures is that in nearly all syntactic environments where the subjunctive is attested in OE, it keeps its ground very firmly against its competitors; its position is weakest in relative clauses. In the following sections I will explore which parameters contribute most to its strength, and I will first consider those parameters that are relevant in all construction types.

6.1.2 *The influence of linguistic and extralinguistic parameters on subjunctive use in all construction types*

6.1.2.1 The parameter second person
Only in the second person does the subjunctive compete with the imperative. Although this holds only for main clauses in OE, verbal syntagms of the second person are worth a closer look (cf. Table 6.2), since it was claimed in earlier publications that subjunctives of the second person were next to non-existent (Mitchell 1985: 378, Rütten 2017: 202).

Compared to the 5,969 verbal syntagms of the whole corpus, those of the second person make up just about 25 per cent, and the great majority of them are imperatives.

The parameter second person has the biggest influence on the realisation of the verbal syntagm in main clauses. In second person verbal syntagms the share of imperatives is more than twice as big as in the whole corpus. With about 90 per cent, it is the most frequent realisation of the verbal syntagm in main clauses, and it expresses root modality more strongly than the subjunctive and modal constructions. Their shares amount to a mere six per cent and a little more than three per cent respectively.

In relative clauses and in adverbial clauses the parameter second person also has a negative influence on subjunctive frequency. It is stronger in relative clauses, where second person verbal syntagms in the subjunctive

---

[2] The preferred realisations are in bold type in the tables of this chapter.
[3] Shaded cells contain frequencies which contribute more to the overall frequency of the measured feature than the frequencies in the other cells.

Table 6.2 The distribution of the subjunctive and its competitors in OE verbal syntagms of the second person in all construction types

Construction type	Subjunctive	Modal	Imperative	Indicative	Total
Main clause	77 6.03%	44 3.45%	1,156 90.52%		1,277 100%
Relative clause		4 14.81%		23 85.19%	27 100%
Noun clause	53 69.74%	11 14.47%		12 15.79%	76 100%
Adverbial clause	57 42.22%	18 13.33%		60 44.45%	135 100%
Total	187 12.35%	77 5.08%	1,156 76.30%	95 6.27%	1,515 100%

do not occur at all. In both construction types the indicative prevails in second person verbal syntagms.

Noun clause is the only construction type where the parameter second person has a positive influence on subjunctive frequency. Its share is about 10 per cent bigger in second person verbal syntagms than in the whole corpus, and this is at the expense of indicative frequency.

From the figures in Table 6.1 and Table 6.2 it is to be concluded that the claim of the subjunctive as the most frequent marker of root modality in OE relies on its occurrence in first and third person verbal syntagms. Only in the construction type noun clause is the subjunctive the most frequent form of the verbal syntagm irrespective of the parameter second person.

6.1.2.2 The parameter date of composition

It is generally agreed that subjunctive use decreased in the history of English. There is less agreement on when this development started and what construction(s) replaced it. So far we have even less knowledge about the contribution of the individual construction types to the overall development. These are the topics at issue in this section (cf. Table 6.3).

The frequency decrease of the subjunctive set in right after the first subperiod, and this development continued all through the OE period. The frequencies of modal constructions and of indicatives increased from subperiod to subperiod, but at the end of the OE period only the indicative had surpassed subjunctive frequency. Of the construction types in which the indicative competed with the subjunctive it was construction type noun clause which contributed least to this development (cf. Table 4.1).

6.1.2.3 The parameter text category

All subcorpora of my OE corpus are coded for the seven text categories distinguished in the HC. Table 6.4 contains the distribution of the realisation possibilities of the verbal syntagms in all text categories in the OE corpus.

Read horizontally, the table shows that in text categories STA, IR, NI and XX the subjunctive is the preferred option. For the category STA this result mirrors that of all OE construction types. The preference of the subjunctive in the three other text categories is due to its dominance in noun clauses. The construction types relative clause and adverbial clause contribute least to the overall result in the text categories IR, NI and XX, since their verbal syntagms are preferably in the indicative mood (cf. Tables 3.5 and 5.3). Read vertically, the most important information is that it is text category STA where the share of subjunctives differs most from the overall share of subjunctives in the OE corpus.

These figures lead to the conclusion that the parameter text category contributes a great deal to the strength of the subjunctive in OE. Text

Table 6.3 The distribution of the realisation possibilities of the verbal syntagm in all construction types across subperiods O1–O4

Subperiod	Subjunctive	Modal	Imperative	Indicative	Total
O1	100 **80.65%**	7 5.65%		17 13.70%	124 100%
O2	900 **58.25%**	113 7.31%	27 17.54%	261 16.90%	1,545 100%
O3	1,599 **44.09%**	437 12.05%	751 20.71%	840 23.15%	3,627 100%
O4	181 26.89%	133 19.76%	135 20.06%	224 **33.29%**	673 100%
Total	2,780 **46.58%**	690 11.56%	1,157 19.38%	1,342 22.48%	5,969 100%

Table 6.4 The distribution of the realisation possibilities of the verbal syntagm in all text categories in the OE corpus

Category	Subjunctive	Modal	Imperative	Indicative	Total
STA	1,446 **78.50%**	190 10.32%	36 1.95%	170 9.23%	1,842 100%
IS	222 27.27%	23 2.83%	508 **62.41%**	61 7.49%	814 100%
IR	345 **37.02%**	149 15.99%	137 14.70%	301 32.29%	932 100%
NI	79 **34.20%**	26 11.25%	68 29.44%	58 25.11%	231 100%
NN	68 22.82%	53 17.79%	66 22.15%	111 **37.24%**	298 100%
EX	37 15.74%	22 9.36%	3 1.28%	173 **73.62%**	235 100%
XX	583 **36.05%**	227 14.04%	339 20.97%	468 28.94%	1,617 100%
Total	2,780 **46.58%**	690 11.56%	1,157 19.38%	1,342 22.48%	5,969 100%

category STA stands out in two ways: it is the category with the biggest share of subjunctives in the OE corpus, and it is the only category in which this holds for all construction types.

6.1.2.4 The parameter format

All four construction types are coded for the parameter format in my OE corpus. The format verse is, however, represented only by six out of the thirty files. This should be borne in mind when interpreting Table 6.5, which shows the distribution of the realisation possibilities of the verbal syntagm in prose and in verse texts.

The preference of the subjunctive in prose texts mirrors the distribution in main clauses, but also that in noun clauses and in adverbial clauses (cf. sections 2.2.5, 4.2.3, 5.2.4). Only in relative clauses is the preferred option in prose texts the indicative (cf. section 3.2.4). The indicative as the preferred option in the verse texts of the whole corpus is the same as in relative clauses and in adverbial clauses individually. Consequently, prose texts contribute more to the strength of the subjunctive than verse texts.

6.1.2.5 The parameter dialect

All construction types are found in the dialect areas Anglian, Kentish and West Saxon. The distribution of the realisation possibilities of their verbal syntagms is presented in Table 6.6.

In all dialect areas the subjunctive is the preferred realisation of the verbal syntagms of the whole OE corpus, and its Kentish texts contribute most to its dominance. However, the weight of the last statement is impaired by the small number of verbal syntagms involved.

6.1.3 The influence of linguistic and extralinguistic parameters on subjunctive use in selected construction types

6.1.3.1 The parameter volition expressed by the form of the matrix verb[4]

Three of the four construction types are dependent clauses, and in their analysis the form of the verbal syntagm in the corresponding matrix clauses proved to have an influence on the relative frequency of the subjunctive in the dependent clauses in such a way that the feature 'volition' in the matrix clause expressed by the subjunctive, the imperative or a modal construction triggered a larger share of subjunctives in the dependent clauses. Table 6.7 shows the cumulative influence of this feature on the form of the verbal syntagm in OE dependent clauses.

---

[4] Note that volition is one of the terms used for reference to the modality expressed by a linguistic form (cf. section 1.2).

Table 6.5 The distribution of the realisation possibilities of the verbal syntagm in OE prose and verse texts of all construction types

Format	Subjunctive	Modal	Imperative	Indicative	Total
Prose	2,630 **49.72%**	507 9.59%	1,055 **19.95%**	1,097 20.74%	5,289 100%
Verse	150 22.06%	183 **26.91%**	102 15.00%	245 **36.03%**	680 100%
Total	2,780 **46.58%**	690 11.56%	1,157 **19.38%**	1,342 22.48%	5,969 100%

Table 6.6 The distribution of the realisation possibilities of the verbal syntagm in different OE dialects of all construction types

Dialect	Subjunctive	Modal	Imperative	Indicative	Total
Anglian	352 **42.93%**	33 4.02%	236 **28.78%**	199 **24.27%**	820 100%
Kentish	70 **76.09%**	9 9.78%		13 14.13%	92 100%
West Saxon	2,358 **46.63%**	648 **12.81%**	921 18.21%	1,130 22.35%	5,057 100%
Total	2,780 **46.58%**	690 11.56%	1,157 19.38%	1,342 22.48%	5,969 100%

Table 6.7 The influence of the feature volition in the verbal syntagm of the matrix clause of all construction types on the form of the verbal syntagm in OE dependent clauses

Dependent \ Matrix	Subjunctive	Modal	Indicative	Total
+ Volition	1,008 **63.28%**	191 11.99%	394 24.73%	1,593 100%
− Volition	517 31.85%	158 9.74%	948 **58.41%**	1,623 100%
Total	1,525 **47.42%**	349 10.85%	1,342 41.73%	3,216 100%

It is a chance effect of the structure of my corpus that it contains nearly as many matrix clauses with verbal syntagms coded + volition as those coded - volition. The influence of the feature volition in the matrix clauses is very obvious; there is a complementary distribution between volitional verbal syntagms in matrix and dependent clauses on the one hand and non-volitional verbal syntagms in matrix and dependent clauses on the other hand. Volitional verbal syntagms in matrix clauses trigger mainly subjunctive verbal syntagms in the dependent clauses, but modal constructions also occur with a higher frequency in the corresponding dependent clauses than in all dependent clauses. The correspondence of the features +/- volition in the matrix and the dependent clause is least prominent in noun clauses (cf. section 4.2.6).

It remains to be shown which type of volitional marking has the strongest subjunctive triggering effect. The amount of this influence can be derived from Table 6.8.

Table 6.8 shows quite clearly that irrespective of the type of the dependent clause a subjunctive in the matrix clause is most likely to trigger a subjunctive in the dependent clause.

The correlations tested in this section prove that the feature volition expressed by the form of the verbal syntagm in the matrix clause has a strong influence on the form of the verbal syntagm in the dependent clause. It triggers large shares of verbal syntagms expressing root modality in the dependent clause, and this influence is most prominent when both verbal syntagms are subjunctive forms. In other words, there is modal harmony between the verbal syntagms in matrix and dependent clause (cf. sections 3.2.7, 4.2.6).

6.1.3.2 The parameters relative marker and antecedent in relative clauses

In Chapter 3 a positive influence on subjunctive frequency was noted in relative clauses introduced by the complex relative marker *se þe*, and in the relevant examples there was a tendency of the verbs in the matrix clause to contain the feature volition. More precisely, out of the thirty relative clauses, twenty-three depend on matrix clauses with a subjunctive verb, two on matrix clauses with an imperative verb form, and only five on matrix clauses with a non-volitional verb form. From this constellation I conclude that it is the combination of a volitional verbal syntagm in the matrix clause and the relative marker *se þe* which raises subjunctive frequency in relative clauses.

Antecedents of the *se, seo, þæt* paradigm were also discovered as subjunctive favouring in relative clauses. Out of the ninety-seven relative clauses with these antecedents, eighty depend on matrix clauses with subjunctive verbal syntagms, in three matrix clauses the verb is an imperative, in another three modal constructions realise the verbal

Table 6.8 The influence of different realisations of the verbal syntagm in matrix clauses on the form of the verbal syntagm in OE dependent clauses of all construction types

Matrix \ Dependent	Subjunctive		Modal		Indicative		Total	
Subjunctive	796	**72.43%**	129	11.74%	174	15.83%	1,099	100%
Imperative	136	**53.13%**	20	7.81%	100	39.06%	256	100%
Modal	76	31.93%	42	17.65%	120	**50.42%**	238	100%
– Volition	517	31.85%	158	9.74%	948	**58.41%**	1,623	100%
Total	1,525	**47.42%**	349	10.85%	1,342	41.73%	3,216	100%

syntagm, and only in eleven matrix clauses is the verbal syntagm of the type non-volitional. So a subjunctive in a relative clause is not primarily caused by an antecedent of the *se, seo, þæt* paradigm, but by the combination of a volitional verbal syntagm in the matrix clause and such an antecedent.

6.1.3.3 The parameters clause type and function of noun clauses

The great majority of noun clauses belongs to the type *that*-clause (580 out of 738 noun clauses = 78 per cent), only *wh*-interrogative clauses and (nominal) relative clauses occur with more than negligible numbers. Therefore it is only natural that most of the overall number of 450 subjunctives in noun clauses occur in *that*-clauses. Their share is even bigger than expected (396 out of 450 subjunctives = 88.00 per cent), so that the clause type *that*-clause is identified as one of the subjunctive favouring parameters in noun clauses.

The largest share of subjunctives was found in noun clauses with the function subject complement. In seventy-four out of the eighty-four subject complement clauses the verbal syntagm is a subjunctive form. Yet the function of these noun clauses is only of secondary importance. The striking observation is that in fifty-one out of the seventy-four subject complement clauses with a subjunctive verbal syntagm the subject is realised by a substantive with the meaning component volition.

In noun clauses with object function the preferred realisation of the verbal syntagm is also the subjunctive, and object clauses with a subjunctive verb (277 tokens) are preferably governed by high-frequency matrix verbs with the meaning component volition (138 tokens = ~50 per cent).

6.1.3.4 The parameter clause type of adverbial clauses

In Chapter 5 it was established that in adverbial clauses the frequency of the subjunctive is a function of the semantic relation between the dependent clause and its matrix clause. Subjunctive favouring relations are concession, condition, and purpose and result. With a share of almost 92 per cent, the subjunctive is the default choice in concessive clauses. In conditional clauses conjunctions other than *gif* contribute most to the subjunctive share of about 63 per cent, and the subjunctive share of about 65 per cent in clauses of purpose and result is mainly due to the subclass of clauses of negative purpose.

6.2 The subjunctive in Middle English

My ME corpus contains thirty-one files with an overall size of 166,390 words. Its relevant verbal syntagms, which are in the second and third person singular present tense, amount to 4,725 tokens. With 1,577 verbal syntagms main clauses contribute most to the overall figure, they are followed by adverbial clauses (1,475 verbal syntagms), relative clauses (885 verbal syntagms) and noun clauses (788 verbal syntagms).

6.2.1 The subjunctive and its competitors

Depending on the construction type, the ME subjunctive has different competitors. These are imperative and modal constructions in main clauses; indicative and modal constructions in relative clauses and adverbial clauses; and imperative, indicative and modal constructions in noun clauses. The distribution of the subjunctive and its competitors in all construction types is entered in Table 6.9 with absolute figures in the first line and percentage shares in the second line of each cell.

A horizontal reading of the table reveals that only in noun clauses is the subjunctive the preferred realisation of the verbal syntagm in ME; in main clauses the top frequency rank is occupied by the imperative; and in the other two construction types the indicative is the preferred realisation of the verbal syntagm. Compared to the OE corpus the preferred realisation of the verbal syntagms in the whole ME corpus has shifted from the subjunctive to the indicative.

A vertical reading shows that in noun clauses and in adverbial clauses the share of subjunctives is greater than in the whole corpus. The other realisations expressing root modality, namely imperatives and modal constructions, dominate in main clauses.

The conclusion to be drawn from these figures is that in ME the subjunctive is next to non-existent in relative clauses and it plays only a minor role in main clauses, but in noun clauses and in adverbial clauses it is used in about one third of the verbal syntagms where it is possible at all. It has its strongest position in noun clauses. In the following sections I will test which parameters contribute most to its strength, and I will first consider those parameters that are relevant in all construction types.

6.2.2 The influence of linguistic and extralinguistic parameters on subjunctive use in all construction types

6.2.2.1 The parameter second person

The realisations of the ME verbal syntagms of the second person are mapped in Table 6.10.

The 1,345 verbal syntagms of the second person singular are only just more than a quarter of all verbal syntagms (~28 per cent), and the majority of them are imperatives. Therefore it is only natural that in the construction types where imperatives occur, namely in main clauses and in noun clauses, the share of subjunctives is smaller in verbal syntagms of the second person singular than when all verbal syntagms are considered.

Table 6.9 The distribution of the subjunctive and its competitors in all construction types of the ME corpus

Construction type	Subjunctive	Modal	Imperative	Indicative	Total
Main clause	227 14.39%	569 36.08%	781 49.53%		1,577 100%
Relative clause	36 4.07%	128 14.46%		721 81.47%	885 100%
Noun clause	302 38.32%	153 19.42%	50 6.35%	283 35.91%	788 100%
Adverbial clause	531 36.00%	233 15.80%		711 48.20%	1,475 100%
Total	1,096 23.19%	1,083 22.92%	831 17.59%	1,715 36.30%	4,725 100%

Table 6.10 The distribution of the subjunctive and its competitors in ME verbal syntagms of the second person singular in all construction types

Construction type	Subjunctive	Modal	Imperative	Indicative	Total
Main clause	30 3.12%	152 15.78%	781 81.10%		963 100%
Relative clause	7 13.46%	8 15.39%		37 71.15%	52 100%
Noun clause	46 32.62%	25 7.73%	50 35.46%	20 14.19%	141 100%
Adverbial clause	79 41.80%	50 26.46%		60 31.74%	189 100%
Total	162 12.05%	235 17.47%	831 61.78%	117 8.70%	1,345 100%

By contrast, in relative clauses and in adverbial clauses the share of subjunctives is greater in verbal syntagms of the second person singular than in the whole corpus. In adverbial clauses the subjunctive is even the preferred realisation of the verbal syntagm.

6.2.2.2 The parameter date of composition
It is the aim of this section to trace the frequency development of the subjunctive and its competitors across the subperiods of ME in the whole corpus (cf. Table 6.11).

None of the realisations of the verbal syntagm does undergo a unidirectional frequency development in the ME period. All in all, apart from the overall frequency rise of modal constructions the relative frequencies of the other realisations of the verbal syntagm do not change much. So, the parameter date of composition plays only a minor role in ME.

6.2.2.3 The parameter text category
This section describes the influence of the text category on the distribution of the subjunctive and its competitors in ME (cf. Table 6.12).

Text category STA is the only one in which the subjunctive is the preferred realisation of the verbal sytagm. At the same time, it is the only one in which subjunctives occur more often than the other realisation possibilities together. This result is not surprising since among the individual construction types it is only in the category STA of relative clauses where the subjunctive is not the preferred realisation of the verbal syntagm. In five out of the other six text categories the indicative is the preferred realisation of the verbal syntagm. Although in three of these five text categories the indicative has a bigger share than the whole ME corpus, it does not reach 50 per cent in any of them.

The obvious conclusion from these figures is that text category STA contributes very much to subjunctive frequency in ME.

6.2.2.4 The parameter format
My ME corpus consists of twenty-six prose files and five verse files. Table 6.13, which contains the distribution of the realisation possibilities of the verbal syntagm in prose and in verse texts, must therefore be interpreted with caution because of the low number of the latter.

The indicative is the preferred realisation of the verbal syntagm both in prose and in verse texts. Among the realisations which express root modality, prose texts contain larger shares of subjunctives and imperatives, and verse texts contain a larger share of modal constructions.

6.2.2.5 The parameter dialect
The dialect areas for which the files of my ME corpus are coded are Northern, East Midland, West Midland, Southern and Kentish. The

Table 6.11 The distribution of the subjunctive and its competitors in all construction types across subperiods M1–M4

Subperiod	Subjunctive	Modal	Imperative	Indicative	Total
M1	265 24.05%	180 16.33%	219 19.87%	438 39.75%	1,102 100%
M2	96 18.86%	142 27.90%	62 12.18%	209 41.06%	509 100%
M3	505 26.99%	390 20.85%	317 16.94%	659 35.22%	1,871 100%
M4	230 18.50%	371 29.85%	233 18.74%	409 32.91%	1,243 100%
Total	1,096 23.19%	1,083 22.92%	831 17.59%	1,715 36.30%	4,725 100%

Table 6.12 The distribution of the realisation possibilities of the verbal syntagm of all construction types in different text categories of the ME corpus

Category	Subjunctive	Modal	Imperative	Indicative	Total
STA	119 53.85%	44 19.91%		58 26.24%	221 100%
IS	174 20.96%	191 23.01%	314 37.83%	151 18.20%	830 100%
IR	373 19.17%	396 20.35%	336 17.27%	841 43.21%	1,946 100%
NI	93 19.54%	152 31.93%	59 12.39%	172 36.14%	476 100%
NN	55 17.13%	66 20.56%	68 21.18%	132 41.13%	321 100%
EX	48 24.62%	51 26.15%	28 14.36%	68 34.87%	195 100%
XX	234 31.79%	183 24.87%	26 3.53%	293 39.81%	736 100%
Total	1,096 23.19%	1,083 22.92%	831 17.59%	1,715 36.30%	4,725 100%

Table 6.13 The distribution of the realisation possibilities of the verbal syntagm of all construction types in ME prose and verse texts

Format	Subjunctive	Modal	Imperative	Indicative	Total
Prose	957 23.76%	873 21.68%	729 18.10%	1,468 36.46%	4,027 100%
Verse	139 19.91%	210 30.09%	102 14.61%	247 35.39%	698 100%
Total	1,096 23.19%	1,083 22.92%	831 17.59%	1,715 36.30%	4,725 100%

distribution of the subjunctive and its competitors in these dialects is shown in Table 6.14.

With the exception of the Southern dialect area, where the imperative is the prevailing realisation of the verbal syntagm, in all other dialect areas the indicative is the most frequent realisation. The share of imperatives in the Southern dialect area is also noteworthy because it is twice as big as that of the whole ME corpus.

6.2.3 *The influence of linguistic and extralinguistic parameters on subjunctive use in selected construction types*

6.2.3.1 The parameter volition expressed by the form of the matrix verb

In the analysis of the OE corpus it was shown that the feature volition in the verbal syntagm of the matrix clause had an effect on the form of the verbal syntagm in all dependent clause types. Table 6.15 shows the result of the corresponding analysis of the ME corpus.

The percentage share of subjunctives in dependent clauses is more than twice as big when the verbal syntagm of the matrix clause is marked by the feature volition. By contrast, the indicative is the preferred realisation of the verbal syntagm in dependent clauses whose matrix clauses are not marked for the feature volition. This distribution is another instance of modal harmony: the verbal syntagms of matrix and dependent clause express the same type of modality.

Verbal syntagms realised by subjunctives, imperatives and modal constructions count as marked by the feature volition. Table 6.16 shows that these different realisations of the verbal syntagm in the matrix clause have different effects on subjunctive use in the dependent clause.

Imperatives in ME matrix clauses have the biggest subjunctive triggering force in dependent clauses, they are followed by subjunctives and modal constructions. Compared to the OE situation the subjunctive changed places with the imperative as the form of the verbal syntagm in the matrix clause which was most likely to be accompanied by a subjunctive in a dependent clause. But it is still the case in ME that the form of the verbal syntagm in the matrix clause has a big influence on the realisation of the verbal syntagm in the dependent clause.

6.2.3.2 The parameters relative marker and antecedent in relative clauses

In ME the most frequent relative marker is *that*, but only in a minority of relative clauses introduced by this marker is the verbal syntagm realised by the subjunctive. The largest share of subjunctives is found in relative clauses introduced by *whom*; however, this occurs in only nineteen relative clauses, and in only five of them is the verbal syntagm realised

Table 6.14 The distribution of the realisation possibilities of the verbal syntagm of all construction types in different ME dialects

Dialect	Subjunctive	Modal	Imperative	Indicative	Total
East Midland	622 24.64%	655 25.95%	294 11.65%	953 **37.76%**	2,524 100%
West Midland	157 18.41%	203 23.80%	100 11.72%	393 **46.07%**	853 100%
Northern	11 14.67%	14 18.67%	9 12.00%	41 **54.66%**	75 100%
Southern	189 21.55%	157 17.90%	321 **36.60%**	210 23.95%	877 100%
Kentish	117 **29.55%**	54 13.64%	107 27.02%	118 **29.79%**	396 100%
Total	1,096 23.19%	1,083 22.92%	831 17.59%	1,715 **36.30%**	4,725 100%

Table 6.15 The influence of the feature volition in the verbal syntagm of the matrix clause of all construction types on the form of the verbal syntagm in the dependent clause in the ME corpus

Dependent / Matrix	Subjunctive	Modal	Indicative	Imperative	Total
+ Volition	402 **44.32%**	154 16.98%	346 38.15%	5 0.55%	907 100%
− Volition	467 20.84%	360 16.06%	1,369 **61.09%**	45 2.01%	2,241 100%
Total	869 27.60%	514 16.33%	1,715 54.48%	50 1.59%	3,148 100%

Table 6.16 The influence of the realisations of the verbal syntagm in the matrix clause of all construction types on the form of the verbal syntagm in the dependent clauses of the ME corpus

Dependent / Matrix	Subjunctive	Modal	Indicative	Imperative	Total
Subjunctive	125 **48.08%**	41 15.77%	93 35.77%	1 0.38%	260 100%
Imperative	164 **52.23%**	38 12.10%	108 34.40%	4 1.27%	314 100%
Modal	113 33.93%	75 22.52%	145 **43.55%**		333 100%
Non-volitional	467 20.84%	360 16.06%	**1,369 61.09%**	45 2.01%	2,241 100%
Total	869 27.60%	514 16.33%	1,715 54.48%	50 1.59%	3,148 100%

by a subjunctive. These small numbers do not justify a hypothesis of an influence of the choice of the relative marker on subjunctive use in ME relative clauses.

The most frequent antecedent of ME relative clauses is a substantival syntagm. Yet the biggest share of subjunctives was found in relative clauses with a deictic or indefinite pronoun as antecedent. In all nine relevant examples the verbal syntagm of the matrix clause is marked by the feature volition. It is therefore the combination of a deictic or indefinite pronoun as antecedent and a matrix verb marked for volition which has a positive influence on subjunctive frequency in ME relative clauses.

6.2.3.3 The parameters clause type and function of noun clauses

That-clauses represent the most frequent clause type of ME noun clauses (518 out of the 788 noun clauses = 65 per cent), they are followed by *wh*-interrogative clauses (103 = 12 per cent) and nominal relative clauses (99 = 13 per cent). As is to be expected from this distribution of clause type frequency, the 260 subjunctives in *that*-clauses represent the largest share (86 per cent) of the 302 subjunctives in ME noun clauses. This is roughly the same distribution as in the OE corpus, so that in ME, too, *that*-clauses have a positive influence on subjunctive frequency in noun clauses.

Only the functions subject (163 examples) and object (544 examples) are realised by a sufficient number of ME noun clauses to attempt generalisations about subjunctive preference. The subjunctive is the preferred realisation only in subject clauses (46 per cent). In object clauses the subjunctive is favoured after matrix clauses with a verbal syntagm expressing the meaning volition and/or is realised by a subjunctive or an imperative.

6.2.3.4 The parameter clause type of adverbial clauses

Among adverbial clauses the following types are distinguished: clauses of time, of place, of reason, of concession, of condition, of purpose and result, of comparison. In ME the preferred realisation of their verbal syntagms is the subjunctive in clauses of concession and in clauses of condition. With more than 93 per cent, the subjunctive is the default option in concessive clauses. The share of almost 69 per cent of subjunctives in conditional clauses results mainly from those introduced by *but (if)*. After *if*, which introduces more than half of the 428 conditional clauses, the subjunctive share is smaller.

6.3 The subjunctive in Early Modern English

My EModE corpus consists of thirty files with an overall size 193,140 words. Its 3,560 relevant verbal syntagms are forms of the second or third person singular, because the subjunctive is formally marked only for these. Adverbial clauses contribute most verbal syntagms (1,126), followed by relative clauses (948), noun clauses (792) and main clauses (694).

6.3.1 *The subjunctive and its competitors*

The number and form of the competitors of the subjunctive depends on the construction type. In EModE main clauses the subjunctive competes with the imperative and modal and semi-modal constructions, in relative clauses and in adverbial clauses with the indicative and modal and semi-modal constructions, and in noun clauses additionally with the imperative. Table 6.17 maps the distribution of the realisation possibilities of the verbal syntagm in the different construction types.[5]

Read horizontally, Table 6.17 shows that apart from main clauses, where it is excluded by definition, the indicative is by far the preferred realisation. In main clauses modal constructions are the preferred realisation. The subjunctive – which in OE and in ME prevailed in noun clauses – has lost much of its popularity, and the same holds for adverbial clauses. A vertical reading shows that in EModE only in adverbial and in main clauses is the share of subjunctives bigger than in the whole corpus.

Overall, we note that the subjunctive stands its ground best in adverbial clauses, but that even in this construction type subjunctives and modal constructions – i.e. the realisations that express root modality – scarcely outnumber indicatives. The following sections will explore which parameters have a positive influence on subjunctive use, and those parameters which are relevant in all construction types will be treated first.

6.3.2 *The influence of linguistic and extralinguistic parameters on subjunctive use in all construction types*

The parameters format and dialect, for which the OE and ME texts were coded, are not analysed in EModE because the few verse texts of the HC in this period are not included in my corpus, and because dialect diversity was greatly reduced through the process of standardisation.

6.3.2.1 The parameter second person

Since verbal syntagms of the second person singular were only counted in the EModE corpus in those texts where the corresponding personal pronoun was realised by a *th*-form, it was to be expected that their number would be much lower than that of third person verbal syntagms. As a matter of fact, second person verbal syntagms amount only to about 6 per cent of the overall number (cf. Table 6.18).

---

[5] Semi-modal constructions are subsumed under 'Modal' in the frequency tables.

Table 6.17 The distribution of the subjunctive and its competitors in all construction types of the EModE corpus

Construction type	Subjunctive	Modal	Imperative	Indicative	Total
Main clause	119 17.15%	498 **71.76%**	77 11.09%		694 100%
Relative clause	16 1.69%	212 22.36%		720 **75.95%**	948 100%
Noun clause	75 9.47%	222 28.03%	15 1.89%	480 **60.61%**	792 100%
Adverbial clause	312 27.71%	257 22.82%		557 **49.47%**	1,126 100%
Total	522 14.66%	1,189 33.40%	92 2.58%	1,757 **49.35%**	3,560 100%

Table 6.18 The distribution of the subjunctive and its competitors in EModE verbal syntagms of the second person in all construction types

Construction type	Subjunctive	Modal	Imperative	Indicative	Total
Main clause	1 7.69%	43 **35.83%**	77 **64.17%**		120 100%
Relative clause		2 15.38%		10 **76.93%**	13 100%
Noun clause	1 2.04%	11 22.45%	14 28.57%	23 **46.94%**	49 100%
Adverbial clause	8 19.05%	7 16.67%		27 **64.28%**	42 100%
Total	10 4.46%	63 28.13%	91 40.63%	60 26.78%	224 100%

The figures of Table 6.18 prove that the parameter second person has a big influence on subjunctive frequency. This is particularly obvious in main clauses and in noun clauses. In main clauses, the negative impact of the second person on subjunctive frequency is so strong that the subjunctive is not used at all in this clause type. In noun clauses with second person verbal syntagms the subjunctive is attested just once. In both construction types this is a consequence of the imperative as a competitor of the subjunctive, which is restricted to the second person. The parameter second person has also a negative effect on the frequency of modal constructions; in verbal syntagms of the second person it is lower than in all verbal syntagms, and this is the case in all construction types.

6.3.2.2 The parameter date of composition

With the expectation that subjunctive frequency would decline throughout the EModE period, I listed the frequency development of the different realisations of the verbal syntagm in Table 6.19.

Subjunctive frequency steadily decreases, whereas the relative frequency of modal constructions equally steadily increases. The conclusion from this complementary development is that the preferred expression of root modality changes from the subjunctive to modal constructions. Yet in all three subperiods there is almost a frequency balance between realisations expressing root modality and those expressing epistemic modality. Indicatives have a share of more than 50 per cent only in E1.

6.3.2.3 The parameter text category

In the previous chapters it was found that different text categories had a positive influence on subjunctive use in the individual construction types. In this section the cumulative influence of the parameter text category on the realisations of the verbal syntagm in EModE is at issue (cf. Table 6.20).

Since the indicative is the preferred realisation in the whole corpus, it is not surprising that it dominates in nearly all text categories. Category STA stands apart: modal constructions are here the preferred realisation, and STA is the only category where verbal syntagms expressing root modality, namely subjunctives and modal constructions, far outnumber indicatives. By way of conclusion we note that the parameter text category has a big influence on the realisation of the verbal syntagm and that the subjunctive occurs with the biggest relative frequency of all text categories in statutory texts.

Table 6.19 The subjunctive and its competitors in all construction types across subperiods E1–E3

Subperiod	Subjunctive	Modal	Imperative	Indicative	Total
E1	224 18.51%	297 24.55%	54 4.46%	635 52.48%	1,210 100%
E2	170 14.78%	426 37.04%	25 2.18%	529 46.00%	1,150 100%
E3	128 10.67%	466 38.83%	13 1.08%	593 49.42%	1,200 100%
Total	522 14.66%	1,189 33.40%	92 2.58%	1,757 49.35%	3,560 100%

Table 6.20 The distribution of the subjunctive and its competitors in all construction types across text categories in the EModE corpus

Category	Subjunctive	Modal	Imperative	Indicative	Total
STA	238 32.92%	362 50.07%		123 17.01%	723 100%
IS	96 15.00%	210 32.81%	8 1.25%	326 50.94%	640 100%
IR	35 9.36%	110 29.41%	21 5.62%	208 55.61%	374 100%
NI	16 12.12%	44 33.33%	24 18.18%	48 36.37%	132 100%
NN	29 14.29%	49 24.14%	5 2.46%	120 59.11%	203 100%
EX	39 7.89%	134 27.13%		321 64.98%	494 100%
XX	69 6.94%	280 28.17%	34 3.42%	611 61.47%	994 100%
Total	522 14.66%	1,189 33.40%	92 2.58%	1,757 49.35%	3,560 100%

6.3.3 *The influence of linguistic and extralinguistic parameters on subjunctive use in selected construction types*

6.3.3.1 The parameter volition expressed by the form of the matrix verb

Verbal syntagms realised by subjunctives, imperatives or modal constructions are interpreted as marked for the feature volition. In this section the influence of matrix verbs marked for the feature volition on subjunctive use in the construction types relative clause, noun clause and adverbial clause will be analysed (cf. Table 6.21).

Irrespective of the form of the verbal syntagm of the matrix clause, the indicative is the preferred realisation of the verbal syntagm in the dependent clause. Nevertheless there is a clear correspondence between matrix clauses with a verbal syntagm marked for the feature volition and dependent clauses with verbal syntagms realised by forms expressing root modality on the one hand, and matrix clauses with a verbal syntagm unmarked for the feature volition and dependent clauses with verbal syntagms realised by forms expresing epistemic modality on the other hand. The percentage share of verbal syntagms expressing root modality in clauses depending on matrix clauses with verbal syntagms marked for the feature volition is almost twice as big as in clauses depending on matrix clauses with verbal syntagms not marked for the feature volition. Next I tested if all markers of volition had the same influence on the realisation of the verbal syntagm in dependent clauses (cf. Table 6.22).

In EModE subjunctive matrix verbs have the strongest subjunctive triggering force in dependent clauses; they are followed by imperatives and modal constructions. The influence of subjunctive matrix verbs on the form of the verbal syntagm in dependent clauses is of particular interest because in the corresponding dependent clauses the share of indicatives is saliently small. This is the same constellation as in OE (cf. Table 6.8).

6.3.3.2 The parameters relative marker and antecedent in relative clauses

The data of my EModE corpus suggest a positive influence of *wh*-relative markers on subjunctive use. Since these relative markers were identified in earlier studies as characteristic of formal style, the salient co-occurrence of *wh*-relative markers and the subjunctive in EModE may have laid the foundation of the association of the subjunctive with formal style in PDE.

Antecedents other than substantival syntagms play only a minor role in EModE, and none of the antecedents triggers a particularly large share of subjunctives.

Table 6.21 The influence of the feature volition in the verbal syntagm of the matrix clause of all construction types on the form of the verbal syntagm in the dependent clauses in the EModE corpus

Dependent / Matrix	Subjunctive	Modal	Imperative	Indicative	Total
+ Volition	169 21.12%	293 36.63%		338 **42.25%**	800 100%
– Volition	234 11.33%	398 19.26%	15 0.73%	1,419 **68.68%**	2,066 100%
Total	403 14.06%	691 24.11%	15 0.52%	1,757 **61.31%**	2,866 100%

Table 6.22 The influence of the realisations of the verbal syntagm in the matrix clause of all construction types on the form of the verbal syntagm in the dependent clause in the EModE corpus

Dependent / Matrix	Subjunctive	Modal	Imperative	Indicative	Total
Subjunctive	72 34.78%	89 **43.00%**		46 22.22%	207 100%
Imperative	12 18.18%	17 25.76%		37 **56.06%**	66 100%
Modal	85 16.13%	187 35.48%		255 **48.39%**	527 100%
Non-volitional	234 11.33%	398 19.26%	15 0.73%	1,419 68.68%	2,066 100%
Total	403 14.06%	691 24.11%	15 0.52%	1,757 **61.31%**	2,866 100%

6.3.3.3 The parameters clause type and function of noun clauses

With 595 examples out of 792 noun clauses *that*-clauses represent the most frequent clause type of EModE noun clauses (= 75 per cent); they are followed by *wh*-interrogative clauses (110 examples, 14 per cent) and nominal relative clauses (49 examples, 6 per cent). The other clause types play only a minor role. The sixty subjunctives in *that*-clauses equal a share of 80 per cent of the 75 subjunctives in EModE noun clauses. As in the previous periods, EModE *that*-clauses are identified as a subjunctive favouring clause type.

Over 90 per cent of the noun clauses realise the functions object (~60 per cent) or subject (~31 per cent), but only in subject clauses is the share of subjunctives bigger than in the whole body of noun clauses. The same is true for the share of modal constructions, which is even larger than that of subjunctives. From this constellation I draw the conclusion that the function subject of noun clauses not only has a positive influence on the frequency of subjunctives but more generally on that of all types of verbal syntagms expressing root modality.

6.3.3.4 The parameter clause type of adverbial clauses

On the basis of the semantic relation between matrix clause and dependent clause the following adverbial clauses are distinguished: clauses of time, of place, of reason, of concession, of condition, of purpose and result, and of comparison. The subjunctive is the preferred realisation of the verbal syntagm in clauses of concession and of condition, where it reaches a share of well above average. The verbal syntagms of clauses of purpose and result are preferably realised by modal constructions. In all other types of EModE adverbial clauses the verbal syntagm is preferably realised by the indicative.

6.4 Subjunctive use from Old English to Early Modern English

Chapters 2 to 5 analysed the use of the subjunctive and its competitors in the construction types main clause, relative clause, noun clause and adverbial clause in three consecutive periods, whereas the first three sections of this chapter provided a synchronic description of subjunctive use in the periods OE, ME and EModE. On the basis of the results achieved so far it is now possible to combine the two approaches and present an overview of the development of subjunctive use in all construction types across the three periods. It will not only contain frequency charts of the subjunctive and its competitors in the individual subperiods but will also single out the parameters that influenced subjunctive use most.

6.4.1 *The frequency development of the subjunctive and its competitors*

The following figures were derived from the percentage values in Tables 6.3, 6.11 and 6.19 for Figure 6.1, in Tables 3.1, 3.11 and 3.20 for Figure 6.3, in Tables 5.1, 5.13 and 5.26 for Figure 6.4, in Tables 4.1, 4.9 and 4.20 for Figure 6.5, and in Tables 2.3, 2.12 and 2.16 for Figure 6.6.

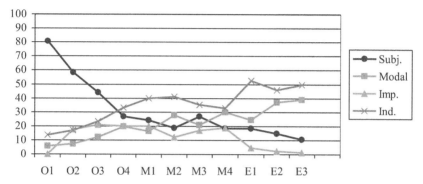

Figure 6.1 The frequency development of the subjunctive and its competitors in all construction types across the periods OE, ME and EModE

The subjunctive shows the expected frequency decrease from the earliest subperiod to the last subperiod, it is only interrupted at subperiod M2. Contrary to general expectation (Fischer 1992: 262, Traugott 1972: 149) it is not replaced by modal constructions but most conspicuously by the indicative. It is true that the indicative and modal constructions follow a general rising trend, but indicative frequency surpasses that of the subjunctive as early as towards the end of the OE period, while the frequency of modal constructions remains below that of the subjunctive until subperiod M2, drops below subjunctive frequency at subperiod M3, and leaves behind subjunctive frequency for good at subperiod M4. M4 is also the only point in time at which the dominance of the indicative over modal constructions is at risk; the percentage values of the construction types are only three per cent apart.

Imperative frequency shows a very characteristic development. It starts to be attested in subperiod O2, and until the end of the ME period it occurs with more or less the same frequency. This development is interrupted only at subperiod M2, before imperative frequency drops drastically at the beginning of the EModE period and then continues its decreasing trend until at the end of the EModE period it realises no more than 1 per cent of all relevant verbal syntagms.

Figure 6.1 shows clearly that subjunctive frequency started at a very high level in the earliest OE texts and declined more or less steadily to reach levels of a little more than 10 per cent at most at the end of the EModE period. The next sections deal with the factors that affected the development of subjunctive use.

6.4.2 *The simplification of the verbal paradigm*

The gradual simplification of the English verbal syntagm through the loss of nearly all endings led to the reduction of the number of forms overtly marked for the subjunctive. This development is reflected in the decreasing relative frequency of relevant verbal syntagms from 21.47/1,000 words in the OE to 9.48/1,000 words in the ME to 3.59/1,000 words in the EModE corpus. Yet the different forms of the verbal paradigm do not contribute the same share to the overall share of the subjunctive in all construction types in the individual subperiods. The contributions of third person singular subjunctives and the other forms of the subjunctive to the overall number of subjunctives are are graphically represented in Figure 6.2.[6]

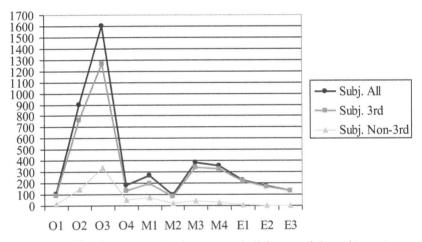

Figure 6.2 The frequency development of all forms of the subjunctive compared to that of third person singular subjunctives and subjunctives of other forms of the verbal paradigm in all construction types across the periods OE, ME and EModE

---

[6] The values for all subjunctives were taken over from the relevant tables in Chapters 2–5. The values of third person singular subunctives are: 83 (O1), 757 (O2), 1,259 (O3), 128 (O4), 193 (M1), 77 (M2), 340 (M3), 324 (M4), 217 (E1), 167 (E2) and 128 (E3). The values for the other forms are the differences between the values for all subjunctives and for third person singular subjunctives.

The small distance between the line representing the frequency development of all subjunctives and that representing the frequency development of third person singular subjunctives indicates that the subjunctives of the other forms of the verbal paradigm play only a minor role in the frequency development of the subjunctive. The difference between the values is greatest in OE, when the subjunctive was marked for the second person singular, the third person singular, and for all persons of the plural. The fewer forms of the verbal paradigm that were available, the smaller became the frequency difference between third person singular subjunctives and all subjunctives. From this distribution of subjunctives, it follows that the impact of the simplification of the verbal paradigm on the frequency development of subjunctive use is much smaller than might be expected from the impact it has on the frequency of verbal syntagms realised by subjunctives and its competitors.

6.4.3 *The parameter construction type*

In Figure 6.1 we saw that the indicative was the strongest competitor of the subjunctive already in the OE period. A closer look at this competition reveals that the cross-over point of indicative over subjunctive frequency differs in the three construction types where these two realisations compete. It is already between O1 and O2 in adjectival relative clauses, between O3 and O4 in adverbial clauses and after several attempts at M4 in noun clauses (cf. Figures 6.3–6.5).

The hypothesis that the subjunctive was replaced by modal constructions in the history of English is only supported by the subjunctive development in main clauses, where it competes only with the imperative and with modal constructions. Here the frequency of modal constructions

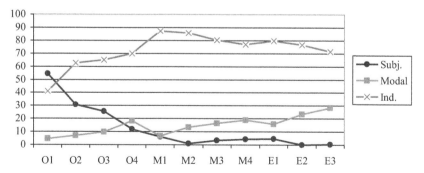

Figure 6.3 The frequency development of the subjunctive and its competitors in adjectival relative clauses across the periods OE, ME and EModE

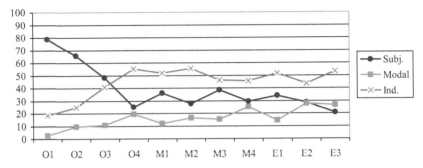

Figure 6.4 The frequency development of the subjunctive and its competitors in adverbial clauses across the periods OE, ME and EModE

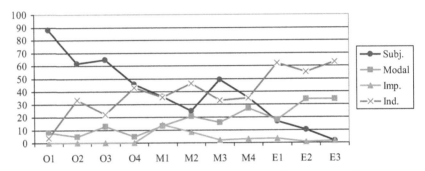

Figure 6.5 The frequency development of the subjunctive and its competitors in noun clauses across the periods OE, ME and EModE

already surpassed that of the subjunctive at the end of the OE period (cf. Figure 6.6).[7]

Another aspect of the impact of the different construction types on the development of subjunctive use becomes obvious when we compare its frequency development in all construction types together and in the individual construction types (cf. Figure 6.7).

Relative clauses contribute next to nothing to the preservation of the subjunctive. The relative frequency of the subjunctive is lower than in all other construction types in all subperiods and reaches the zero point in E2. The relative frequencies of the subjunctive in all other construction types stay close together from O1 to O2, then only main clauses and adverbial clauses continue their subjunctive frequency decrease together until the end of the OE period. From O4 onwards subjunctive frequency develops differently in the individual construction types to reach a maximum divergence at M3. This is the moment when its final

---

[7] The values for 'Modal' include those of all periphrastic constructions.

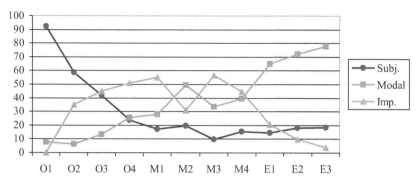

Figure 6.6 The frequency development of the subjunctive and its competitors in main clauses across the periods OE, ME and EModE

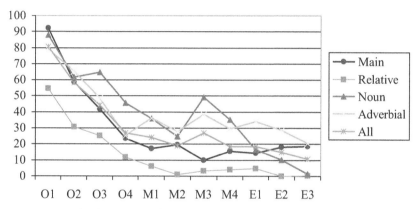

Figure 6.7 The frequency development of the subjunctive in different construction types across the periods OE, ME and EModE

decreasing trend starts in noun clauses and in adverbial clauses, whereas an unexpected increase sets in in main clauses. If grammar books and our own experience did not tell us that the subjunctive is still used in PDE adverbial clauses, and if many recent publications did not prove that the subjunctive 'seems to be alive and kicking' in noun clauses (Serpollet 2001), Figure 6.7 would nourish the expectation that the subjunctive in these two construction types would reach point zero not long after the end of the EModE period.

6.4.4 *The parameter text category*

The seven prototypical text categories, for which I coded my corpus, were taken over from the HC. Rissanen points out that 'although these categories can be defined by extra-linguistic criteria, they have been specified with distinctive linguistic features in mind' (Rissanen 1996: 232). It is therefore not surprising that subjunctive use should turn out to be one of those linguistic features characterising a particular text category.

This is the case for category STA, which stands out from all other text categories in all construction types and in all three periods. Texts of category STA have the largest shares of subjunctives among all categories across all three periods. In OE and in ME the subjunctive is the preferred realisation of the verbal syntagm in the texts of this category, and in EModE it shares this place with modal constructions. Two conclusions can be drawn from this distribution of subjunctive use. In texts up to the beginning of the eighteenth century the subjunctive was a style-marker of statutory texts, and the changing preferences of the realisation of the verbal syntagm in statutory texts in the EModE period suggest a change in the genre conventions of this text category. As a matter of fact, this concerns the form and the arrangement of the text structure elements, or in Swales's terminology the arrangement of the moves 'identification of the legislator' and 'provisions' (Swales 1990: 140). In OE law-codes they are clearly recognisable as separate moves. From the end of the ME period onwards the identification of the legislator is integrated in the so-called promulgation formula in the form of a *by*-phrase in a matrix clause, which governs a *that*-clause containing the provision(s) (Moessner forthcoming: sections 6.1.1, 6.1.2 and 7.2.1).[8]

[6.1]   *þis is seo woruldcunde gerædnes, þe ic wylle mid minan witenan ræde,*
        þæt man healde ofer eall Englaland.
        ðæt is þonne ærest, þæt ic wylle, þæt man rihte laga upp arære &
        æghwylce unlaga georne afylle, & þæt man aweodige & awyrtwalige
        æghwylce unriht, swa man geornost mæge, of þysum earde, & arære
        up Godes riht. (O3 STA LAW LAW11C, p. 308)
        'This is the secular decree, which I [= King Cnut] with the council of my advisors wish that one shall obey all over England.
        That is foremost, that I wish that one shall establish right laws and eagerly abolish unrightful laws and that one shall root out and extirpate all wrong from this earth as completely as one can and establish God's right.'
[6.2]   *Be yt therfor ordeyned by auctorite of this present parliament that if*
        eny Capteyn ..., he shall for suche defaute forfeite to the King all his
        goodes and catalles (M4 STA LAW STAT2, p. II, 549)
        'Be it therefore ordained by the authority of this present parliament

---

[8] The different distribution of subject forms of first person personal pronouns detected by Rissanen (1996: 215–216) is another consequence of this change of genre conventions in statutory texts.

that if any captain ..., he shall for this default forfeit all his goods and livestock'

Examples [6.1] and [6.2] illustrate that this change of genre conventions goes along with the replacement of the subjunctive in the provisions part by modal constructions, and they are also in line with the observation that it takes rather a long time before the frequency of modal constructions surpasses that of the subjunctive (cf. section 6.4.1).

An influence of a change in genre conventions on the use of the subjunctive was also detected in OE wills. In the wills of the first two OE subperiods the focus was on the inheritance, and the linguistic expression of this convention was a main clause with a subjunctive verb. In the last two OE subperiods the focus shifted to the testator, and the default linguistic expression was a complex sentence with a matrix clause with an indicative verb followed by an object clause with a subjunctive verb.

6.4.5 *The expression of modality*

Following the model of the subjunctive outlined in section 1.2, in simple sentences root modality can be expressed only by one verbal syntagm, and here by the subjunctive, the imperative or by a modal construction.[9] From the definition of the subjunctive as a realisation of the morphological category mood and an expression of root modality it follows that main clauses with indicative verbal syntagms are not included in my corpus. This is the reason why the indicative could not replace the subjunctive as in the other construction types. In OE and in ME, when subjunctive and imperative singular were formally distinguished, there was a trend towards complementary distribution between imperative for the realisation of second person verbal syntagms expressing root modality and subjunctive for the third person verbal syntagms expressing root modality. Only in EModE, when the formal distinction between subjunctive and imperative was given up, had the subjunctive no other competitor besides modal constructions. This explains the late replacement of subjunctives by modal constructions in main clauses. So the development of subjunctive use in main clauses can only be explained by the combination of several factors: the non-availability of the indicative due to the definition of the subjunctive as an expression of root modality; the more than average contribution of third person verbal syntagms to the overall subjunctive share; and the late loss of the formal distinction between subjunctive and imperative singular.

---

[9] Expressions of modality by constituents other than the verbal syntagm, e.g. adverbs, are not considered here.

In complex sentences modality can be expressed in more than one verbal syntagm. In adverbial clauses the subjunctive was replaced by the indicative as the preferred mood after O3. Then there are no more cross-overs, and both frequency lines run more or less parallel up to E3 (cf. Figure 6.4). This corresponds to the finding that the subjunctive is the preferred realisation of the verbal syntagm in the same types of adverbial clauses in all three periods; these are concessive clauses and conditional clauses, in OE additionally clauses of purpose and result. The indicative is the preferred realisation of the verbal syntagm in clauses of time, place, reason and comparison in all three periods. This complementary distribution becomes understandable when we consider the meaning relations which hold between the matrix clause and the adverbial clause, and which is expressed by the introductory conjunction. It is our experience that reasons are usually expressed by statements of facts, and the appropriate linguistic form for statements of facts is the indicative. In this manner of representation, words are intended to match the world (= epistemic modality). If this was the only possibility of stating reasons, the indicative should occur with a share of 100 per cent. This is not quite the case. In my whole corpus I found one single example of a clause of reason with a subjunctive verbal syntagm, and the share of modal constructions varies between 8.86 per cent in OE and 15.79 per cent in EModE. In these clauses the reason for the state of affairs expressed in the matrix clause is presented as a non-fact, cf. example [6.3]:

[6.3]   *Ond ic nu þas þing write to þe gemænelice & to olimphiade minre meder & minum geswustrum forþon incer lufu sceal beon somod gemæne* (O2/3 NI TRAV ALEX, p. 3) 'And now I write these things jointly to you and to my mother Olympia and to my sisters, because your love shall be common to both of you'

My corpus contains very few clauses of reason in which the verbal syntagm expresses root modality so unambiguously. In the majority of clauses of reason with modal constructions the interpretation of the meaning of the verbal syntagm is not without problems, cf. example [6.4]:

[6.4]   *þis he deð þonne, forðam þe he ne mæg locian on þæt sar and on þone micelan wop* (O3/4 IR HOM SUND6, p. 169) 'he does this then, because he may not look at the sorrow and big weeping'

It is not quite clear if he (= St Peter) is not allowed to look at the misery of the people in hell or if it is possible that he turns his eyes away from what goes on in hell. In the first interpretation his looking into hell is presented as a negated permission (an instance of root modality), in the second interpretation his look into hell is presented as an improbable possibility (a weak type of epistemic possibility). The conversational background of all the examples of my corpus would have to be established in detail if one wanted to find out in how many of them the modal construction was a 'real' competitor of the subjunctive in the sense that it not only occurs in the same syntactic environment as the subunctive but also expresses root modality. This, however, would require a separate study on the modality of modal auxiliaries.

The analysis of the meaning of the verbal syntagm of the other types of adverbial clauses in terms of root vs. epistemic modality will also go a long way in the explanation of the distribution of the realisation possibilities of their verbal syntagms. Promising canditates are the clauses of time and the clauses of purpose and result.

In the analysis of the clauses of time in my corpus it proved helpful to distinguish clauses of subsequent action (clauses of posteriority) on the one hand from clauses of contemporaneous and antecedent action on the other. The former have a bigger share of subjunctives than the other subclasses in all periods. This corresponds to the presentation of the state of affairs in these clauses as non-fact at the time of the matrix clause. The meaning of the introductory conjunction would be enough to indicate the non-factuality of the state of affairs in the clause of subsequent action, the form of the verbal syntagm merely underlines this signification. Since the subjunctive did not contribute an additional meaning component, the replacement of the subjunctive by the indicative as a consequence of the simplification of the verbal paradigm did not change the meaning of the adverbial clause.

Whereas clauses of subsequent action are introduced by special conjunctions that can take over the function of indicating that the state of affairs in the adverbial clause is expressed as non-fact, this is not possible in clauses of purpose and result. With the exception of some specialised conjunctions like *þy læs þe* in OE or *lest* in ME and EModE, which introduce clauses of negative purpose and are usually followed by the subjunctive, the vast majority of clauses of purpose and result are introduced by the conjunction *that*. The analysis of the meaning of these clauses must therefore rely on other elements. Since the state of affairs in clauses of purpose and in clauses of result is not a fact at the time of the time of the production of the matrix clause, the discrimination of the two types of adverbial clause can only rely on whether the state of affairs in the adverbial clause is presented as the intention of the speaker (= root modality) or as a consequence of the state of affairs at issue in the matrix clause. This is where the speaker's world experience is helpful, cf. examples [6.5] and [6.6]:

[6.5]   *But I haue prayed for the to thentent that thy faythe do not fayle* (E1
         IR SERM FISHER, p. 1317)

[6.6]   *we staid so long to take our leave of your Huntsmen this morning,*
that the Sun is got so high, and shines so clear, that I will not under-
take the catching of a Trout (E3 IS HANDO WALTON, p. 215)

It is our experience that people who say a prayer do so with a special
purpose in mind. In the adverbial clause of example [6.5] the state of
affairs of 'not losing one's faith' is the purpose of the speaker's prayer. The
analysis of the adverbial clause in [6.5] as a clause of purpose is motivated
by our experience, and it is supported by the subjunctive *do*. The subjunctive does not contribute an additional meaning component; its expression
of root modality is redundant under the given circumstances. It is also our
experience that the rising of the sun, the state of affairs in the adverbial
clause in [6.6], is beyond the influence of mankind. It happens as a consequence of the passing of time, and it is represented as a fact (epistemic
modality). From our experience we derive the analysis of the adverbial
clause in [6.6] as a clause of result. This is in line with the indicative form
of the verbal syntagm, which also expresses epistemic modality.[10]

In complex sentences containing noun clauses there are also two verbal
syntagms available for the expression of modality. In this construction
type the subjunctive was replaced by the indicative, and this replacement
took place only after the ME period. A little bit later, in the first EModE
subperiod, the frequency of modal construction also surpassed that of
subjunctives, yet without ever reaching the frequency of the indicative
(cf. Figure 6.5). The analysis of my corpus revealed various expressions
of root modality in the matrix clause as a feature influencing the realisation of the verbal syntagm in noun clauses. Subjunctive frequency was
found to be raised in OE and in ME by root modality expressed by the
meaning of matrix verbs of object clauses (sections 4.2.5.1 and 4.4.5.1)
and by root modality expressed by the subjunctive as a realisation of the
verbal syntagm in the matrix verb (sections 4.2.6 and 4.4.5.2), in OE
additionally by root modality expressed by the meaning of the subjects
of sentences containing subject complement clauses (section 4.2.5.2). For
the agreement in the type of modality between matrix clause and noun
clause the term modal harmony was taken over from the *Cambridge
Grammar*. As noticed above in the adverbial clauses, when root modality is already expressed in the matrix clause the subjunctive in the noun
clause does not contribute an additional meaning component, but simply
supports the meaning root modality of the matrix clause. In the EModE
corpus fewer instances of modal harmony were found than in the periods
before. EModE is also the period when indicative and subjunctive frequencies drift further and further apart. So, it could be assumed that the

---

[10] Note that in my model of the subjunctive the indicative is not an unmodalised form
but a form that expresses epistemic modality.

rising indicative frequency was the reason for the decreasing frequency of modal harmony. Another reason, which would be worth a long-term diachronic study, is the rising frequency of *to*-infinitive constructions. In their study on complement selection López-Couso and Méndez-Naya (2006) compared *that*-clauses and infinitive constructions after the high-frequency verbs *beodan* and *biddan* in the OE and the ME parts of the HC, and they found that the relative frequency of infinitive constructions was at least three times as high as that of subjunctive *that*-clauses from the first ME subperiod onwards, whereas in OE infinitives played only a minor role. It may be problematic to derive generalisations on this result because only complements of two verbs were analysed. But based on evidence from a comparison of the two versions of Wærferth's translation of *Gregory's Dialogues*, Los (2005) claims a replacement of subjunctive *that*-clauses by infinitive constructions already for OE. Her claim has the flaw that she subsumes under the label 'subjunctive *that*-clause' 'a clause with a subjunctive form or "neutralized" subjunctive forms which are ambiguous between subjunctive and indicative but can be expected to be subjunctive because of the putative nature of the clause, and clauses with modals, indicative or subjunctive' (Los 2005: 180). In the examples from Gregory's *Dialogues*, which are supposed to show the replacement of subjunctive *that*-clauses in the earlier manuscript by *to*-infinitives in the later manuscript, the verb forms in the *that*-clauses are either ambiguous (examples 47, 49 [*hæfde*], 51 [*licode*], 54 [*wunedon*]), indicatives (examples 56 [*wæs*], 58 [*gehyreð*]), or they contain a modal (examples 52 [*scoldon*], 60 [*mihte*]). Among the quoted examples there is not one with a morphologically marked subjunctive in the *that*-clause. Even if one does not accept Los's argument that the *to*-infinitive replaced sub-junctive *that*-clauses, there is no doubt that she provided evidence for the more general claim established before by Manabe (1989) for ME, namely that infinitive constructions gradually replaced *that*-clauses (irrespective of the realisation of their verbal syntagms).[11] If more evidence can be produced that the frequency of infinitive constructions increased at the expense of *that*-clauses with finite verbal syntagms, this would explain the decreasing frequency of modal harmony. From this perspective the replacement of the subjunctive by the indicative in noun clauses and the concomitant decrease of modal harmony can then be interpreted as a contribution to the reduction of redundancy, which can be observed in other parts of English syntax as well.

[11] Cf. Manabe's Table 2:

	13th century		14th century		15th century	
That-clause	1,438	40.9%	1,311	37.7%	1,027	27.5%
Infinitive	2,075	59.1%	2,169	62.3%	2,702	72.5%

In relative clauses the subjunctive was replaced by the indicative already after the first OE subperiod. Therefore, the question of which factors contributed most to its preservation proved irrelevant. Consequently, the expression of root modality in the matrix clause was found to raise subjunctive frequency only in combination with other factors: in OE relative clauses in combination with the relative marker *se þe* and with antecedents of the *se, seo, þæt* paradigm; in ME in combination with deictic and indefinite pronouns as antecedents.

Epilogue

Summary and outlook

My understanding of the concept of the subjunctive combines the categories mood and modality. It is identified by its form as a realisation of the category mood, and it expresses one of several kinds of root modality. Depending on its occurrence in one of the periods OE, ME or EModE it is overtly marked for different persons and numbers in lexical verbs. The verb *be* distinguishes more forms than the lexical verbs. These additional forms and all forms of past tense were excluded from the analysis. The number of relevant forms drops from period to period. The subjunctive is attested in the construction types main clause, relative clause, noun clause and adverbial clause. The verb forms or verbal syntagms which compete with the subjunctive differ in these construction types and also in the individual periods.

My treatment of the subjunctive is strictly corpus based. The data of my corpus come from the HC and amount to 487,730 words. They have been coded for the extralinguistic parameters text, number in text, (sub) period, region (only for OE and ME), prose vs. verse (only for OE and ME) and for several linguistic parameters according to the construction type. The quantitative analysis of my data was carried out with the statistics program SPSS. It is presented in the form of tables and illustrated by corpus examples. The tables contain absolute and relative frequencies, usually as percentage figures. Reasons for this strategy are given in Chapter 1.

Chapters 2–5 provide descriptions of the use of the subjunctive and its competitors in the construction types main clause, relative clause, noun clause and adverbial clause in the periods OE, ME and EModE. Here the scope of the book surpasses that of earlier studies, which neglected subjunctive use in main clauses and in relative clauses. Furthermore, the publications which focused on one of the construction types noun clause or adverbial clause dealt with one period only. A detailed presentation of the hypotheses and findings of earlier studies and their evaluation in light of the results of my analysis is to be found at the beginning and end of each chapter.

Chapter 6 approaches subjunctive use from a different point of view.

Its first three parts are synchronic descriptions of the use of the subjunctive and its competitors in all construction types in the three periods OE, ME and EModE, and the last part traces the long-term development of subjunctive use from the earliest English texts to the beginning of the eighteenth century. These descriptions rely on the results of the earlier fine-grained analyses, and they reveal the linguistic and extralinguistic parameters that affected the distribution of the realisation possibilities of the relevant verbal syntagms, in particular those that contributed to the preservation of the subjunctive.

One of these parameters is construction type (cf. Figure 6.7). Relative clauses contribute next to nothing to the preservation of the subjunctive until EModE. Subperiod M3 is the moment when subjunctive frequency differs most between all construction types, and at the same time it is the turning point when subjunctive frequency in noun clauses and adverbial clauses starts decreasing until the end of the EModE period, whereas an unexpected rise sets in in relative clauses and main clauses. This development is reversed at subperiod E1, when subjunctives nearly disappear from relative clauses. By contrast, the rising trend of subjunctive frequency in main clauses continues. To explore the further development of subjunctive use in main clauses from the eighteenth century onwards is one of the attractive topics awaiting further study. It remains to be shown whether the subjunctive in main clauses really becomes restricted to set phrases like *God save the Queen* as PDE grammars want to make us believe (Quirk et al. 1985: 157–158, Huddleston and Pullum 2002: 944) or whether it never lost its productivity as PDE corpus examples suggest (Waller 2017: 24).

The changing structure of the verbal paradigm also proved a parameter with an interesting influence on the development of subjunctive use. The general way of describing it is that its morphological simplification was responsible for the frequency decrease of the subjunctive. This is the case when all forms of the subjunctive are taken into account. The picture changes when the frequency of individual forms is compared to the frequency of all forms of the subjunctive. My data show that third person singular subjunctive frequency was always above that of all other subjunctive forms together (cf. Figure 6.2). This constellation supports a different hypothesis, namely that third person singular subjunctives contributed more to the preservation of the subjunctive up to the EModE period than the subjunctives of all other forms of the verbal paradigm, and that the impact of the simplification of the verbal paradigm on the development of subjunctive use is less than might be expected. It would be fascinating to investigate if third person singular verb forms differ from other verb forms in other respects as well.

The text category STA, which contains written formal legislative texts, favours the use of the subjunctive in all periods. It is the purpose of these texts to regulate societal behaviour, and this accounts for their directive nature. Since they share the feature directivity with the text categories IS and IR, another explanation had to be sought for the exceptionally large share of subjunctives in STA texts. The changing structure of their moves 'identification of the legislator' and 'provisions' was identified as this explanation. More research is necessary to find out if later changes of the move structure of statutory texts had a similar influence on their linguistic profile. From a cursory look at the Acts of Parliament of the nineteenth century I have the impression that this is another point in time when both the move structure and the linguistic profile of statutory texts changed.

An influence of a change in genre conventions on the use of the subjunctive was also detected in OE wills. Here the shift of the focus from the inheritance to the testator was shown to correspond to a change in the linguistic profile of the genre: subjunctives moved from main clauses to noun clauses.

Although modality is an elusive concept when it comes to definition (Huddleston and Pullum 2002: 172–173), it proved a parameter with a significant influence on subjunctive use in different ways in different periods. My model, which defines the subjunctive as a realisation of the morphological category mood expressing the semantic/pragmatic category modality allowed me to propose answers for a number of questions about the development of subjunctive use in the history of the English language:

Subjunctive use developed differently in main clauses from other clauses, because in main clauses the indicative, which expresses epistemic modality, did not compete with the subjunctive. The replacement of the subjunctive by modal constructions happened so late because the formal distinction between the subjunctive and its only other competitor, the imperative, was given up so late.

In adverbial clauses, there is little change in the preferred realisation of the verbal syntagm in individual clause types across the periods OE, ME and EModE. There is a complementary distribution between the subjunctive as the preferred realisation in clauses of concession and condition, in OE additionally in clauses of purpose and result on the one hand and the indicative in clauses of time, place, reason and comparison on the other. This distribution was explained as resulting from different representations of our world experience. The explanation was outlined in some detail with the examples of clauses of reason, clauses of time, and clauses of purpose and result. It was argued that the subjunctive was replaced by the indicative in the environments where it did not add a meaning component. This change contributed to the reduction of redundancy or, in other words, to the growth of economy.

The expression of root modality in the matrix clause of noun clauses – and to a lesser degree also in relative clauses – was identified as the most important factor to contribute to the preservation of the subjunctive in these construction types. It results in modal harmony. Since my data also indicate that modal harmony lost some of its importance after the ME period, it was suggested that one of the reasons for this change could be the increasing frequency of infinitive constructions, which do not express modality at all, at the expense of *that*-clauses with finite verbal syntagms.

A detailed study of the parameters construction type, structure of the verbal paradigm, text category, and modality, and their influence on subjunctive frequency, will be particularly rewarding for the period(s) following EModE. It should explore in particular: if there is support for the hypothesis that the subjunctive in main clauses is still productive today; if its decreasing frequency in adverbial clauses continued after EModE, and if so why; and finally why and how its decreasing frequency trend in noun clauses was reversed in PDE. It should also discuss how far other word classes (e.g. modal adverbs like *probably*, *possibly*, etc.) can combine with the subjunctive or in the long run partially or wholly replace it for the expression of root modality.

Appendix I

Matrix verbs of Old English object clauses

Verb	Subjunctive	Indicative	Modal	Total
adreogan			1	1
aredian	1			1
ascian	1			1
asecan			1	1
aþencan		1		1
bebeodan	15			15
behealdan	1			1
beladian	1			1
beodan	10			10
beorgan	3			3
besprecan	1			1
betan	1			1
beteon	2			2
beþencan		1		1
bidan			1	1
biddan	46		8	54
ceorian		1		1
ceosan	4		1	5
cepan		1		1
cnawan		3		3
cunnan	1	1	4	6
cweþan	6	4	1	11
cyþan	4	3		7
don	6	4		10
eahtan	1			1
earnian	4		1	5
fæstnian			1	1
findan			4	4
forbeodan	3			3
forberan	2			2
forewitan	1			1
forgiefan			1	1
forgieman	1			1
forhelan	1			1

Verb	Subjunctive	Indicative	Modal	Total
frignan	1			1
fultuman	1			1
fylstan			1	1
giefan	2			2
gieman	4			4
giernan			1	1
habban	2	1		3
halsian	6			6
hatan	1			1
healdan			1	1
hedan	3			3
hieran		2		2
hogian		1		1
hycgan			1	1
hyhtan			1	1
læran	18		1	19
leornian	1	1		2
liefan	5	3	1	9
locian	2	1		3
munnan		1		1
myndgian	2			2
mynian	2			2
niedan		1		1
oncnawan		3		3
ondrædan	1			1
ongietan	1	2		3
reccan	1	2		3
samnian	1			1
scamian	2			2
sceawian	2	1	1	4
secgan	15	49	3	67
sellan			1	1
seon	2	6	2	10
settan	1			1
singan	1			1
smeagan			2	2
sorgian	1			1
sprecan	1	1		2
sweotolian	1	2	1	4
tacnian		1	1	2
tellan		1		1
teohhian	1			1
teon	1			1
tilian	1			1
þafian	2			2
þencan	5	7		12

Verb	Subjunctive	Indicative	Modal	Total
þingian	2			2
þristian	1			1
þristlæcan	1			1
tocnawan		1		1
treowsian			1	1
understandan	2	5	2	9
unnan	2			2
wafian	1	2		3
warnian	1			1
wenan	9	1	4	14
willan	29	1	2	32
wilnian			2	2
wisian		1		1
witan	16	27	6	49
wundrian	2	3	1	6
wunian	2			2
wyrcan	2			2
ymbhycgan	1			1
ymbþencan		1		1
Total	277	147	60	484

Appendix II

Matrix verbs of Middle English object clauses

Verb	Subjunctive	Indicative	Modal	Imperative	Total
acordin			1		1
agreen			1		1
andræden	1				1
angieten		1			1
anginnen	1				1
askien		3			3
awarden			3		3
bediglien		1			1
beoden		1			1
beon		1			1
beren		2			2
beren on hand		1			1
beware	4				4
bidden	5			1	6
bihaten			1		1
bihealden		3			3
bileven		2			2
bisechen	7		1		8
bitacnen		2	1		3
biþenchen		1	1		2
bringen		1			1
causen		1			1
certifie		1			1
chargin	1			1	2
cnawen	2	13	11		26
comanden	5	1			6
complain		1			1
consideren		3	3		6
cüðen	1	2			3
cweðen	4		3	29	36
demen	1	1			2
don	1	7			8
dræden	2				2
drawen			1		1

Verb	Subjunctive	Indicative	Modal	Imperative	Total
enact	3		1		4
enqvere	1				1
espien		1			1
felen		2			2
finden	1	1			2
forlæten	1				1
forswigien	1				1
freinen	1				1
geþavien		1			1
gifen		1			1
granten		1	2		3
halsien	3				3
haten	2	3			5
healden		1			1
heren	1	4			5
herkien		4			4
hlüsten		2			2
hopien	1		5		6
informin	1	2			3
kepen	3				3
læsten		1			1
læten			2		2
leanien	1				1
letten			2		2
leven	1				1
liken		1			1
lokien	30	5			35
lufien	1	1			2
manien	1				1
meten		1			1
misliken		1			1
ofersen	1				1
ordenen	33		3		36
pardone	1				1
perceiven			1		1
preien	7		5		12
proven		2			2
putten		1			1
ræden			1		1
recchen	1	1			2
remembren		1	4		5
reportin		1			1
scheawen	1	4	2		7
schilden	1				1
sechen			1		1
seggen	1	28	26	18	73

Verb	Subjunctive	Indicative	Modal	Imperative	Total
seon		10	1		11
setten		2			2
singen				1	1
smakin	1				1
suffren	2				2
sutelin			1		1
swerien			1		1
taken		1			1
taken hede	3	5			8
tellen	1	4			5
þankien		2			2
þenchen	3	13	3		19
þolien		1			1
traversen		1			1
treowen	1				1
trukien		1			1
trusten		2	1		3
understanden	1	7	3		11
warnien	1				1
wenen	4	4			8
willen	34	1	1		36
witen	7	19	13		39
witnessen		1	1		2
writen		1			1
Total	192	195	107	50	544

Appendix III

Matrix verbs of Early Modern English object clauses

Verb	Subjunctive	Indicative	Modal	Imperative	Total
acknowledge		1			1
add		1	2		3
admit		1	1		2
affirm		1			1
agree		3			3
allow		1			1
answer		1			1
appoint		1			1
argue		1			1
ascertain		1			1
ask		1			1
assure			2		2
beg		1			1
behold		5	1		6
believe		3	4		7
bring		1			1
charge	1			2	3
comprehend			1		1
conceive		1			1
conclude		7	2		9
confess		12	1		13
confirm		1			1
conjecture		1			1
consider	1	6	1		8
contradict		1			1
cry out		1			1
declare		5			5
demonstrate		1	2		3
deny		2			2
deserve		1			1
determine	2				2
do	1	1			2
doubt		3	2		5
drink	1				1

Verb	Subjunctive	Indicative	Modal	Imperative	Total
eat		1			1
enact	3				3
establish		1			1
examine			1		1
express		1			1
find		6	3		9
follow		2			2
gather		4			4
get		1			1
give		1			1
give out		1	1		2
grant		6	3		9
have		2			2
hear		11			11
hold		2			2
hold true			1		1
hope		1	1		2
imagine		2	1		3
judge	2	3	1		6
keep		2			2
know	2	38	8		48
lack		1			1
learn		2	2		4
look	1	6			7
make			2		2
marvel	1				1
matter	1				1
note		2	1		3
nourish		1			1
nurse		1			1
ordain	4		7		11
own		1			1
perceive		11	1		12
pray		1	3	3	7
presume		2			2
prove		3	1		4
quoth	1		2	3	6
receive			1		1
respect		1			1
say	1	49	20	7	77
see	4	21	7		32
set			1		1
show		18	5		23
speak		1			1
suppose		3	2		5
swear		2			2

Verb	Subjunctive	Indicative	Modal	Imperative	Total
take	1				1
taste		1			1
tell		14	5		19
testify		1			1
think	2	19	9		30
touch			1		1
trow		1	1		2
trust		1			1
try			2		2
understand		7			7
warn	1				1
wish		1			1
wonder		1	1		2
write		2			2
yield		1			1
Total	30	326	113	15	484

References

Aarts, Bas (2012), 'The subjunctive conundrum in English', *Folia Linguistica*, 46: 1, pp. 1–20.

Algeo, John (1992), 'British and American mandative constructions', in Claudia Blank (ed.), *Language and Civilization. A Concerted Profusion of Essays and Studies in Honour of Otto Hietsch*, Paris: Peter Lang Publishers, pp. 599–617.

Algeo, John (1988), 'English and American differences', *International Journal of Lexicography*, 1, pp. 1–31.

Anderson, John M. (2007), 'Finiteness, mood and morphosyntax', *Journal of Linguistics*, 43, pp. 1–32.

Anderson, John M. (2001), 'Modals, subjunctives, and (non)-finiteness', *English Language and Linguistics*, 5: 1, pp. 159–166.

Anklam, Ernst (1908), *Das englische Relativ im 11. und 12. Jahrhundert*, Berlin diss.

Auer, Anita (2008), '*Lest* the situation deteriorates – a study of *lest* as a trigger of the inflectional subjunctive', in Miriam A. Locher and Jürg Strässler (eds), *Standards and Norms in the English Language*, Berlin and New York: Mouton de Gruyter, pp. 149–173.

Auer, Anita (2006), 'Precept and practice: The influence of prescriptivism on the english subjunctive', in Christiane Dalton-Puffer, Dieter Kastovsky, Nikolaus Ritt and Herbert Schendl (eds), *Syntax, Style and Grammatical Norms: English from 1500–2000*, Frankfurt and Bern: Peter Lang, pp. 33–53.

Auer, Anita (2005), *Language Standardisation and Prescription in the Eighteenth Century. The Subjunctive in English and (Austrian) German*, University of Manchester, PhD thesis.

Barber, Charles (1997), *Early Modern English*, Edinburgh: Edinburgh University Press.

Behre, Frank (1934), *The Subjunctive in Old English Poetry*, Göteborg: Elanders Boktryckeri Aktiebolag.

Biber, Douglas (1993), 'Representativeness in corpus design', *Literary and Linguistic Computing*, 8: 4, pp. 243–257.

Biber, Douglas, Edward Finegan and Dwight Atkinson (1994), 'ARCHER and its challenges: Compiling and exploring a representative corpus of historical English registers', in Udo Fries, Gunnel Tottie and Peter Schneider (eds),

Creating and Using English Language Corpora. Papers from the Fourteenth International Conference on English Language Research on Computerized Corpora, Zürich 1993, Amsterdam and Atlanta, GA: Rodopi, pp. 1–13.

Biber, Douglas, Susan Conrad and Randi Reppen (1998), *Corpus Linguistics. Investigating Language Structure and Use*, Cambridge: Cambridge University Press.

Biber, Douglas, Stig Johansson, Geoffrey Leech, Susan Conrad and Edward Finegan (1999), *Longman Grammar of Spoken and Written English*, Harlow: Longman [LGSWE].

Blum-Kulka, Shoshana, Juliane House and Gabriele Kasper (1989), 'Investigating cross-cultural pragmatics: An introductory overview', in Shoshana Blum-Kulka, Juliane House and Gabriele Kasper (eds), *Cross-cultural Pragmatics. Requests and Apologies*, Norwood, NJ: Ablex, pp. 1–34.

Bradley, Sidney Arthur James (1982), *Anglo-Saxon Poetry. An Anthology of Old English Poems in Prose Translation with Introduction and Headnotes*, London, Melbourne and Toronto: Dent.

Bullokar, William (1977, reprint), *Bref Grammar for English*, Delmar: Scholars' Facsimiles and Reprints. Original edition, London: Bollifant, 1586.

Bungarten, Theo (1979), 'Das Korpus als empirische Grundlage in der Linguistik und Literaturwissenschaft', in Henning Bergenholtz and Burkhard Schaeder (eds), *Empirische Textwissenschaft: Ausbau und Auswertung von Text-Corpora*, Königstein: Scriptor, pp. 28–51.

Burrow, John Anthony and Thorlac Turville-Petre (1992), *A Book of Middle English*, Oxford, UK and Cambridge, MA: Blackwell.

Butler, Charles (1910, reprint), *The English Grammar*, Halle/Saale: Niemeyer. Original edition, Oxford: Turner, 1634.

Callaway, Morgan (1933), *The Consecutive Subjunctive in Old English*, Boston, MA: D. C. Heath and Co.

Callaway, Morgan (1931), *The Temporal Subjunctive in Old English*, Austin: The University of Texas Press.

Campbell, Alistair John (1959), *Old English Grammar*, Oxford: Clarendon Press.

Claridge, Claudia (2007), 'Conditionals in Early Modern English texts', in Ursula Lenker and Anneli Meurman-Solin (eds), *Connectives in the History of English*, Amsterdam and Philadelphia: John Benjamins, pp. 229–254.

Collins, Peter (2015), 'Diachronic variation in the grammar of Australian English. Corpus-based explorations', in P. Peters, P. Collins and A. Smith (eds), *Grammatical Change in English World-Wide*, Amsterdam and Philadelphia: John Benjamins, pp. 15–42.

Collins, Peter, Ariane Macalinga Borlongan, Joo-Hyuk Lim and Xinyue Yao (2014), 'The subjunctive mood in English. A diachronic analysis', in S. E. Pfenninger, O. Timofeeva, A. C. Gardner, A. Honkapohja, M. Hundt and D. Schreier (eds), *Contact, Variation and Change in the History of English*, Amsterdam and Philadelphia: John Benjamins, pp. 259–280.

Corpus of Early English Correspondence Sampler (CEECS), <http://www.hels inki.fi/varieng/domains/CEEC.html>.

Corpus of English Religious Prose, <http://coerp.uni-koeln.de>.

Crawford, William J. (2009), 'The mandative subjunctive', in Günter Rohdenburg and Julia Schlüter (eds), *One Language, Two Grammars?*, Cambridge: Cambridge University Press, pp. 257–276.

Culpeper, Jonathan and Dawn Archer (2008), 'Requests and directness in Early Modern English trial proceedings and play texts', in Andreas Jucker and Irma Taavitsainen (eds), *Speech Acts in the History of English*, Amsterdam and Philadelphia: John Benjamins, pp. 45–84.

Dekeyser, Xavier (1984), 'Relativizers in Early Modern English. A dynamic quantitative study', in Jacek Fisiak (ed.), *Historical Syntax*, Berlin and New York: Mouton de Gruyter, pp. 61–87.

Denison, David (1998), 'Syntax', in Romaine, Suzanne (ed.), *The Cambridge History of the English Language. Vol. IV. 1776–1997*, Cambridge: Cambridge University Press, pp. 92–329.

Denison, David (1993), *English Historical Syntax: Verbal Constructions*, London and New York: Longman.

Diani, Giuliana (2001), 'Modality and speech acts in English acts of parliament', in Maurizio Gotti and Marina Dossena (eds), *Modality in Specialized Discourse*, Bern: Peter Lang, pp. 175–191.

Dons, Ute (2004), *Descriptive Adequacy of Early Modern English Grammars*, Berlin and New York: Mouton de Gruyter.

Ervin-Tripp, Susan (1976), 'Is Sybil there? The structure of some American English directives', *Language in Society*, 5: 1, pp. 25–66.

Facchinetti, Roberta (2001), 'Conditional Constructions in Modern English Legal Texts', in Maurizio Gotti and Marina Dossena (eds), *Modality in Specialized Texts. Selected Papers of the 1st CERLIS Conference*, Bern, Berlin and Brüssel: Peter Lang, pp. 133–150.

Faulkner, William Harrison (2004), *The Subjunctive Mood in the Old English Version of Bede's Ecclesiastical History*, diss. [Reprint from the collections of the University of California Libraries, 2011.]

Fillbrandt, Eva-Liisa (2006), 'The development of the mandative subjunctive in the Early Modern English Period', *Trames*, 10: 2, pp. 135–151.

Fischer, Olga (1992), 'Syntax', in Norman Blake (ed.), *The Cambridge History of the English Language. Vol. II. 1066–1476*, Cambridge: Cambridge University Press, pp. 207–408.

Fleischhauer, W. (1886), *Ueber den Gebrauch des Conjunctivs in Alfred's Altenglischer Uebersetzung von Gregor's Cura Pastoralis*, Göttingen diss., Erlangen.

Fowler, Henry (1926), *A Dictionary of Modern English Usage*, 2nd edn. Revised by Ernest Gowers, Oxford: Clarendon Press, 1965.

Francis, Winthrop Nelson (1979), 'Problems of assembling and computerizing large corpora', in Henning Bergenholtz and Burkhard Schaeder (eds),

Empirische Textwissenschaft: Ausbau und Auswertung von Text-Corpora, Königstein: Scriptor, pp. 110–123.

Franz, Wilhelm (1939), *Die Sprache Shakespeares in Vers und Prosa*, 4th edn. [Nachdruck Tübingen, Halle/Saale: Niemeyer, 1986.]

Glunz, Hans Hermann (1929), *Die Verwendung des Konjunktivs im Altenglischen*, Leipzig: Tauchnitz.

González-Álvarez, Dolores (2003), 'If he come vs. if he comes, if he shall come: Some remarks on the subjunctive in conditional protases in Early and Late Modern English', *Neuphilologische Mitteilungen*, 3: 104, pp. 303–313.

Görlach, Manfred (1991), *Introduction to Early Modern English*, Cambridge: Cambridge University Press.

Gorrell, Joseph Hendren (1895), *Indirect Discourse in Anglo-Saxon*, Baltimore: The Modern Language Association of America.

Greenbaum, Sidney (1977), 'Judgments of syntactic acceptability and frequency', *Studia Linguistica*, 31, pp. 83–105.

Hacquard, Valentine (2012), 'Modality', in Claudia Maienborn, Klaus von Heusinger and Paul Portner (eds), *Semantics: An International Handbook of Natural Language Meaning*, Berlin, etc.: De Gruyter Mouton, 2012, Vol. 2, pp. 1448–1515.

Harmer, Florence Elizabeth (ed.) (1914), *Select English Historical Documents of the Ninth and Tenth Centuries*, London and Edinburgh: Cambridge University Press.

Harsh, Wayne (1968), *The Subjunctive in English*, Alabama: University of Alabama Press.

Henshaw, Alonzo Norton (1894), *The Syntax of the Indicative and Subjunctive Moods in the Anglo-Saxon Gospels*, Leipzig diss.

Hintikka, Jaakko (1962), *Knowledge and Belief. An Introduction to the Logic of the Two Notions*, Ithaca, NY and London: Cornell University Press.

Hoffmann, Sebastian (1997), *Mandative Sentences. A Study of Variation on the Basis of the British National Corpus*, Universität Zürich: unpublished Lizentiats-Arbeit.

Hogg, Richard Milne (1992), 'Phonology and morphology', in Richard M. Hogg (ed.), *The Cambridge History of the English Language. Vol. 1: The Beginnings to 1066*, Cambridge: Cambridge University Press, pp. 67–167.

Huddleston, Rodney and Geoffrey Keith Pullum (2002), *The Cambridge Grammar of the English Language*, Cambridge: Cambridge University Press.

Hundt, Marianne (2019), 'It is important that mandatives *(should) be studied* across different world Englishes and from a construction grammar perspective', in Paloma Núñez Pertejo, María José López-Couso, Belén Méndez-Naya and Ignacio Palacios Martínez (eds), *Crossing Linguistic Boundaries: Systemic, Synchronic and Diachronic Variation in English*, London: Bloomsbury, pp. 211–238.

Hundt, Marianne (2018), 'It is time that this *(should)* be studied across a broader range of Englishes: A global trip around mandative subjunctives', in Sandra C. Dehors (ed.), *Modeling World Englishes: Assessing the Interplay of Emancipation and Globalization of ESL Varieties*, Amsterdam and Philadelphia: John Benjamins, pp. 217–244.

Hundt, Marianne (2009), 'Colonial lag, colonial innovation, or simply language change?', in Günter Rohdenburg and Julia Schlüter (eds), *One Language, Two Grammars?: Differences Between British and American English*, Cambridge: Cambridge University Press, pp. 13–37.

Hundt, Marianne (1998a), *New Zealand English Grammar: Fact or Fiction*, Amsterdam: John Benjamins.

Hundt, Marianne (1998b), 'It is important that this study (*should*) be based on the analysis of parallel corpora: On the use of the mandative subjunctive in four major varieties of English', in Hans Lindquist, Staffan Klintborg, Magnus Levin and Maria Estling (eds), *The Major Varieties of English. Papers from Maven 97, Växjö 20–22 November 1997, Acta Wexionensia Humaniora*, 1, Växjö University, pp. 159–175.

Hundt, Marianne and Anne-Christine Gardner (2017), 'Corpus-based approaches: Watching English change', in Laurel Brinton (ed.), *English Historical Linguistics: Approaches and Perspectives*, Cambridge: Cambridge University Press, pp. 96–130.

Jacobsson, Bengt (1975), 'How dead is the English subjunctive?', *Moderna Språk*, 69, pp. 218–231.

James, Francis (1986), *Semantics of the English Subjunctive*, Vancouver: University of British Columbia Press.

Jespersen, Otto (1909–1949), *A Modern English Grammar on Historical Principles I–VII*, Copenhagen: Munksgaard. [MEG]

Johansson, Christine (2017), 'Relativization', in Alexander Bergs and Laurel Brinton (eds), *The History of English. Volume 4: Early Modern English*, Berlin: Mouton de Gruyter, pp. 267–286.

Johansson, Stig (1979), 'American and British English grammar: An elicitation experiment', *English Studies*, 60, pp. 195–215.

Johansson, Stig (in collaboration with G. Leech and H. Goodluck) (1978), *Manual of Information to Accompany the Lancaster-Oslo/Bergen Corpus of British English for use with Digital Computers*, Oslo: University of Oslo, Department of English.

Johansson, Stig and Else Helene Norheim (1988), 'The subjunctive in British and American English', *ICAME Journal*, 12, pp. 27–36.

Kampers-Manhe, Brigitte (1991), *L'opposition subjonctif/indicatif dans les relatives*, Amsterdam and Atlanta, GA: Rodopi.

Kastronic, Laura and Shana Poplack (2014), 'The North-American English mandative subjunctive in the 21st century. Revival or remnant?', *University of Pennsylvania Working Papers in Linguistics*, 20: 2, pp. 71–80.

Kellner, Leon (1892), *Historical Outlines of Englis Syntax*, London: Macmillan and Co.

Kihlbom, Asta (1939), 'Present subjunctive in conditional clauses', *Studia Neophilologica*, 11, pp. 257–266.

Kikusawa, Namiko (2012), 'The subjunctive vs. modal auxiliaries: *Lest*-clauses in Late Middle English', in Manfred Markus, Yoko Iyeiri, Reinhard Heuberger and Emil Chamson (eds), *Middle and Modern English Corpus Linguistics*, Amsterdam and Philadelphia: John Benjamins, pp. 127–139.

Kjellmer, Göran (2009), 'The revived subjunctive', in Günter Rohdenburg and Julia Schlüter (eds), *One Language, Two Grammars? Differences Between British and American English*, Cambridge: Cambridge University Press, pp. 246–256.

Kohnen, Thomas (2008a), 'Directives in Old English: Beyond politeness?', in Andreas Jucker and Irma Taavitsainen (eds), *Speech Acts in the History of English*, Amsterdam and Philadelphia: John Benjamins, pp. 27–44.

Kohnen, Thomas (2008b), 'Tracing directives through text and time: Towards a methodology of corpus-based diachronic speech-act analysis', in Andreas Jucker and Irma Taavitsainen (eds), *Speech Acts in the History of English*, Amsterdam and Philadelphia: John Benjamins, pp. 295–310.

Kohnen, Thomas (2007), 'Text types and the methodology of diachronic speech act analysis', in Susan Fitzmaurice and Irma Taavitsainen (eds), *Methods in Historical Pragmatics*, Berlin and New York: Mouton de Gruyter, pp. 139–166.

Kohnen, Thomas (2004), '"Let mee bee so bold to request you to tell me". Constructions with *let me* and the history of English directives', *Journal of Historical Pragmatics*, 5: 1, pp. 159–173.

Kohnen, Thomas (2002), 'Towards a history of English directives', in Andreas Fischer, Gunnel Tottie and Hans Martin Lehmann (eds), *Text Types and Corpora: Studies in Honour of Udo Fries*, Tübingen: Gunter Narr, pp. 165–175.

Kohnen, Thomas (2000), 'Explicit performatives in Old English: A corpus-based study of directives', *Journal of Historical Pragmatics*, 1, pp. 301–321.

Kortmann, Bernd (1997), *Adverbial Subordination. A Typology and History of Adverbial Subordinators Based on European Languages*, Berlin and New York: Mouton de Gruyter.

Kovács, Éva (2010), 'The Subjunctive in Old English and Middle English', *Eger Journal of English Studies*, 10, pp. 57–69.

Kovács, Éva (2009), 'On the development of the subjunctive from Early Modern English to Present-Day English', *Eger Journal of English Studies*, 9, pp. 79–90.

Kratzer, Angelika (1991), 'Modality', in Armin v. Stechow and Dieter Wunderlich (eds), *Semantik: Ein internationales Handbuch zeitgenössischer Forschung*, Berlin: Mouton de Gruyter, pp. 639–650.

Kroch, Anthony and Ann Taylor (2000), *Penn-Helsinki Parsed Corpus of Middle English*, second edition, <http://www.ling.upenn.edu/hist-corpora/PPCME2-RELEASE-4/index.html>.

Kroch, Anthony, Beatrice Santorini and Lauren Delfs (2004), *Penn-Helsinki*

Parsed Corpus of Early Modern English, Department of Lingistics, University of Pennsylvania. CD-ROM, first edition, release 3, <http://www.ling.upenn. edu/ppche/ppche-release-2016/PPCEME-RELEASE-3>.

Kroch, Anthony, Beatrice Santorini and Ariel Diertani (2016), *The Penn Parsed Corpus of Modern British English* (PPCMBE2), Department of Linguistics, University of Pennsylvania. CD-ROM, second edition, release 1, <http://www. ling.upenn.edu/ppche/ppche-release-2016/PPCMBE2-RELEASE-1>.

Kytö, Merja (comp. 1996), *Manual to the Diachronic Part of The Helsinki Corpus of English Texts. Coding Conventions and Lists of Source Texts*, 3rd edn, Helsinki: Department of English, University of Helsinki.

Kytö, Merja and Matti Rissanen (1993), 'General introduction', in Matti Rissanen, Merja Kytö and Minna Palander-Collin (eds), *Early English in the Computer Age. Explorations through the Helsinki Corpus*, Berlin and New York: Mouton de Gruyter, pp. 1–17.

Lass, Roger (1999), 'Phonology and morphology', in Roger Lass (ed.), *The Cambridge History of the English Language. Vol. III. 1476–1776*, Cambridge: Cambridge University Press, pp. 56–186.

Lass, Roger (1992), 'Phonology and morphology', in Norman Blake (ed.), *The Cambridge History of the English Language. Vol. II. 1066–1476*, Cambridge: Cambridge University Press, pp. 23–155.

Leech, Geoffrey (2007), 'New resources, or just better old ones? The Holy Grail of representativeness', in Marianne Hundt, Nadja Nesselhauf and Carolin Biewer (eds), *Corpus Linguistics and the Web*, Amsterdam and New York: Rodopi, pp. 133–149.

Leech, Geoffrey and Nicholas Smith (2005) 'Extending the possibilities of corpus-based research in the twentieth century: A prequel to LOB and FLOB', *ICAME Journal*, 29, pp. 83–98.

Leech, Geoffrey, Marianne Hundt, Christian Mair and Nicholas Smith (2009), *Change in Contemporary English. A Grammatical Study*, Cambridge: Cambridge University Press.

López-Couso, María José and Belén Méndez-Naya (2012), 'Compiling British English legal texts: A contribution to ARCHER', in Nila Vázquez González (ed), *Creation and Use of Historical English Corpora in Spain*, Newcastle upon Tyne: Cambridge Scholars Publishing, pp. 5–19.

López-Couso, María José and Belén Mendez-Naya (2006), 'Complement selection in Early English dependent desires: A look at commands and requests', *Estudios Ingleses de la Universidad Complutense*, 14, pp. 33–53.

López-Couso, María José and Belén Mendez-Naya (1996), 'On the use of the subjunctive and modals in Old and Middle English dependent commands and requests. Evidence from the Helsinki Corpus', *Neuphilologische Mitteilungen*, XCVII, pp. 411–421.

Los, Bettelou (2005), *The Rise of the 'To'-Infinitive*, Oxford: Oxford University Press.

Louw, B. (1993), 'Irony in the text or insincerity in the writer? The diagnostic potential of semantic prosodies', in M. Baker, G. Francis and E. Tognini-Bonelli (eds), *Text and Technology: In Honour of John Sinclair*, Amsterdam: John Benjamins, pp. 157–176.

Manabe, Kazumi (1989), *The Syntactic and Stylistic Development of the Infinitive in Middle English*, Kukuoka: Kyushu University Press.

Mindt, Ilka (2008), 'Adjective complementation by *that*-clauses: The relation between the semantics of adjectives and the verb phrase in the *that*-clause', *International Journal of English Studies*, 19: 1, pp. 141–155.

Mitchell, Bruce (1985), *Old English Syntax*, two vols, Oxford: Clarendon Press.

Moessner, Lilo (2020), 'Old English law-codes: A synchronic-diachronic study', *Journal of Historical Pragmatics*, 21:1, pp. 28–52.

Moessner, Lilo (2018), 'Old English wills: A genre study', in Peter Petré, Hubert Cuyckens and Frauke D'hoedt (eds), *Sociocultural Dimensions of Lexis and Text in the History of English*, Amsterdam: John Benjamins, pp. 103–124.

Moessner, Lilo (2017), 'Standardization', in Alexander Bergs and Laurel Brinton (eds), *The History of English. Volume 4: Early Modern English*, Berlin: Mouton de Gruyter, pp. 167–187.

Moessner, Lilo (2010a), 'Mandative constructions in Middle English', *ICAME Journal. Computers in English Linguistics*, 34, pp. 151–168.

Moessner, Lilo (2010b), 'Directive speech acts. A cross-generic diachronic study', *Journal of Historical Pragmatics*, 11: 2, pp. 219–249.

Moessner, Lilo (2009), 'The influence of the Royal Society on 17th-century scientific writing', *ICAME Journal. Computers in English Linguistics*, 33, pp. 65–87.

Moessner, Lilo (2007), 'The mandative subjunctive in Middle English', in Gabriella Mazzon (ed.), *Studies in Middle English Forms and Meanings*, Frankfurt/Main: Peter Lang, pp. 209–26.

Moessner, Lilo (2006), 'The subjunctive in Early Modern English adverbial clauses', in Christian Mair and Reinhard Heuberger (eds), *Corpora and the History of English. Papers Dedicated to Manfred Markus on the Occasion of His Sixty-Fifth Birthday*, Heidelberg: Winter, pp. 249–63.

Moessner, Lilo (2005), 'The verbal syntagm in ME conditional clauses', in Nikolaus Ritt and Herbert Schendl (eds), *Rethinking Middle English. Linguistic and Literary Approaches*, Frankfurt/Main, etc.: Peter Lang, pp. 216–227.

Moessner, Lilo (1999), 'The negative relative marker *but*. A case of syntactic borrowing', in Guy A. J. Tops, Betty Devriendt and Steven Geukens (eds), *Thinking English Grammar. To Honour Xavier Dekeyser, Professor Emeritus*, Leuven and Paris: Peeters, pp. 65–77.

Moessner, Lilo (1992), 'Relative constructions and functional amalgamation in Early Modern English', in Matti Rissanen, Ossi Ihalainen, Terttu Nevalainen and Irma Taavitsainen (eds), *History of Englishes. New Methods and Interpretations in Historical Linguistics*, Berlin and New York: Mouton de Gruyter, pp. 336–351.

Moessner, Lilo and Ursula Schaefer (1987), *Proseminar Mittelenglisch*, 2nd edn, Tübingen: Francke Verlag.

Morris, Richard (1880), *The Blickling Homilies, Edited with a Translation and Index of Words*, London: Trübner. [Early English Text Society. OS 73]

Mossé, Fernand (1952), *A Handbook of Middle English*, Baltimore, MA: The John Hopkins Press.

Mossé, Fernand (1945), *Manuel de l'anglais du moyen âge des origines du xive siècle, I. Vieil-anglais*, Paris: Aubier.

Mourek, Václav Emanuel (1908), 'Zur Syntax des Konjunktivs im Beowulf', in Carl von Kraus und August Sauer (eds), *Prager deutsche Studien, Achtes Heft*, Prag: Carl Bellmann, pp. 121–137.

Mustanoja, Tauno F. (1960), *A Middle English Syntax*, Helsinki: Société Néophilologique.

Nevalainen, Terttu (2006), *An Introduction to Early Modern English*, Edinburgh: Edinburgh University Press.

Nichols, Ann Eljenholm (1987), 'The suasive subjunctive: Alive and well in the upper Midwest', *American Speech*, 62, pp. 140–153.

Ogawa, Hiroshi (1989), *Old English Modal Verbs: A Syntactical Study*, Copenhagen: Rosenkilde and Bagger.

Övergaard, Gerd (1995), *The Mandative Subjunctive in American and British English in the 20th Century*, Uppsala: Studia Anglistica Upsaliensia 94.

Oxford English Dictionary (*OED*), available at <httpl/:www.oed.com>.

Palmer, Frank Robert (2001), *Mood and Modality*, 2nd edn, Cambridge: Cambridge University Press.

Palmer, Frank Robert (1979), *Modality and the English Modals*, London and New York: Longman.

Palmer, Frank Robert (1974), *The English Verb*, 2nd edn, London: Longman.

Panzeri, Francesca (2006), 'Subjunctive relative clauses', in Pascal Denis, Eric McCready, Alexis Palmer and Brian Reese (eds), *Proceedings of the 2004 Texas Linguistics Society Conference: Issues at the Semantics-Pragmatics Interface*, Somerville, MA: Cascadilla Press, pp. 60–68.

Peters, Pam (2009), 'The mandative subjunctive in spoken English', in Pam Peters, Peter Collins and A. Smith (eds), *Comparative Studies in Australian and New Zealand English: Grammar and Beyond*, Amsterdam: John Benjamins, pp. 125–138.

Peters, Pam (1998), 'The survival of the subjunctive: Evidence of its use in Australia and elsewhere', *English World-Wide*, 19: 1, pp. 87–103.

Pilch, Herbert (1970), *Altenglische Grammatik*, München: Hueber.

Pintzuk, Susan and Leendert Plug (s.d.), *The York-Helsinki Parsed Corpus of Old English Poetry*, York: University of York, Department of Language and Linguistic Science.

Poole, Joshua ([1646] 1967), *The English Accidence*, Menston: The Scolar Press Limited. Original edition, London: Seile and Lownes.

Portner, Paul (2012), 'Verbal mood', in Claudia Maienborn, Klaus von Heusinger and Paul Portner (eds), *Semantics: An International Handbook of Natural Language Meaning*, Berlin, etc.: Mouton de Gruyter, Vol. 2, pp. 1262–1291.

Quirk, Randolph, Sidney Greenbaum, Geoffrey Leech and Jan Svartvik (1985), *A Comprehensive Grammar of the English Language*, London: Longman.

Radford, Andrew (1988), *Transformational Grammar: A First Course*, Cambridge: Cambridge University Press.

Rieger, Burghard (1979), 'Repräsentativität: von der Unangemessenheit eines Begriffs zur Kennzeichnung eines Problems linguistischer Korpusbildung', in Henning Bergenholtz and Burkhard Schaeder (eds), *Empirische Textwissenschaft: Ausbau und Auswertung von Text-Corpora*, Königstein: Scriptor, pp. 52–70.

Rissanen, Matti (1999), 'Syntax', in Roger Lass (ed.), *The Cambridge History of the English Language. Vol. III. 1476–1776*, Cambridge: Cambridge University Press, pp. 187–331.

Rissanen, Matti (1996), 'Genres, texts and corpora in the study of Medieval English', in J. Klein and D. Vanderbeke (eds), *Anglistentag 1995 Greifswald. Proceedings*, Tübingen: Niemeyer, pp. 229–242.

Rissanen, Matti (1994), 'The Helsinki Corpus of English texts', in Merja Kytö, Matti Rissanen and Susan Wright (eds), *Corpora Across the Centuries. Proceedings of the First International Colloquium on English Diachronic Corpora. St Catherine's College Cambridge, 25–27 March 1993*, Amsterdam and Atlanta, GA: Rodopi, pp. 73–79.

Robertson, Agnes Jane (1956), *Anglo-Saxon Charters. Edited with Translation and Notes*, Cambridge: Cambridge University Press.

Ruohonen, Juho (2017), 'Mandative sentences in British English: Diachronic developments in newswriting between the 1990s and the 2010s', *Neuphilologische Mitteilungen*, 118: 1, pp. 171–200.

Rütten, Tanja (2017), 'Speech, texts, and choices from the modal system: Mood distribution in Old English sermons', *Nordic Journal of English Studies*, 16: 1, pp. 190–213.

Rütten, Tanja (2015), 'For whom the bell tolls, or: why we predicted the death of the mandative subjunctive', in Christina Sanchez-Stockhammer (ed.), *Can we Predict Linguistic Change?*, VARIENG e-journal, vol. 16.

Rütten, Tanja (2014), 'Comparing apples and oranges – the study of diachronic change based on variant forms', in Silvia Mergenthal and Reingard Nischik (eds), *Anglistentag 2013 Konstanz: Proceedings*, Trier: Wissenschaftlicher Verlag, pp. 373–385.

Rydén, Mats (1966), *Relative Constructions in Early Sixteenth Century English. With Special Reference to Sir Thomas Elyot*, Uppsala: Acta Universitatis Upsaliensis.

Sayder, S. (1989), 'The subjunctive in Indian, British and American English: A corpus-based study', *Linguistische Arbeiten*, 69, pp. 58–66.

Schlüter, Julia (2009), 'The conditional subjunctive', in Günter Rohdenburg and Julia Schlüter (eds), *One Language, Two Grammars?*, Cambridge: Cambridge University Press, pp. 277–305.

Schneider, Edgar Werner (2011), 'The subjunctive in Philippine English – An updated assessment', in Maria Lourdes S. Bautista (ed.), *Studies in Philippine English: Exploring the Philippine Component of the International Corpus of English*, Mandaluyong City: Anvil Publishing, pp. 159–173.

Schneider, Edgar Werner (2007), *Postcolonial English: Varieties of English around the World*, Cambridge: Cambridge University Press.

Schneider, Edgar Werner (2005), 'The subjunctive in Philippine English', in Danilo T. Dayag and Stephen Quakenbusch (eds), *Linguistics and Language Education in the Philippines and Beyond. A Festschrift in Honour of Ma. Lourdes S. Bautista*, Manila: Linguistic Society of the Philippines, pp. 27–40.

Schneider, Edgar Werner (2000), 'Corpus linguistics in the Asian context: Examplary analyses of the Kolhapur corpus of Indian English', in Maria Lourdes Bautista, Teodoro A. Llamzon and Bonifacio P. Sibayan (eds), *Parangal cang Brother Andrew: Festschrift for Andrew Gonzalez*, Manila: Linguistic Society of the Philippines, pp. 115–137.

Searle, John Rogers (1976), 'A classification of illocutionary acts', *Language in Society*, 5, pp. 1–23.

Serpollet, Noëlle (2001), 'The mandative subjunctive in British English seems to be alive and kicking . . . Is this due to the influence of American English?', in *Proceedings of the Corpus Linguistics 2001 Conference. Technical Papers*, Vol. 13, Lancaster: University Centre for Computer Corpus Research on Language, pp. 531–542.

Swales, John Malcolm (1990), *Genre Analysis. English in Academic and Research Settings*, Cambridge: Cambridge University Press.

Swanton, Michael (1993), *Anglo-Saxon Prose, Translated and Edited*, London: Dent.

Taylor, Ann, Anthony Warner, Susan Pintzuk and Frank Beths (2003), *The York-Toronto-Helsinki Parsed Corpus of Old English Prose*, York: University of York.

The British English 2006 Corpus (BEO6), compiled by Paul Baker.

The Helsinki Corpus of English Texts (HC) (1991), compiled by Matti Rissanen, Merja Kytö, Leena Kahlas-Tarkka, Matti Kilpiö, Saara Nevanlinna, Irma Taavitsainen, Terttu Nevalainen, and Helena Raumolin-Brunberg, Department of Modern Languages, University of Helsinki.

The Helsinki Corpus of Older Scots (1995), compiled by Anneli Meurman-Solin, Department of Modern Languages, University of Helsinki.

Traugott, Elizabeth Closs (1992), 'Syntax', in Richard Milne Hogg (ed.), *The Cambridge History of the English Language, Volume I. The Beginnings to 1066*, Cambridge: Cambridge University Press, pp. 168–289.

Traugott, Elizabeth Closs (1972), *A History of English Syntax*, New York: Holt, Rinehart and Winstron, Inc.

Trnka, Bohumil (1930), *On the Syntax of the English Verb from Caxton to Dryden*, Prague. [Kraus Reprint Nendeln/Liechtenstein, 1978.]

Trosborg, Anna (1995), 'Statutes and contracts: An analysis of legal speech acts in the English language of the law', *Journal of Pragmatics*, 23, pp. 31–53.

Turner, John F. (1980), 'The marked subjunctive in contemporary English', *Studia Neophilologica*, 52, pp. 271–277.

Van Linden, An and Kristin Davidse (2009), 'The clausal complementation of deontic-evaluative adjectives in extraposition constructions: A synchronic-diachronic approach', *Folia Linguistica*, 43: 1, pp. 171–211.

Visser, Frederik Theodoor (1963–1973), *An Historical Syntax of the English Language*, 3 vols, Leiden: Brill.

Vogt, Andreas (1930), *Beiträge zum Konjunktivgebrauch im Altenglischen*, Borna-Leipzig: Noske.

Waller, Tim (2017), *The Subjunctive in Present-Day English. A Critical Analysis of Recent Research, Leading to a New Diachronic Investigation of the Mandative Subjunctive*, London, UCL PhD thesis.

Wharton, Jeremiah ([1654] 1970), *The English Grammar*, Menston: The Scolar Press Limited. Original edition, London: Du-Gard.

Whitelock, Dorothy (1930), *Anglo-Saxon Wills, Edited with Translation and Notes*, Cambridge: Cambridge University Press.

Wilde, H.-O. (1939/1940), 'Aufforderung, Wunsch und Möglichkeit', *Anglia*, 63, pp. 209–391 and *Anglia*, 64, pp. 10–105.

Wischer, Ilse (2008), '*Will* and *shall* as markers of modality and/or futurity in Middle English', *Folia Linguistica Historica*, 29, pp. 125–143.

Yañez-Bouza, Nuria (2011), 'ARCHER past and present (1990–2010)', *ICAME Journal*, 35, pp. 205–236.

Yerkes, David (1976), *Studies in the Manuscripts of the Old English Translation of the 'Dialogues' of Gregory the Great*, Oxford diss.

Name index

General index

Printed and bound by CPI Group (UK) Ltd, Croydon, CR0 4YY

20/11/2024

01791642-0004